Secret Sauce Contents

FOREWORD

The Secret Sauce should be used as part of a rigorous study program. Its purpose is to focus your attention on topics that I feel are integral to a thorough understanding of the CFA® Level 3 Curriculum. As such, it is assumed that, at a minimum, you have thoroughly read the Schweser 2008 Level 3 Study Notes and the CFA Institute Standards of Practice Handbook. Also, if you have access to the Level 3 blog, be sure you keep a file of those to review.

You will see several places where I have noted that you should know one or more formulas; be sure you know those formulas and can perform the related calculations.

Due to the nature of the Level 3 CFA curriculum and the fact that only the essay portions of recent exams are available for public review, it is virtually impossible for a study provider to write sample exam questions that will mimic the actual exam with any significant degree of certainty or even know exactly which topics will be tested. The point is that you must learn the underlying material and be able to apply that knowledge to the questions that are asked on exam day.

Some Level 3 candidates fall into a trap when they study only questions from sample exams or test banks and fail to learn the underlying concepts. This strategy makes it extremely difficult to apply your knowledge to actual exam questions that you have never seen before. So, as you read the Sauce, you will notice that each section is referenced to our study notes. If you come across concepts you can't recall, be sure to go back to the study notes to flesh them out.

Part of the difficulty of the Level 3 exam is its form; it is quite different from the other CFA exams. At Level 1, you more or less memorized facts and then regurgitated them on the exam. At Level 2, the topical coverage was more difficult, but each topic was tested in a stand-alone item set in much the way it was presented in the curriculum.

At Level 3, you will be expected to combine different topics from different parts of the curriculum into a single, multi-part question. For example, questions on Study Sessions 3, 4, and 7 (Behavioral Finance, Private Wealth Management, and Asset Allocation) can easily be combined in a single morning case for an individual investor. Of course, many other combinations are also possible, both in item sets and essay questions.

Another challenge with Level 3 is that many of the topics (e.g., Study Session 6, Economic Concepts for Portfolio Management) can be tested along with several other topics as part of an item set or case (essay), or they can be tested as the only topic in a stand-alone, multi-part question. In other words, it is difficult to determine the depth of knowledge required for each topic; you must know each topic thoroughly enough to answer several questions about it but also be able to integrate a small part of it with other topics.

As you can imagine, the Level 3 exam is a grueling mental challenge and not to be taken lightly. Your hard work and dedication combined with our quality products, however, will see you through.

I wish you all the best on exam day.

Bruce Kuhlman

Bruce Kuhlman, Ph.D., CFA, CAIA
Level 3 Manager

Kaplan Schweser

ETHICS

Topic Weight on Exam	10%
Study Notes Reference	Book 1, Pages 15–158
Video CD Reference	CD 1
Audio CD Reference	CDs 1–3

STUDY SESSION 1 – ETHICAL AND PROFESSIONAL STANDARDS

CFA INSTITUTE CODE OF ETHICS AND STANDARDS OF PROFESSIONAL CONDUCT
Cross-Reference to CFA Institute Assigned Readings #1 & 2

This topic will probably be tested in selected response item set format. The distracters (incorrect choices) will all appear indistinguishable unless you have learned to think in the spirit of the Code and Standards. The best way to do this is through the practice questions contained in the *Handbook* and Book 1 of the Study Notes.

As you read this material, keep in mind that it is assumed you have already read/studied the Code and Standards and our coverage in the Schweser Study Notes. As such, this material represents a "downsizing" of the material in our Study Notes without the LOS, concept checkers, applications (examples), and cases. Given a familiarity with the Code and Standards, this "critical core" of the Code and Standards should be all you need for that last push before the exam.

Code of Ethics

Members of CFA Institute, including Chartered Financial Analyst® (CFA®) charterholders, and candidates for the CFA designation ("Members and Candidates") must:[1]

- Act with integrity, competence, diligence, respect, and in an ethical manner with the public, clients, prospective clients, employers, employees, colleagues in the investment profession, and other participants in the global capital markets.

---

1. Copyright 2005, CFA Institute. Reproduced and republished from "The Code of Ethics," from Standards of Practice Handbook, 9th Ed., 2005, with permission from CFA Institute. All rights reserved.

- Place the integrity of the investment profession and the interests of clients above their own personal interests.
- Use reasonable care and exercise independent professional judgment when conducting investment analysis, making investment recommendations, taking investment actions, and engaging in other professional activities.
- Practice and encourage others to practice in a professional and ethical manner that will reflect credit on themselves and the profession.
- Promote the integrity of, and uphold the rules governing, capital markets.
- Maintain and improve their professional competence and strive to maintain and improve the competence of other investment professionals.

Standards of Professional Conduct[2]

The Standards of Professional Conduct are organized into seven standards:

I.   Professionalism.
II.   Integrity of Capital Markets.
III.   Duties to Clients.
IV.   Duties to Employers.
V.   Investment Analysis, Recommendations, and Action.
VI.   Conflicts of Interest.
VII.   Responsibilities as a CFA Institute Member or CFA Candidate.

I.   **Professionalism**

        A.   **Knowledge of the Law.** Understand and comply with all applicable laws, rules, and regulations (including the CFA Institute Code of Ethics and Standards of Professional Conduct) of any government, regulatory organization, licensing agency, or professional association governing your professional activities. In the event of conflict, comply with the more strict law, rule, or regulation.

        B.   **Independence and Objectivity.** Use reasonable care and judgment to achieve and maintain independence and objectivity in professional activities. Do not offer, solicit, or accept any gift, benefit, compensation, or consideration that could be expected to compromise your or another's independence and objectivity.

        C.   **Misrepresentation.** Do not knowingly make any misrepresentations relating to investment analysis, recommendations, actions, or other professional activities.

---

2. Copyright 2005, CFA Institute. Reproduced and republished from "Standards of Professional Conduct," from Standards of Practice Handbook, 9th Ed., 2005, with permission from CFA Institute. All rights reserved.

D. **Misconduct.** Do not engage in any professional conduct involving dishonesty, fraud, or deceit, or commit any act that reflects adversely on your professional reputation, integrity, or competence.

II. **Integrity of Capital Markets**

A. **Material Nonpublic Information.** Members and Candidates must not act or cause others to act on material nonpublic information.

B. **Market Manipulation.** Do not engage in practices that distort prices or artificially inflate trading volume with the intent to mislead market participants.

III. **Duties to Clients**

A. **Loyalty, Prudence, and Care.** Members and Candidates have a duty of loyalty to their clients and must act with reasonable care and exercise prudent judgment. Always act for the benefit of clients and place clients' interests before your employer's or your own interests.

B. **Fair Dealing.** Deal fairly and objectively with all clients when providing investment analysis, making investment recommendations, taking investment action, or engaging in other professional activities.

C. **Suitability.**

1. When Members and Candidates are in an advisory relationship with a client, they must:

   a. Make a reasonable inquiry into a client's or prospective client's investment experience, risk and return objectives, and financial constraints prior to making any investment recommendation or taking investment action and update this information regularly.

   b. Determine that an investment is suitable to the client's financial situation.

   c. Judge the suitability of investments in the context of the client's total portfolio.

  2. Make only investment recommendations or take investment actions that are consistent with the stated objectives and constraints of the portfolio.

 D. **Performance Presentation.** Must make reasonable efforts to ensure performance information is fair, accurate, and complete.

 E. **Preservation of Confidentiality.** Keep information about current, former, and prospective clients confidential unless:

  1. The information concerns illegal activities,

  2. Disclosure is required by law, or

  3. The client or prospective client permits disclosure.

IV. **Duties to Employers**

 A. **Loyalty.** Act for the benefit of your employer. Do not deprive your employer of your skills and abilities, divulge confidential information, or otherwise cause harm to your employer.

 B. **Additional Compensation Arrangements.** Do not accept gifts, benefits, compensation, or consideration that competes with, or might reasonably be expected to create a conflict of interest with, your employer's interests unless you obtain written consent from all parties involved.

 C. **Responsibilities of Supervisors.** Make reasonable efforts to detect and prevent violations of applicable laws, rules, regulations, and the Code and Standards by anyone subject to your supervision.

V. **Investment Analysis, Recommendations, and Action**

 A. **Diligence and Reasonable Basis.** Members and Candidates must:

  1. Exercise diligence, independence, and thoroughness in analyzing investments.

  2. Have a reasonable and adequate basis, supported by appropriate research and investigation.

B. **Communication With Clients and Prospective Clients.** Members and Candidates must:

1. Disclose the basic format and general principles of the investment processes used to analyze investments, select securities, and construct portfolios and promptly disclose any changes that might materially affect those processes.

2. Identify which factors are important to their investment analyses, recommendations, or actions, and include those factors in communications with clients and prospective clients.

3. Distinguish between fact and opinion.

C. **Record Retention.** Develop and maintain appropriate records to support their investment analysis, recommendations, actions, and other investment-related communications.

VI. **Conflicts of Interest**

A. **Disclosure of Conflicts.** Members and Candidates must make full and fair disclosure of all matters that could reasonably be expected to impair their independence and objectivity or interfere with respective duties to their clients, prospective clients, and employer. Disclosures should be prominent, delivered in plain language, and communicate the information effectively.

B. **Priority of Transactions.** Investment transactions for clients and employers must have priority over investment transactions in which a Member or Candidate is the beneficial owner.

C. **Referral Fees.** Disclose to employer, clients, and prospective clients, as appropriate, any compensation, consideration, or benefit received by, or paid to, others for the recommendation of products or services.

VII. **Responsibilities as a CFA Institute Member or CFA Candidate**

A. **Conduct as Members and Candidates in the CFA Program.** Do not engage in any conduct that compromises the reputation or integrity of CFA Institute or the CFA designation or the integrity, validity, or security of the CFA examinations.

B. **Reference to CFA Institute, the CFA Designation, and the CFA Program.** When referring to CFA Institute, CFA Institute membership, the CFA designation, or candidacy in the CFA Program, do not misrepresent or exaggerate the meaning or implications of membership in CFA Institute, holding the CFA designation, or candidacy in the CFA Program.

GUIDANCE FOR STANDARDS I–VII

I.   Professionalism

Professor's Note: The term "members" in the following applies to candidates as well.

I(A).   Knowledge of the Law. Members must understand and comply with laws, rules, regulations, and Code and Standards of any authority governing their activities. In the event of a conflict, follow the more strict law, rule, or regulation.

Guidance

Members must know the laws and regulations relating to their professional activities in all countries in which they conduct business. Do not violate Code or Standards even if the activity is otherwise legal. Always adhere to the most strict rules and requirements (law or CFA Institute Standards) that apply.

Dissociate from any ongoing client or employee activity that is illegal or unethical, even if it involves leaving an employer (an extreme case). While a member may confront the involved individual first, he must approach his supervisor or compliance department. Inaction with continued association may be construed as knowing participation.

Recommended Procedures for Compliance

Members should keep up with changes in applicable laws, rules, and regulations:
* Review compliance procedures on an ongoing basis to assure that they address current law, CFAI Standards, and regulations.
* Maintain current reference materials.
* Seek advice of counsel or compliance department when in doubt.
* Document any violations when they disassociate themselves from prohibited activity and encourage employers to bring an end to such activities.
* There is no requirement under the Standards to report violations to governmental authorities, but this may be advisable in some circumstances and required by law in others.

Members should encourage their firms to:

- Develop and/or adopt a code of ethics.
- Make information available that highlights applicable laws and regulations.
- Establish written procedures for reporting suspected violations.

I(B).   Independence and Objectivity. Use reasonable care to exercise independence and objectivity in professional activities. Do not offer, solicit, or accept any gift, benefit, compensation, or consideration that would compromise independence and objectivity.

Guidance

Do not let the investment process be influenced by any external sources. Modest gifts are permitted. Allocation of shares in oversubscribed IPOs to personal accounts is NOT permitted. Distinguish between gifts from clients and gifts from entities seeking influence to the detriment of the client. Gifts must be disclosed to the member's employer in any case.

Guidance—Investment-Banking Relationships

Do not be pressured by sell-side firms to issue favorable research on current or prospective investment-banking clients. It is appropriate to have analysts work with investment bankers in "road shows" only when the conflicts are adequately and effectively managed and disclosed. Be sure there are effective "firewalls" between research/investment management and investment banking activities.

Guidance—Public Companies

Analysts should not be pressured to issue favorable research by the companies they follow. Do not confine research to discussions with company management, but rather use a variety of sources, including suppliers, customers, and competitors.

Guidance—Buy-Side Clients

Buy-side clients may try to pressure sell-side analysts. Portfolio managers may have large positions in a particular security, and a rating downgrade may have an effect on the portfolio performance. As a portfolio manager, there is a responsibility to respect and foster intellectual honesty of sell-side research.

Guidance—Issuer-Paid Research

Analysts' compensation for preparing such research should be limited, and the preference is for a flat fee, without regard to conclusions or the report's recommendations.

Recommended Procedures for Compliance

- Protect the integrity of opinions—make sure they are unbiased.
- Create a restricted list and distribute only factual information about companies on the list.
- Restrict special cost arrangements—pay for one's own commercial transportation and hotel; limit use of corporate aircraft to cases in which commercial transportation is not available.
- Limit gifts—token items only. Business-related entertainment is okay if it does not influence a member's independence or objectivity.
- Restrict employee investments in equity IPOs and private placements.
- Have effective supervisory and review procedures.
- Firms should have formal written policies.

I(C). Misrepresentation. Do not misrepresent facts regarding investment analysis, recommendations, actions, or other professional activities.

Guidance

Do not make misrepresentations or give false impressions. This includes oral and electronic communications. Misrepresentations include guaranteeing investment performance and plagiarism. Plagiarism encompasses using someone else's work without giving credit.

Recommended Procedures for Compliance

Avoid misrepresentation by providing employees who deal with clients or prospects a written list of the firm's available services and a description of the firm's qualifications. Employee qualifications should be accurately presented as well. To avoid plagiarism, maintain records of all materials used to generate reports or other firm products and properly cite sources. Information from recognized financial and statistical reporting services need not be cited.

I(D). Misconduct. Do not engage in any professional conduct which involves dishonesty, fraud, or deceit. Do not do anything that reflects poorly on your integrity, good reputation, trustworthiness, or professional competence.

Guidance

CFA Institute discourages unethical behavior in all aspects of members' and candidates' lives. Do not abuse CFA Institute's Professional Conduct Program by seeking enforcement of this Standard to settle personal, political, or other disputes that are not related to professional ethics.

Recommended Procedures for Compliance

Firms are encouraged to adopt these policies and procedures:

- Develop and adopt a code of ethics and make clear that unethical behavior will not be tolerated.
- Give employees a list of potential violations and sanctions, including dismissal.
- Check references of potential employees.

II.   Integrity of Capital Markets

II(A).   Material Nonpublic Information. Members and Candidates in possession of material nonpublic information must not act or induce someone else to act on the information.

Guidance

Information is "material" if its disclosure would impact the price of a security or if reasonable investors would want the information before making an investment decision. Information is "non-public" until it has been made available to the marketplace.

Guidance—Mosaic Theory

There is no violation when a perceptive analyst reaches an investment conclusion about a corporate action or event through an analysis of public information together with items of non-material non-public information.

Recommended Procedures for Compliance

Make reasonable efforts to achieve public dissemination of the information. Encourage firms to adopt procedures to prevent misuse of material nonpublic information. Use a "firewall" within the firm, with elements including:

- Substantial control of relevant interdepartmental communications.
- Review employee trades—maintain "watch," "restricted," and "rumor" lists.
- Monitor and restrict proprietary trading while a firm is in possession of material nonpublic information.

Prohibition of all proprietary trading while a firm is in possession of material nonpublic information may be inappropriate, because it may send a signal to the market. In these cases, firms should take the contra side of only unsolicited customer trades.

II(B).   Market Manipulation. Do not engage in any practices intended to mislead market participants through distorted prices or artificially inflated trading volume.

Guidance

This Standard applies to transactions that deceive the market by distorting the price-setting mechanism of financial instruments or by securing a controlling position to manipulate the price of a related derivative and/or the asset itself. Spreading false rumors is also prohibited.

III. Duties to Clients and Prospective Clients

III(A). Loyalty, Prudence, and Care. Members must always act for the benefit of clients and place clients' interests before their employer's or their own interests. Members must be loyal to clients, use reasonable care, exercise prudent judgment, and determine and comply with their applicable fiduciary duty to clients.

Guidance

Client interests always come first.

- Exercise prudence, care, skill, and diligence.
- Manage pools of client assets in accordance with the terms of the governing documents.
- Make investment decisions in the context of the total portfolio.
- Vote proxies in an informed and responsible manner. Due to cost benefit considerations, it may not be necessary to vote all proxies.
- Client brokerage, or "soft dollars" or "soft commissions" must be used to benefit the client.

Recommended Procedures of Compliance

Submit to clients, at least quarterly, itemized statements showing all securities in custody and all debits, credits, and transactions.

Encourage firms to address these topics when drafting policies and procedures regarding fiduciary duty:

- Follow applicable rules and laws.
- Establish client's investment objectives. Consider suitability of portfolio relative to client's needs and circumstances, the investment's basic characteristics, or the basic characteristics of the total portfolio.
- Diversify.
- Deal fairly with all clients in regards to investment actions.
- Disclose conflicts.
- Disclose compensation arrangements.
- Vote proxies in the best interest of clients and ultimate beneficiaries.
- Maintain confidentiality.
- Seek best execution.
- Place client interests first.

III(B).   Fair Dealing. Members must deal fairly and objectively with all clients and prospects.

Guidance

Do not discriminate against any clients when disseminating recommendations or taking investment action. Fairly does not mean equally. In the normal course of business, there will be differences in the time emails, faxes, et cetera, are received by different clients. Different service levels are okay, but they must not negatively affect or disadvantage any clients. Disclose the different service levels to all clients and prospects, and make premium levels of service available to all who wish to pay for them.

Give all clients a fair opportunity to act upon every recommendation. Clients who are unaware of a change in a recommendation should be advised before the order is accepted.

Treat all clients fairly in light of their investment objectives and circumstances. Members and Candidates should not take advantage of their position in the industry to disadvantage clients.

Recommended Procedures for Compliance

Encourage firms to establish compliance procedures requiring proper dissemination of investment recommendations and fair treatment of all customers and clients.

- Limit the number of people who are aware that a change in recommendation will be made.
- Shorten the time frame between decision and dissemination.
- Have in place published guidelines prohibiting personnel who have prior knowledge of a recommendation from discussing it or taking action on the pending recommendation.
- Simultaneous dissemination.
- Maintain list of clients and holdings to ensure that all are treated fairly.
- Develop written trade allocation procedures—ensure fairness to clients, timely and efficient order execution, and accuracy of client positions.
- Disclose trade allocation procedures.
- Establish systematic account review—to ensure that no client is given preferred treatment and that investment actions are consistent with the account's objectives.
- Disclose available levels of service.

III(C).   Suitability

    1. When in an advisory relationship with client or prospect:
        a. Make reasonable inquiry into clients' investment experience, risk and return objectives, and constraints prior to making any recommendations or taking investment action. Reassess information and update regularly.

      b. Be sure recommendations and investments are suitable to a client's financial situation and consistent with client objectives.

      c. Make sure investments are suitable in the context of a client's total portfolio.

  2. When managing a portfolio, investment recommendations and actions must be consistent with stated portfolio objectives and constraints.

Guidance

In advisory relationships, be sure to gather client information at the beginning of the relationship, in the form of an investment policy statement (IPS). If a member is responsible for managing a fund to an index or other stated mandate, be sure investments are consistent with the stated mandate.

Recommended Procedures for Compliance

- Put the needs and circumstances of each client and the client's investment objectives into a written IPS.
- Consider the type of client and whether there are separate beneficiaries, investor objectives, investor constraints, and performance measurement benchmarks.
- Review investor's objectives and constraints periodically to reflect any changes in client circumstances.

III(D). Performance Presentation. Presentations of investment performance information must be fair, accurate, and complete.

Guidance

Avoid misstating performance or misleading clients/prospects about investment performance. Do not misrepresent past performance or reasonably expected performance. Do not state or imply the ability to achieve a rate of return similar to that achieved in the past.

Recommended Procedures for Compliance

Encourage firms to adhere to Global Investment Performance Standards. Obligations under this Standard may also be met by:

- Considering the sophistication of the audience.
- Presenting performance of weighted composite of similar portfolios rather than a single account.
- Including terminated accounts as part of historical performance.
- Including all appropriate disclosures to fully explain results.
- Maintaining data and records used.

III(E). Preservation of Confidentiality. All information about current and former clients and prospects must be kept confidential unless it pertains to illegal activities, disclosure is required by law, or the client or prospect gives permission for the information to be disclosed.

Guidance

If illegal activities by a client are suspected, members may have an obligation to report the activities to authorities. The requirements of this Standard are not intended to prevent Members and Candidates from cooperating with a CFA Institute Professional Conduct Program (PCP) investigation.

Recommended Procedures for Compliance

Members should avoid disclosing information received from a client, except to authorized co-workers who are also working for the client.

IV. Duties to Employers

IV(A). Loyalty. Members and Candidates must place their employer's interest before their own and must not deprive their employer of their skills and abilities, divulge confidential information, or otherwise harm their employer.

Guidance

Members must not engage in activities which would injure the firm, deprive it of profit, or deprive it of the advantage of employees' skills and abilities. Always place client interests above employer interests.

Guidance—Independent Practice

Independent practice for compensation is allowed if a notification is provided to the employer fully describing all aspects of the services, including compensation, duration, and the nature of the activities and if the employer consents to all terms of the proposed independent practice before it begins.

Guidance—Leaving an Employer

Members must continue to act in their employer's best interests until resignation is effective. Activities which may constitute a violation include:

- Misappropriation of trade secrets.
- Misuse of confidential information.
- Soliciting employer's clients prior to leaving.

©2008 Kaplan Schweser

- Self-dealing.
- Misappropriation of client lists.

Once an employee has left a firm, simple knowledge of names and existence of former clients is generally not confidential. Also, there is no prohibition on the use of experience or knowledge gained while with a former employer.

Guidance—Whistleblowing

There may be isolated cases where a duty to one's employer may be violated in order to protect clients or the integrity of the market, and not for personal gain.

Guidance—Nature of Employment

The applicability of this Standard is based on the nature of the employment— employee versus independent contractor. If Members and Candidates are independent contractors, they still have a duty to abide by the terms of the agreement.

IV(B). Additional Compensation Arrangements. Accept no gifts, benefits, compensation or consideration which may create a conflict of interest with the employer's interest unless written consent is received from all parties.

Guidance

Compensation includes direct and indirect compensation from a client and other benefits received from third parties. Written consent from a member's employer includes e-mail communication.

Recommended Procedures for Compliance

Make an immediate written report to employer detailing proposed compensation and services, if additional to that provided by employer.

IV(C). Responsibilities of Supervisors. All Members and Candidates must make reasonable efforts to detect and prevent violations of laws, rules, regulations, and the Code and Standards by any person under their authority.

Guidance

Take steps to prevent employees from violating laws, rules, regulations, or the Code and Standards and make reasonable efforts to detect violations.

Guidance—Compliance Procedures

An adequate compliance system must meet industry standards, regulatory requirements, and the requirements of the Code and Standards. Members with supervisory responsibilities have an obligation to bring an inadequate compliance system to the attention of firm's management and recommend corrective action. While investigating a possible breach of compliance procedures, it is appropriate to limit the suspected employee's activities.

Recommended Procedures for Compliance

A member should recommend that his employer adopt a code of ethics. Employers should not commingle compliance procedures with the firm's code of ethics—this can dilute the goal of reinforcing one's ethical obligations. Members should encourage employers to provide their code of ethics to clients.

Adequate compliance procedures should:

- Be clearly written.
- Be easy to understand.
- Designate a compliance officer with authority clearly defined.
- Have a system of checks and balances.
- Outline the scope of procedures.
- Outline what conduct is permitted.
- Contain procedures for reporting violations and sanctions.

Once the compliance program is instituted, the supervisor should:

- Distribute it to the proper personnel.
- Update it as needed.
- Continually educate staff regarding procedures.
- Issue reminders as necessary.
- Require professional conduct evaluations.
- Review employee actions to monitor compliance and identify violations.
- Enforce procedures once a violation occurs.

If there is a violation, respond promptly and conduct a thorough investigation while placing limitations on the wrongdoer's activities.

V.   Investment Analysis, Recommendations, and Action

V(A).   Diligence and Reasonable Basis

1. When analyzing investments, making recommendations, and taking investment actions, use diligence, independence, and thoroughness.
2. Analysis, recommendations, and actions should have a reasonable and adequate basis, supported by research and investigation.

Guidance

The application of this Standard depends on the investment philosophy adhered to, members' and candidates' roles in the investment decision-making process, and the resources and support provided by employers. These factors dictate the degree of diligence, thoroughness of research, and the proper level of investigation required.

Guidance—Using Secondary or Third-Party Research

See that the research is sound. Examples of criteria to use to evaluate:

- Review assumptions used.
- How rigorous was the analysis?
- How timely is the research?
- Evaluate objectivity and independence of the recommendations.

Guidance—Group Research and Decision Making

Even if a member does not agree with the independent and objective view of the group, he does not necessarily have to decline to be identified with the report, as long as there is a reasonable and adequate basis.

Recommended Procedures for Compliance

Encourage firms to consider the policies and procedures supporting this Standard:

- Have a policy requiring that research reports and recommendations have a basis that can be substantiated as reasonable and adequate.
- Have detailed, written guidance for proper research and due diligence.
- Have measurable criteria for judging the quality of research.

V(B). **Communication With Clients and Prospective Clients**

1. Disclose to clients and prospects basic format and general principles of investment processes used to analyze and select securities and construct portfolios. Promptly disclose any process changes.
2. Use reasonable judgment in identifying relevant factors important to investment analyses, recommendations, or actions, and include factors when communicating with clients and prospects.
3. Investment analyses and recommendations should clearly differentiate facts from opinions.

Guidance

Proper communication with clients is critical to provide quality financial services. Distinguish between opinions and facts and always include the basic characteristics of the security being analyzed in a research report.

Members must illustrate to clients and prospects the investment decision-making process utilized. The suitability of each investment is important in the context of the entire portfolio.

All means of communication are included here, not just research reports.

Recommended Procedures for Compliance

Selection of relevant factors in a report can be a judgment call. Be sure to maintain records, and be able to supply additional information if it is requested by the client or other users of the report.

V(C).   Record Retention. Maintain all records supporting analysis, recommendations, actions, and all other investment-related communications with clients and prospects.

Guidance

Members must maintain research records that support the reasons for the analyst's conclusions and any investment actions taken. Such records are the property of the firm. If no other regulatory standards are in place, CFA Institute recommends at least a 7-year holding period.

Recommended Procedures for Compliance

This record-keeping requirement is generally the firm's responsibility.

VI.   Conflicts of Interest

VI(A).   Disclosure of Conflicts. Members and Candidates must make full and fair disclosure of all matters which may impair their independence or objectivity or interfere with their duties to employer, clients, and prospects. Disclosures must be prominent, in plain language, and effectively communicate the information.

Guidance—Disclosure to Clients

The requirement allows clients and prospects to judge motives and potential biases for themselves. Disclosure of broker/dealer market-making activities would be included here. Board service is another area of potential conflict. The most common conflict that requires disclosure is actual ownership of stock in companies the member recommends or clients hold.

©2008 Kaplan Schweser

Guidance—Disclosure of Conflicts to Employers

Members must promptly report potential conflicts and give the employer enough information to judge the impact of the conflict. Take reasonable steps to avoid conflicts.

Recommended Procedures of Compliance

Disclose any special compensation arrangements, bonus programs, commissions, and incentives.

VI(B). Priority of Transactions. Investment transactions for clients and employers must have priority over those in which a Member or Candidate is a beneficial owner.

Guidance

Client transactions take priority over personal transactions and over transactions made on behalf of the member's firm. Personal transactions include situations where the member is a "beneficial owner." Personal transactions may be undertaken only after clients and the member's employer have had an adequate opportunity to act on a recommendation. Note that family-member accounts that are client accounts should be treated just like any client account; they should not be disadvantaged.

Recommended Procedures for Compliance

All firms should have in place basic procedures that address conflicts created by personal investing. The following areas should be included:

- Limited participation in equity IPOs. Members can avoid these conflicts by not participating in IPOs.
- Restrictions on private placements. Strict limits should be placed on employee acquisition of these securities and proper supervisory procedures should be in place.
- Establish blackout/restricted periods. Employees involved in investment decision making should have blackout periods prior to trading for clients—no "front running." The size of the firm and the type of security should help dictate how severe the blackout requirement should be.
- Reporting requirements. Supervisors should establish reporting procedures, including duplicate trade confirmations, disclosure of personal holdings/ beneficial ownership positions, and pre-clearance procedures.
- Disclosure of policies. When requested, members must fully disclose to investors their firm's personal trading policies.

VI(C). Referral Fees. Members and Candidates must disclose to their employers, clients, and prospects any compensation consideration or benefit received by, or paid to, others for recommendations of products and services.

Guidance

Members must inform employers, clients, and prospects of any benefit received for referrals of customers and clients, allowing them to evaluate the full cost of the service as well as any potential partiality.

VII. Responsibilities as a CFA Institute Member or CFA Candidate

VII(A). Conduct as Members and Candidates in the CFA Program. Members and Candidates must not engage in conduct that compromises the reputation or integrity of CFA Institute or the CFA designation or the integrity, validity, or security of the CFA exams.

Members must not engage in any activity that undermines the integrity of the CFA charter. This Standard applies to conduct which includes:

- Cheating on the CFA exam or any exam.
- Not following rules and policies of the CFA program.
- Giving confidential information on the CFA program to anyone.
- Improperly using the designation for personal gain.
- Misrepresenting information on the Professional Conduct Statement (PCS) or the CFA Institute Professional Development Program.

Members and candidates are not precluded from expressing their opinions regarding the exam program or CFA Institute.

VII(B). Reference to CFA Institute, the CFA designation, and the CFA Program. Members and Candidates must not misrepresent or exaggerate the meaning or implications of membership in CFA Institute, holding the CFA designation, or candidacy in the program.

Guidance

Members must not make promotional promises or guarantees tied to the CFA designation. Do not:

- Over-promise individual competence.
- Over-promise investment results in the future.

Guidance—CFA Institute Membership

Members must sign PCS annually and pay CFA Institute membership dues annually. If they fail to do this, they are no longer active members.

Guidance—Using the CFA Designation

Do not misrepresent or exaggerate the meaning of the designation.

Guidance—Referencing Candidacy in the CFA Program

There is no partial designation. It is acceptable to state that a Candidate successfully completed the program in three years, if in fact they did, but claiming superior ability because of this is not permitted.

Guidance—Proper Usage of the CFA Marks

The Chartered Financial Analyst and CFA marks must always be used either after a charterholder's name or as adjectives, but not as nouns.

Recommended Procedures for Compliance

Make sure that members' and candidates' firms are aware of the proper references to a member's CFA designation or candidacy.

STUDY SESSION 2 – ETHICAL AND PROFESSIONAL STANDARDS

ETHICS IN PRACTICE
Cross-Reference to CFA Institute Assigned Reading #3

ETHICAL RESPONSIBILITIES

The Code of Ethics identifies six provisions that promote ethical standards among individuals in the investment profession.

1. The first provision focuses on the actions of investment professionals by stating that they should act with integrity, competence, diligence, and respect. They should also convey their actions in an ethical manner to their clients, potential clients, and employers.

2. The second provision calls for investment professionals to place personal interests below the interest of clients and the integrity of the investment profession.

---

3. The third provision asks investment professionals to act with care and maintain independent judgment when applying investment analysis, recommendations, and actions. Analysts must use independent judgment when engaging in activities that will ultimately affect client interests.

4. The fourth provision relates to the practice of the analyst and the practice of others within the investment profession. The analyst should not only act in an ethical manner, but should also promote ethical actions to others within the profession.

5. The fifth provision asks investment professionals to contribute to well functioning markets by respecting the applicable rules and promoting those rules to others.

6. The sixth provision indicates that investment professionals should strive to maintain and improve their professional competence, as well as the competence of others within the investment profession.

STANDARDS OF PROFESSIONAL CONDUCT

Standard I: Professionalism

This Standard covers the following four topics: knowledge of the law, independence and objectivity, misrepresentation, and misconduct.

Standard I(A) Knowledge of the Law

- Know the law, and when confronted with differences between the applicable law or regulation and the Code and Standards, honor the stricter of the two.
- Do not participate/assist in violations. If needed, dissociate.
- In cases of observed violations, report it to a supervisor and compliance officer, if necessary. Extreme cases may require resignation and/or reporting the violation to the proper authorities.

Standard I(B) Independence and Objectivity

- The client's best interest always comes first. Maintaining independence and objectivity is paramount. Do not accept any consideration which may interfere with this. Use judgment concerning what is a "threshold" of improper consideration.
- This Standard applies not only to investment managers, but to plan sponsors, investment consultants, investment bankers, and dealmakers.

Standard I(C) Misrepresentation

- An analyst has a duty of competence and diligence to make sure that her analysis is properly documented and supported. There should be no guarantees or assurances. An accurate description of facts is permitted.

- Plagiarism is prohibited. Give credit and cite the sources of ideas, facts, and opinions taken from others.
- Do not misrepresent your own or your firm's experience or qualifications.

Standard I(D) Misconduct

- Investment professionals must not do anything that reflects poorly on their professional reputation, integrity, or competence.
- Trust must not be violated.

Standard II: Integrity of Capital Markets

Standard II(A) Material Non-Public Information

- Defined as "information that could affect an investment's value." Covered persons must not act or cause others to act on material, nonpublic information.
- To gain unfair profits is wrong, and it erodes confidence in the financial markets.
- Combining non-material, nonpublic information routinely from inside sources with material public information can form a mosaic and is an acceptable basis for trading.
- If accidentally encountering material non-public information, encourage the public release of the information from the subject firm.

Standard II(B) Market Manipulation

- This Standard prohibits any practices that inflate or misstate trading volume or mislead market participants.
- Deceptive practices interfere with fair/efficient financial markets.

Standard III: Duties to Clients

Part of the definition of a profession is dedication to a greater good
(i.e., performance in the best interests of clients rather than the practitioner).

Standard III(A) Loyalty, Prudence, and Care

- Always act with the client's best interest in mind, even if the employer is disadvantaged. There is a duty of loyalty to clients, and investment recommendations and actions must be sound.
- Fiduciary responsibility is needed. Client loyalty also extends to mutual fund managers.

Standard III(B) Fair Dealing

- There can be no special treatment for favored clients.
- It is acceptable to offer premium services as long as the availability, nature, and cost of these services are fully disclosed.
- Premium services should benefit those who utilize them but cannot unfairly disadvantage any other investor classes.

Standard III(C) Suitability

- Before giving any investment advice or taking investment action, inquire about the client's investment experience and objectives and constraints.
- Judge investments in the context of the total portfolio. The importance of diversification must be stressed. If a client suggests imprudent investment actions, the investment advisor must advise the client in plain language.

Standard III(D) Performance Presentation

Performance results must be presented fairly, accurately, and completely. Adherence to GIPS is strongly encouraged.

Standard III(E) Preservation of Confidentiality

All information concerning past, present, or prospective clients must be kept confidential unless it concerns illegal activities.

Standard IV: Duties to Employers

Standard IV(A) Loyalty

- Covered persons must always act for the benefit of their employer.
- If an employee chooses to join another firm, the employee cannot remove or copy the firm's property and represent it as his own. Furthermore, the employee cannot take client lists, software, files, et cetera, with the intent of competing with the former employer.

Standard IV(B) Additional Compensation Arrangements

Covered individuals should not accept any form of additional compensation that competes with the employer's interest and may produce a conflict. Written consent must be obtained from all parties involved.

Standard IV(C) Responsibilities of Supervisors

- A covered person who is a supervisor must make reasonable efforts to detect and prevent violations of laws and regulations.
- Adequate training and continuing education of employees subject to supervision is crucial.
- Advise subordinates of the provisions of the Code and Standards.
- Delegation of work responsibilities does not relieve the supervisor of his or her responsibilities.

Standard V: Investment Analysis, Recommendations, and Actions

Standard V(A) Diligence and Reasonable Basis

- Covered persons must strive to protect their independent professional judgment and must be diligent and thorough in their work.

- Investment conclusions must be supported by facts, and analysts should make reasonable inquiries regarding reliability of sources.

Standard V(B) Communication With Clients and Prospective Clients

It is important that any communication with a client regarding investment decisions is not biased or misleading in any way and that all decisions are based upon the client's interests. The analyst should ascertain that all relevant information is included.

- Part 1: Covered persons must explain their investment decision-making process.
- Part 2: Covered persons must include relevant factors in their analyses, recommendations, or investment actions. The "communication" should include the reasonable and adequate basis for the conclusion reached. When deciding what topics to cover, consider the audience.
- Part 3: Covered persons must separate fact from opinion in presenting analysis and recommendations.

Standard V(C) Record Retention

Records must be retained to support analyses and recommendations.

Standard VI: Conflicts of Interest

Conflicts of interest, perceived or real, can undermine clients' trust in investment professionals and the entire investment profession.

Standard VI(A) Disclosure of Conflicts

- Covered persons must disclose any matters that would adversely affect their independence and objectivity.
- Disclosures must be in clearly understood, plain language.

Standard VI(B) Priority of Transactions

Transactions for clients and employers always come before the investment professional's transactions.

Standard VI(C) Referral Fees

Compensation received by covered persons as a result of referring or recommending a product or service must be disclosed.

Standard VII: Responsibilities as a CFA Institute Member or CFA Candidate

Standard VII(A) Conduct as Members and Candidates in the CFA Program

Covered persons may not do anything to compromise the reputation/integrity of CFA Institute, the designation, or the CFA exam.

Standard VII(B) Reference to CFA Institute, the CFA Designation, and the CFA Program

Covered individuals are barred from misrepresenting or exaggerating the CFA designation and program.

INTERPRETING THE CODE AND STANDARDS

Following the Code and Standards and interpreting and applying them to real situations often involves real investments, strategies, and several different, perhaps competing, parties at interest. Real, ethical wisdom may be needed. Practice is needed to determine the principles/values at stake, come up with alternatives, and decide a course of action. Here are a few helpful guidelines:

1. Is the course of action consistent with the intent of the Code and Standards?

2. Would the client agree that this action is the best alternative?

3. Once the circumstances of the situation are disclosed, will the firm's reputation for fair dealing be enhanced or compromised?

4. Is the decision consistent with what would be expected from a leader?

VIOLATIONS AND CORRECTIVE ACTIONS

The assigned article concludes with several cases designed to demonstrate how to recognize violations of the Code and Standards and determine what actions are necessary to correct the violations. It is instructive to review the cases in order to develop your ability to spot violations and suggest corrective measures.

Argent Capital Management

Case Facts

Francoise Vandezande, CFA, senior relationship manager in Argent's New York office, must meet with a defined benefit pension client whose portfolio has lost value over the last quarter due to foreign currency transactions that may have violated portfolio restrictions. She first calls the client's portfolio manager, Aidan McNamara, CFA, who explains that the Global Markets group manipulated the Investment Council into taking a large bet on the euro-yen exchange rate (long euro/short yen) that turned out to be wrong and negatively affected all portfolios. During the call McNamara was unable to say if the strategy was consistent with his client's investment policy statement (IPS).

Vandezande reviews the client's IPS and determines that:

- The portfolio benchmark is the MSCI EAFE® Index.
- Currency risk may be managed, but no currency speculation is allowed. Futures and forwards hedges are limited to 100% of underlying exposure.
- The portfolio must be managed according to original mandate. No extreme positions that would be inconsistent with the original mandate are allowed.

Case Discussion

The portfolio manager is unfamiliar with the IPS, which is a violation of Standard III(C.1.b) related to suitability. The benchmark does not hold short currency positions, and the IPS prohibits speculation. McNamara has not respected the constraints of the client's IPS.

Suggested Actions

Vandezande should:

- Give the client a thorough explanation of the events, investment decision-making process, and rationale for recommending the unusual foreign exchange position.
- Explain how the situation will not be repeated in the future.

Senior management should:

- Modify the investment decision process to exclude certain portfolios.
- Re-educate portfolio managers on the importance of complying with the IPS.
- Periodically audit portfolios for compliance with client guidelines.

River City Pension Fund

Case Facts

Jack Aldred, CFA, is Chief Investment Officer of the River City Pension Fund. He must decide what to do about Northwest Capital Advisors, a small-cap value equity manager used by the pension fund.

Roger Gray, CFA, is Northwest's CEO. Northwest employees have contributed large amounts to local election campaigns (including Aldred's manager, the city

Treasurer), a practice which, a few years ago, was made illegal for corporate officers doing business with the municipality.

Northwest's always mediocre performance has become substantially worse. Aldred observes that the returns calculated by Northwest do not match the returns calculated by the custodian bank (Northwest's figures are higher) and that Northwest has strayed from its small-cap value mandate (value being an out-of-favor style) to include growth stocks.

Aldred was also concerned that one of Northwest's three original principals left the firm. Gray has personally assumed responsibility for River City's pension plan. Aldred expressed his concerns to his manager and stated that he felt action was necessary. He further stated that he had some suggestions as to how to proceed but would do whatever the manager wished.

Case Discussion

Jack Aldred, CFA: Aldred may have violated Standard III(A) – Loyalty, Prudence, and Care by suggesting that he would do whatever the manager wants (must fulfill fiduciary duty and act for pension beneficiaries' benefit). He may also have violated Code and Standard I(B) – Independence and Objectivity by compromising his independent judgment.

Roger Gray, CFA: Gray may have violated Standard III(D) – Performance Presentation for not presenting fair, accurate, and complete performance. Gray may have violated Standard III(C.2) related to suitability by not taking action consistent with the portfolio mandate. He may also have violated Standard I(A) – Knowledge of the Law (if he himself made illegal campaign contributions) and Standard IV(C) – Responsibilities of Supervisors. Gray may have also misstated asset values in violation of Standard III(D).

Suggested Actions

Jack Aldred, CFA, should:

- Decide which performance figures to use.
- Assess the portfolio's compliance with its mandate.
- Evaluate the impact of the principal's departure on future results.

Roger Gray, CFA, should:

- Review pricing sources and methods to assess their fairness and accuracy.
- Ensure portfolio holdings are consistent with the portfolio mandate.
- Stop the illegal campaign contributions from employees and/or himself.

Macroeconomic Asset Management

Case Facts

Alice Chapman, CFA, Director of Marketing for Macroeconomic Asset Management (MAM) is reviewing a letter from Arlington Verification Service stating that Arlington cannot issue a verification report for MAM since the review of policies, processes, sample portfolios, and composites revealed the following:

- Poor quality or missing documentation.
- Fee-paying discretionary portfolios excluded from composites.
- Inconsistent implementation of policies on asset valuation and external cash flows.
- Incomplete performance presentations.

Chapman considers continuing to claim compliance while challenging the verifier's report.

Case Discussion

Macroeconomic Asset Management claims compliance with GIPS as a firm, but Chapman can determine whether a compliance claim is true when deciding to communicate such information to clients and prospects. She may not be able to withdraw a compliance claim but can recommend to senior management that the claim be removed. If the verifier is correct, Chapman would violate Standard I(A) – Knowledge of the Law by helping the firm make a false claim and would also violate Standard I(C) – Misrepresentation. Standard III(D) – Performance Presentation doesn't require compliance with GIPS but does require that Chapman not convey performance information to potential clients without determining that the information is a fair, accurate, and complete representation of MAM's performance. Chapman is aware of the significant shortcomings of MAM's performance presentation.

Suggested Actions

Alice Chapman should:

- Determine whether Arlington Verification Service's report is correct.
- Not make statements claiming compliance with GIPS unless the firm meets all requirements.
- Make a reasonable effort to ensure performance presentations are fair, accurate, and complete.

Bob Ehrlich

Case Facts

Bob Ehrlich, a performance analyst for a custodial bank's U.K. division, went to a lunch meeting for investment professionals. While at the luncheon, Ehrlich met Peter Neustadt who suggested they meet later at a pub. At the pub, Neustadt explained that his small firm has many contacts and a promising future but lacks technological support. Neustadt suggests that Ehrlich work for him as a part-time consultant, since he has analytical talent and access to information. Neustadt explains that his business represents newly created investment management firms with portfolio management and trading experience but no marketing or performance analytics skills. Neustadt states that he can put together the necessary marketing packages but needs performance data (benchmark returns, attributions, style analyses, etc.) that Ehrlich and his firm are good at producing.

Case Discussion

Neustadt's proposal is unacceptable, since it requires the use of assets belonging to Ehrlich's employer (for Ehrlich's personal benefit). If Ehrlich were to use his employer's assets for personal benefit without authorization, he would violate Standard I(D) – Misconduct and Standard IV(A) – Loyalty (to employer) by violating his employer's trust for personal gain and misusing the employer's physical and intellectual property. He also risks divulging confidential information, which could compromise his employer's financial position and damage his employer's reputation. Distributing research purchased by his employer may violate legal restrictions and allow Neustadt to represent the data or research as his own.

Standard IV(B) – Additional Compensation Arrangements requires members and candidates to obtain their employer's consent before accepting additional compensation. To avoid violating the Standard, Ehrlich must disclose Neustadt's proposal in full, including the use of the employer's resources.

Standard VI(A) – Disclosure of Conflicts requires Ehrlich to disclose the proposed arrangement to his employer, since it can reasonably be expected to interfere with his duties to his employer, such as protecting the firm's intellectual property. In addition, the arrangement with Neustadt would compete directly with the services of Ehrlich's firm.

Suggested Actions

Ehrlich should not accept Neustadt's proposal.

Alex Kaye

Case Facts

Alex Kaye, CFA, heads the performance measurement advisory services department for a consulting firm. Kaye has promoted Derek Nelson (who has nine month's verification analysis experience) to project manager. With clients getting impatient, Kaye asked four team leaders to submit status reports and shortened time frames for completion.

Nelson responded with an email to Kaye. The email stated that before he could revise the timeline for Argent Asset Management, he needed guidance on two issues:

1. Documentation for two-thirds of the accounts is not available. The available one-third meet the discretionary status, and Argent maintains that the remaining two-thirds do as well. Nelson is unsure whether to wait for the documents, use what is available, or take Argent's word.

2. Treatment of several large external cash flows was inconsistent with stated policy for specific composites. These instances would have produced higher or lower composite returns if the cash flows were treated properly. Nelson wants to know if he can assume the errors are offsetting, making the composite returns reasonably correct.

Case Discussion

The Code requires Kaye and Nelson to act with competence and diligence, exercise reasonable care and independent judgment in their professional activities, and maintain and improve their professional competence. Standard I(A) – Knowledge of the Law requires Kaye and Nelson to understand and comply with applicable laws, rules, and regulations governing their professional activities. In this case, GIPS requirements, recommendations, and verification procedures would be applicable regulation. Two GIPS standards are applicable:

1. Verifiers must be sure that all discretionary-fee-based portfolios are included in a composite and that the discretion distinction is applied consistently over time.

2. Verifiers must sample from the entire list (not just a sub-sample) of discretionary portfolios to determine the consistency of discretionary/ non-discretionary classification as evidenced by the account agreement and the firm's guidelines.

Poor planning or intentional deception may be the reason Argent's account documents are unavailable, and taking Argent's word doesn't fulfill the duty to exercise care and independent judgment. In addition, GIPS indicate a larger sample is warranted or additional verification procedures are needed in light of the inconsistent external cash flow treatment.

Standard III(A) – Loyalty, Prudence, and Care requires Kaye and Nelson to act for the benefit of their clients. Kaye is potentially telling employees to shortcut their verification in the interest of time, placing his and his employer's interests ahead of the clients' interests.

Standard IV(C) – Responsibilities of Supervisors requires Kaye to take reasonable measures to detect violations of laws, rules, regulations, and the Code and Standards. Kaye must prevent Nelson from violating the Code and Standards as well as GIPS.

Suggested Actions

Alex Kaye should:

- Stop taking on new clients until capacity warrants it.
- Make sure the staff is properly trained in GIPS verification procedures.
- Inform the staff that every assignment must receive due care.
- Give Nelson appropriate guidance to the issues raised in his e-mail.

ASSET MANAGER CODE OF PROFESSIONAL CONDUCT

There are six components to the (voluntary) Asset Manager Code of Professional Conduct (the "Code"): (1) Loyalty to Clients, (2) Investment Process and Actions, (3) Trading, (4) Compliance and Support, (5) Performance and Valuation, and (6) Disclosures.[3] Related to these six components are ethical responsibilities:

- Always act ethically and professionally.
- Act in the best interest of the client.
- Act in an objective and independent manner.
- Perform actions using skill, competence, and diligence.
- Communicate accurately with clients on a regular basis.
- Comply with all legal and regulatory requirements.

PREVENTING VIOLATIONS

Loyalty to clients deals with always putting the client's interests before your own, maintaining the confidentiality of client information, and not engaging in any business relationship or accepting gifts from others that could affect your judgment and objectivity. Appropriate procedures include:

- Designing salary arrangements that align the interests of the client with those of the manager without the manager taking undue risks that would conflict with the client's interests.

---

3. CFA Institute. Asset Manager Code of Professional Conduct, including Appendix A. CFA Institute, Centre for Financial Market Integrity, 2005.

- Creating a procedure that delineates how confidential client information should be collected, utilized, and stored. The confidential information policy does not preclude disseminating necessary information to legal authorities in the event of an investigation.
- Creating an anti-money-laundering policy to detect and help prevent firms from being used for money laundering or other illegal activities.
- Determining what constitutes a token gift and allowing only token gifts from outside business relationships as to limit the influence of these individuals over the asset manager. Cash should never be accepted, and employees should always notify their supervisor in writing when they accept any gifts.

Investment process and actions deals with being competent and taking reasonable action that would not cause any harm to the client while still balancing the client's risk and return objectives:

- Never engage in market manipulation of security prices.
- Deal fairly with all clients when disseminating information, making recommendations, and placing trades as to not favor or disadvantage one client over another.
- Thoroughly investigate and research different investment options to have a reasonable basis for a recommendation.

Appropriate procedures include having different levels of service and products available to all clients as long as they are fully disclosed. The manager must analyze and understand the different investment options available and can also rely on third party research as long as the manager has verified that this research is correct. When using complex derivative products, the manager should conduct stress testing to determine how the investment will react under different scenarios.

Compliance and support deals with:

- Ensuring compliance with the Code and legal and regulatory requirements and appointing a compliance officer.
- Ensuring that portfolio information disseminated to clients is accurate and complete and reviewed by an independent third party.
- Appropriately maintaining records.
- Employing qualified staff along with adequate resources.
- Instituting a contingency plan in the event of a natural disaster.

Procedures include having documentation that ensures adherence to the Code, along with internal controls and self assessment mechanisms. A compliance officer who reports directly to the CEO or board of directors and who is responsible for making sure compliance procedures are in place and followed should be designated. The compliance officer is also responsible for employee training related to compliance procedures and policies and on-going self evaluations. They should also review employee trading practices to ensure client trades are placed before employee trades. The compliance officer should also provide a copy of the Code to all employees and document that the employees have read and understand the Code.

Companies should develop contingency plans, also called disaster-recovery planning or business-continuity planning, in the event of a disruption in normal business operations such as a power outage, fire, natural disaster, or acts of terrorism.

Disclosures

Suggested disclosures deal with many issues related to disseminating pertinent information to the client. Some of these disclosures are:

- Communicate with the client on a timely basis in an understandable manner that does not misrepresent any information.
- Disclose to the client any information she would need to know to be able to make an informed decision regarding the investment manager, the organization, investment options, or the investment process.
- Disclose potential conflicts of interest such as soft or bundled commissions, referral fees, sales incentive programs, brokerage arrangements, and stocks held by clients that are also held by firm employees.
- Any regulatory disciplinary actions taken against the manager or his organization.
- The investment decision-making process and strategies, including inherent risks associated with a particular strategy or investment.
- Returns both gross and net of fees, the fee schedule, a projection of fees charged, and make available an itemized list of actual costs and fees.
- A discussion of any soft or bundled commissions, how those commissions are being spent, and the benefits to the client.
- Performance of the client's account at least quarterly and within 30 days of the end of the quarter.
- The method used to determine the value of the client's assets.
- Proxy voting policies of the manager.
- How shares of stock are allocated.
- The results of any audits performed on the client's account or fund.

Behavioral Finance

Topic Weight on Exam	5% or less
Study Notes Reference	Book 1, Pages 159–205
Video CD Reference	CD 2
Audio CD Reference	CD 4

Look for behavioral finance to show up in the morning session as part of a case. You also might see it in an afternoon item set.

Heuristic-Driven Bias: The First Theme; Frame Dependence: The Second Theme; Inefficient Markets: The Third Theme
Cross-Reference to CFA Institute Assigned Readings #7, 8, & 9

A **heuristic learning process** is one in which people develop investment decision making rules through experiment, trial and error, or personal experience. Rather than research financial statements and other relevant data, individuals form investment rules and make investments using information that is most prominent in the media or otherwise most readily *available*.

Representativeness is a heuristic process by which investors base expectations upon past experience, applying stereotypes. For example, investors might feel that all firms whose managements espouse environmental awareness are "good" firms (i.e., good investments). Another example is interpreting all good earnings announcements as predictors of good future performance, without determining whether the performance will continue for the individual firm making the announcement. Any time an investor bases expectations on some past or current characteristic or measure, the individual is applying an "if-then" heuristic. That is, *if* this has happened, *then* that will happen.

Overconfidence means that people tend to place too much confidence in their ability to predict. They tend to systematically underestimate the risk (standard deviation) of the returns on the stock. Overconfidence can lead to *surprises*. Since investors continually underestimate the range of possible returns, there is a higher than normal probability of a return outside the confidence interval (i.e., a surprise).

Anchoring refers to the inability to fully incorporate (adjust) the impact of new information on projections (i.e., conservatism). Like overconfidence, anchoring can

---

lead to surprises. In this instance, however, the surprises tend to be biased in the direction of the announcement.

Aversion to ambiguity can be loosely described as "fear of the unknown." Following a momentum strategy, for example, investors buy in an up-trending market and sell in a down-trending market. In an up-trending market, investors might see the odds as greater than 50% that prices will continue moving up. In a down-trending market they might see the odds as greater than 50% that the market will continue down. A non-trending market, however, presents individual with ambiguity. They might not be able to base their expected odds on anything, so they might shy away or at least leave the stock picking to the experts.

FRAME DEPENDENCE

Frame dependence implies that individuals make decisions and take actions according to the framework within which information is received (i.e., the media) or the individual's circumstances at the time (i.e., emotional state). If investors acted with frame *independence*, they would make purely economic decisions, and the form within which information is received and the individual's current circumstances would have no effect on their decision-making. They would base each decision purely on its expected merits.

Loss aversion refers to the individual's reluctance to accept a loss. A stock may be down considerably from its purchase price, but the investor holds on to it hoping that it will recover. You can relate this to the gambler who keeps throwing the dice hoping to break even. Loss aversion can also lead to *risk-seeking behavior*.

Self-control (i.e., controlling one's emotions) is related to frame dependence. Frame dependence implies that individuals' reactions to information are affected by the framework within which the information is received. And the framework is the media carrying the information as well as the individual's circumstances when the information is received.

For example, consider stage of life and dividends. A younger, affluent investor may totally avoid high dividend paying stocks because of the related tax consequences and the effect on the overall portfolio return. A retired investor, however, might use dividends as a self-imposed *control mechanism* to avoid spending the capital in his retirement account.

In an investment framework, regret is the feeling (in hindsight) associated with making a bad decision. **Regret minimization** can lead to two common situations. First, to avoid the possibility of feeling regret, investors can tend to stay in comfortable investments, such as stocks and bonds (i.e., regret minimization can lead to lack of variety in investments). Next, rather than sell profitable investments, investors may tend to use their cash flows, such as interest payments and dividends, for living expenses.

Money illusion refers to the way individuals react to *inflation* and its impact on investment performance. People tend to think in terms of nominal amounts. That is, they look at the overall investment return without regard for the level of inflation and the resulting real return. This leads to positive reactions to high returns no matter what the level of inflation and resulting real return. Of course, the opposite is also true. Investors tend to react negatively to low returns, even if inflation is more or less nonexistent.

Inefficient Markets

Market efficiency assumes all investors have the same information, interpret it the same, and make the same forecasts. This would imply that all assets are priced efficiently (i.e., there is no bias in stock prices). *Representativeness, anchoring-and-adjustment, frame dependence,* and *overconfidence*, however, can all lead to inefficiently priced stocks.

The **representativeness** heuristic can lead investors to make incorrect projections based upon *stereotypes*. Since investors' perceptions are based upon current or historical information rather than unbiased expectations, stocks can be temporarily mispriced. An example is assuming a stock will perform well in the future because the firm just unexpectedly announced good earnings over the last period. Assuming the good announcement implies good future performance (a winner), investors buy the stock and push its price up. Likewise, a bad earnings announcement (a loser) may be met with selling pressure, which drives the price down. The result is that overpriced "winners" will tend to underperform and underpriced "losers" will tend to outperform, as their prices return to their intrinsic values.

Conservatism. As discussed previously, conservatism refers to the inability of analysts to fully incorporate the impact of new information (e.g., earnings surprises) on their projections. The implication is that negative adjustments in price forecasts (e.g., from a lower-than-expected earnings announcement) tend to be followed by negative surprises (i.e., a further decline in price). Positive adjustments (e.g., from a higher-than-expected earnings announcement) tend to be followed by positive surprises (i.e., a further increase in price). These "patterns" in price performance imply a market inefficiency with an accompanying investment strategy: buy stocks which have experienced positive earnings surprises; sell (short) stocks which have experienced negative surprises.

Empirical tests have shown that these strategies out-perform the market and, in fact, the greater the earnings surprise, the greater the potential excess return. Behavioral finance attributes the excess returns to conservatism, while traditional finance explains the results by saying stocks with positive earnings surprises are riskier and, thus, should earn a greater return.

Frame dependence refers to investors' tendency to change (frame) their risk tolerance according to the direction of the market. Loss aversion predicts investors will be hesitant to enter the market. This applies when the market is flat or falling.

When the market is in an upward trend, investors' loss aversion falls and they jump in, further pushing prices up.

There are two important implications of **overconfidence** and the resulting failure to recognize the true risk of an investment. First, investors tend to make unjustified "bets." Second, investors tend to trade more frequently than can be justified by the information.

Portfolios, Pyramids, Emotions, and Biases and the Folly of Forecasting: Ignore All Economists, Strategists, and Analysts

Cross-Reference to CFA Institute Assigned Readings #10 & 12

Hope, Fear, and Risk Tolerance

Fear makes people focus on the downside and strive for *security*. Hope, the focus on *potential gains*, is positive and drives *aspirations* (i.e., the investor's desire for wealth and material gains). A natural by-product of these emotions is that they drive investors' tolerance for risk, which in turn affects the way they structure their portfolios. Investors who are driven mostly by fear tend to focus on investment risk and are naturally more risk averse. Those who focus on hope tend to focus more on potential gains and are somewhat less risk averse. The relative trade off between fear and hope ultimately determines the investor's risk aversion and resulting allocation to risky versus secure investments.

Pyramids. Rather than approach portfolio construction from a diversification perspective, varying perceptions of risk and segmentation of goals lead investors to structure their portfolios like pyramids, with secure investments on the bottom (i.e., the wide foundation of the pyramid). This bottom layer, which typically includes bonds and money market securities, is utilized to fund important goals, like the children's education. Once this first, secure layer is established, investors start adding layers to the pyramid, with each successive layer of the pyramid containing riskier investments than the previous layer and each layer dedicated to a different goal.

The pyramid structure can be viewed (and further rationalized) from another perspective by considering aspirations. Aspirations provide a minimum focus for the investor. For example, an investor's first aspiration may be for his children to go to college. Before considering any other goals, the investor will focus on at least meeting his children's college expenses. After this goal is securely reached (i.e., the first layer of the pyramid is constructed), the investor turns to meeting other, less critical goals and constructs another layer of the pyramid.

REGRET, SELF-ATTRIBUTION BIAS, AND FINANCIAL ADVISORS

Regret is a backward-looking behavioral characteristic based upon feelings associated with making a bad decision. Regret can influence investors' decisions to trade and even the types of investments they make. Regret can even make investors stay out of certain investments, which can lead to concentrated (i.e., undiversified) portfolios.

By following the advice of a financial advisor, an investor can shift blame and avoid the feeling of regret associated with making bad investment decisions. Shefrin[1] refers to this as being long a *psychological call option*. The investor can exercise the call and take credit for good investments or not exercise the call and let the advisor take the blame for poor investments. This behavioral characteristic is referred to as *self-attribution bias*; attributing good investments to skill while blaming others (e.g., financial advisors) or totally unforeseen events (e.g., just plain bad luck) for negative outcomes.

Individuals, possibly in a subconscious attempt to avoid *cognitive dissonance*, also tend to remember only the good investments they have made. For example, when asked about their investment track record, most individuals will remember, or at least emphasize, the periods during which they beat the market. This is known as *hindsight bias*, and it is common both to professionals and individuals.

OPTIMISM AND OVERCONFIDENCE

Optimism is a well documented trait among (particularly young) individuals who feel the odds of something bad occurring in their lives are very low or even non-existent. Or they simply do not even entertain the idea that something could go wrong. As evidence Shefrin[2] offers data suggesting that young adults are far more likely to become disabled than they are of dying, yet the vast majority does not carry disability insurance. This common psychological trait leads to *overconfidence* in an investment setting.

Increased Trading

Overconfidence in an investment setting is the belief that you can interpret information better than the average investor and thus select superior investments. Overconfidence often leads to excessive trading and undiversified portfolios. Empirical studies have shown that the increase in return attributed to selecting superior investments and self-trading is more than outweighed by the increased costs. The result is a net return less than that of an indexed portfolio.

---

1   Hersh Shefrin, *Portfolios, Pyramids, Emotions, and Biases,* Reading 10, 2008 Level 3 Curriculum, CFA Institute.

2   Ibid.

Portfolio Structure

1/n diversification is also known as *naïve diversification*. Employees put equal amounts into each of the alternative funds provided in their defined contribution retirement fund. The employer must be sure to provide an adequate number of alternatives for employees using 1/n diversification to achieve an acceptable level of diversification.

Familiarity. Employers must be cognizant of their employees' tendency to invest in securities with which they are familiar. If allowed, employees would typically invest heavily in the sponsor firm's stocks, placing the employee in a particularly risky position. Familiarity also leads to *home bias*.

OVERCONFIDENCE IN FORECASTERS

The primary factor leading to overconfidence in professionals is *knowledge* (education or experience) which leads them to think they know more than they do and can produce better forecasts than they do. They feel their forecasts are based upon skill (i.e., an *illusion of knowledge*), so when their forecasts are inaccurate the blame is usually placed on some outside factor. In addition, all individuals, not just professionals, seem to suffer from a form of selective recall. When asked how well they performed over a given period, for example, analysts tend to consistently overstate their performance (i.e., only recall where they performed well).

FORECASTER DEFENSE MECHANISMS

There are five common ego defense mechanisms (excuses) used by analysts to justify inaccurate forecasts:

1. The *"if-only"* defense.

2. The *"ceteris-paribus"* defense.

3. The *"almost right"* defense.

4. The *"it hasn't happened yet"* defense.

5. The *"single predictor"* defense.

WHY ARE FORECASTS USED?

A driving force with most investors is the desire for more and better information. Even faced with typically poor forecasts, investors want to be able to base investment decisions on some perceived expert's forecast. This is a form of *anchoring*. In this case, anchoring refers to the (subconscious) need to grab onto anything when faced with uncertainty. Investors have a psychological need to have some sort of justification for their decisions.

INVESTMENT DECISION MAKING IN DEFINED CONTRIBUTION PENSION PLANS

Cross-Reference to CFA Institute Assigned Reading #11

In recent times, there has been a significant shift away from *defined benefit* pension plans (DB) to *defined contribution* pension plans (DC). In a DB plan, the employer promises to deliver retirement benefits to the retired worker, based upon some formula concerning years of employment and level of wages. The employer faces all the risk of sufficiently funding and investing plan assets to meet retirement liabilities. In a DC plan, in contrast, the employer only promises to make contributions to the employee's pension plan and provide sufficient investment education and alternatives. The employee in the DC plan faces the challenge of allocating assets appropriately to fund their own retirement (i.e., they face the investment risk).

In a defined contribution pension plan, the plan sponsor (i.e., the employer) is obligated to make promised contributions to employees' retirement funds and provide a list of eligible investment alternatives (i.e., mutual funds). Plan participants (i.e., the employees) must decide how much to deposit each period as well as how to allocate their funds among the mutual funds. Unfortunately, plan participants often exhibit behavioral traits such as *limited knowledge, bounded rationality, bounded self-control,* and *bounded self-interest.*

Status quo bias refers to DC plan participants' tendency to make an original allocation and not change it. Also, participants can be overwhelmed by the number of alternative fund choices, particularly as the number increases. The result is that, without being forced to regularly evaluate their allocation, investors tend toward a buy-and-hold (do nothing) strategy.

Myopic loss aversion refers to investors' focus on short-term performance and their aversion to losses. When they are shown short-term (i.e., annual) performance data for stocks and bonds, the short-term variability of equity returns increases their risk aversion and they allocate more heavily to fixed income. The resulting portfolio allocation exposes them to less risk than they can tolerate given their long (e.g., retirement) time horizons. When they are shown long-term (e.g., 15- to 20-year) performance data and asked to determine a portfolio allocation, the higher average equity returns make them less risk averse and they allocate more heavily to equity.

The **endorsement effect** refers to the misconception by plan participants that, by providing a list of investment alternatives, the sponsor is implicitly endorsing them as good investments. This is particularly prevalent if and when the sponsor adds new alternatives.

Even without direct encouragement by the plan sponsor, employees tend to invest more in their company's stock than would be warranted from a diversification standpoint. Also, sponsors will sometimes offer stock ownership plans, and this act can be seen by participants as an *endorsement* of the stock as a good investment.

Another factor leading to over investment in the plan sponsor's stock is *familiarity*. Individual investors tend to invest in stocks with which they are comfortable (i.e., they are familiar with). Familiarity is sometimes bred by proximity. A local firm is often seen as a sound investment, even if investors know nothing of the firm's future prospects.

A Survey of Behavioral Finance
Cross-Reference to CFA Institute Assigned Reading #13

Fundamental Values

Behavioral finance indicates that security prices can deviate from their fundamental values due to irrational traders. A classic objection to this view suggests that rational traders will undo any mispricings caused by the actions of irrational investors.

The logic behind this objection deals with how securities are handled once they become mispriced. If irrational investors drive the price of a security below its fundamental value, then a buying opportunity will present itself and rational investors will conduct a pair trading arbitrage strategy. This strategy involves going long the security that is undervalued and taking a short position in a similar security. Behavioral finance argues, however, that exploiting mispricings in this manner may be too risky and costly for rational investors, and that the mispricing can persist.

No Free Lunch

If a market is performing rationally (i.e., efficiently), there should be no free lunches as all assets should be continuously priced at their true, intrinsic values.

In an inefficient market, behavioral concepts may push assets away from their intrinsic values, but the same factors generate uncertainty that the assets will ever reach their intrinsic values. The fact that in an inefficient market, prices can vary from intrinsic values and very slowly or even never return means that identifying an over- or under-priced asset is no guarantee of a free lunch.

In an efficient market, no free lunches implies that prices are right (and vice versa). In an inefficient market, however, no free lunches does NOT imply that prices are right.

IMPLEMENTATION COSTS AND RISKS

Fundamental and Noise Trader Risks

In a pair-trade, the portfolio manager tries to combine offsetting long and short positions in *perfect substitutes*. The two securities are affected by the same macro- and micro-economic factors, so their values always move together. Identifying over-priced and under-priced perfect substitutes, the manager shorts the over-priced security and purchases the under-priced security. As both securities return to their intrinsic (i.e., fundamental) values, the manager captures both alphas.

Unless the securities used in a pair trade are perfect substitutes, the manager faces **fundamental risk.** That is, if the two securities are not perfect substitutes, they are not sensitive to the same risk factors and they do not always move in the same direction or by the same amount.

Noise traders are (irrational) investors who base investment decisions on non-fundamental factors, including psychological factors and/or technical trading data. One reason arbitrageurs may see mispricing opportunities is that noise traders have grown averse to a security, and their aversion has caused the security's market price to fall below its fundamental value. Then, since noise traders do not act in predictable ways, they may grow even more averse to the security, and its price will fall even further, causing considerable losses for the arbitrageur in the short run.

If this is the case, the short-run hit taken by the arbitrageur could cause investors to pull their funds from the portfolio, causing the arbitrageur to sell at severely depressed prices. This demonstrates how noise trader risk differs from fundamental risk [i.e., the difference between an arbitrageur's estimate of fundamental value and market price can grow larger for reasons not necessarily associated with cash flow and discount rate (fundamental) assumptions].

Implementation costs are any costs, including commissions, that impair the ability of the manager to exploit perceived asset mispricings. Constraints on short-selling such as borrowing fees, insufficient supply of the borrowed asset, and legal constraints against short sales are additional costs. Finally, effort is required to determine the degree of mispricing. This effort requires investor time and resources that could be used for other activities.

Persistent Mispricing

Two general conditions allow the persistence of mispriced securities: (1) *risk-averse arbitrageurs* and (2) *systematic fundamental risk.*

Incorporating the presence of noise traders and implementation costs only exacerbates the limits to arbitrage opportunities. The reduction of profitable opportunities allows deviations from fundamental value (i.e., mispricing situations) to persist longer, and possibly to a greater degree, than would reasonably be expected.

ALPHA HUNTERS AND BETA GRAZERS

Cross-Reference to CFA Institute Assigned Reading #14

Investors who believe securities markets are efficient will pursue a passive strategy which typically tracks a particular index. These investors are sometimes called "beta grazers." Conversely, investors who believe inefficiencies exist will pursue an active strategy in search of alpha. Alpha, also referred to as active alpha, is achieved through trading in response to perceived market anomalies. These "alpha hunters" research anomalies that are persistent as well as occasional in nature.

Acute market inefficiencies are very transient in nature and relatively easily identified. They can be exploited using an arbitrage strategy, and any uncertainty can usually be hedged away.

Chronic market inefficiencies are less easily identified and are longer-term in nature. They are resistant to investor strategies that focus on identifying mispricings and their subsequent corrections. Despite being less discernible, a majority of investors (including hedge funds) concentrate their resources on finding chronic inefficiencies.

Chronic inefficiencies can be **structural** or **behavioral**. Examples of structural sources include frictions on trading, organizational barriers, and capital flow imbalances. Examples of behavioral sources are process versus outcome, herding behavior, rigid views, price target revisions, and correlating emotions with the market.

Process versus outcome. In this behavioral bias, investors overemphasize their recent performance and let it drive future investment decisions.

Herding (a.k.a. **convoy**) **behavior.** Investors may be influenced by the masses and as a result, will keep their investment decisions in line with the rest of their peer group.

Rigid views (a.k.a. **Bayesian Rigidity**). Investors who exhibit this behavioral bias hold onto their old views despite the presence of new information. These investors formulate goals and policies at a point in time and then focus on staying true to those original policies even when conditions change.

Price target revisions. After purchasing a security, an investor may set a price target (i.e., maximum expected price) for that security. When the security's price moves towards the target, the investor becomes overconfident in her investment abilities and may revise the original price target upwards and even purchase additional shares.

Correlating emotions with the market (a.k.a. "The Ebullience Cycle"). In a downward market, investors may be disinclined to evaluate their portfolio's performance. This will result in inaction as investors hold on to losers too long. In an upward market, the opposite occurs. Investors exhibit exuberance and become too active with their positions, resulting in investments that are too aggressive.

REBALANCING DECISIONS

Holders tend not to adjust their portfolio allocations with changes in equity values. They generally have little impact on market movements since they practice a true buy-and-hold strategy and don't trade when equity values (and their portfolio allocations) change.

Rebalancers have rigid portfolio allocations. Any deviation from the target allocation results in rebalancing back to the original weights. These actions tend to smooth market movements, because rebalancers buy as the market falls and sell as the market rises.

Valuators base their rebalancing decisions on whether the market is "cheap" or "rich." Depending on their views, they may act as contrarians (e.g., buy in a down trending market) or momentum players (e.g., sell in a down trending market). The impact on market movements will then also depend on their views. If they act as contrarians, they will tend to smooth market movements. If they act as momentum players, they will tend to further exacerbate market movements.

Shifters typically rebalance their portfolios in response to some non-market value related event. Any investor has the potential to become a shifter, although institutional investors are much less prone to do so.

REBALANCING IN AN EFFICIENT MARKET

Formulaic rebalancing involves setting an optimal asset allocation and rebalancing the portfolio back to the target weights when the portfolio deviates from its initial (policy) allocation. Those who advocate formulaic rebalancing argue that they are responding to efficient markets by buying securities at a cheaper price in a down market (i.e., when they are cheap) and selling securities in an up market (i.e., when they are rich). Notice, however, that formulaic rebalancers only rebalance back to the original allocation.

Rebalancing using judgmental flexibility can be conducted when a portfolio allocation is allowed to change somewhat with fluctuating market conditions. Institutional investors, however, normally are not allowed to use such flexibility in their decision making process since they are fixed to a predetermined policy allocation.

PRIVATE WEALTH MANAGEMENT

Topic Weight on Exam	Up to 30%
Study Notes Reference	Book 1, Pages 206–282
Video CD Reference	CDs 3 & 4
Audio CD Reference	CDs 5 & 6

Study Sessions 4 and 5 are the heart of the Level 3 exam. You *will* see at least one morning case on an individual investor. In fact, I would expect two or more questions dealing with the same or different investors worth 40 to 50 points!

The material in the following pages does not contain any of the example scenarios/cases from the Study Notes. This material does, however, cover all the core concepts associated with Study Session 4, so they will be fresh in your mind when you enter the exam room.

MANAGING INDIVIDUAL INVESTOR PORTFOLIOS[1]
Cross-Reference to CFA Institute Assigned Reading #15

Situational profiling places individuals into categories according to stage of life or economic circumstances.

Source of wealth. The manner in which an investor acquired wealth is likely to affect the investor's stance on risk. For example, wealth created through entrepreneurial activity probably indicates investor knowledge and experience with risk-taking decisions. Wealth acquired through inheritance or one-time windfalls, or wealth accumulated over a long period of secure employment, may indicate an individual who has *less* familiarity with risk-taking activity.

Measure of wealth. The key to measuring wealth is the perception an individual has regarding his wealth level. In general, a positive correlation exists between the *perception* of portfolio size and the willingness to take risk.

Stage of life. In general, an inverse relationship exists between age and risk tolerance.

---

1   Much of the terminology in this section is convention as presented in *Managing Individual Investor Portfolios*, by James W. Bronson, Matthew H. Scanlan, and Jan R. Squires.

PSYCHOLOGICAL PROFILING AND BEHAVIORAL FINANCE

According to Behavioral Finance advocates, investors exhibit three psychological characteristics:

1. *Loss aversion.*
2. *Biased expectations.*
3. *Asset segregation.* This is also referred to as *mental accounting.*

Individuals tend to construct portfolios one asset at a time rather than from a portfolio perspective. Wealth creation is determined by making investment decisions that relate to specific goals (e.g., investing in eco-friendly stocks, etc.).

INVESTOR PERSONALITY TYPES

Cautious investors exhibit a strong desire for financial security and are the most risk averse. They tend to over-analyze investment opportunities. Their portfolios exhibit low turnover and low volatility.

Methodical investors do their own research and rarely form emotional attachments to investments. Their investment decisions tend to be conservative, and they are more risk averse than individualistic investors.

Individualistic investors are not afraid of doing their own research and are confident in their abilities. Their confidence makes them capable of questioning inconsistencies in analysts' recommendations.

Spontaneous investors tend to buy the latest hot investment, so their portfolios exhibit high turnover levels and trading costs. Risk considerations take a back seat in their investment decision-making process.

INDIVIDUAL INVESTOR OBJECTIVES

Return objective. The distinction between *required* and *desired* return levels should be discussed with the client:

- *Required returns* are those necessary to meet an investor's major long-term financial objectives (e.g., retirement spending).
- *Desired returns* are associated with non-primary goals and objectives (e.g., second home, charitable gift).

Risk objective. *Ability* to take risk is related to the size of the portfolio relative to the investor's objectives and time horizon. The individual's willingness to take risk is based on psychological factors.

INDIVIDUAL INVESTOR CONSTRAINTS

Time horizons shorter than three years are considered short-term. Time horizons longer than 10–20 years are long-term. You will likely see two time horizons: the preretirement period and the years of retirement.

Tax Rates will be provided on the exam by:

- Income tax.
- Capital gains tax.
- Transfer tax.
- Wealth tax or personal property tax.

The **liquidity** constraints of a portfolio relate to spending needs the portfolio must meet. These can include *normal everyday expenses (if the client's salary isn't enough), sufficient surplus, major planned events, et cetera.*

> *Professor's Note: Look for statements regarding the individual's desire to maintain a surplus (cash reserves) sufficient to cover a period of unemployment, et cetera. If no statement is made, always minimize cash but maintain enough for meeting emergencies (e.g., three months' salary).*

The **legal and regulatory** constraints that apply to individuals are mainly associated with taxes and transfer of personal property, typically call for **legal advice**.

Personal trusts. A *trust document* states the purpose of the trust and names the *trustee*, who is responsible for administering the trust. There are two types of personal trusts: *revocable trusts* and *irrevocable trusts*.

Unique circumstances. Miscellaneous information or requests that should be kept in mind, such as future *out of the ordinary* expenditures, *disallowed investments, large holding of an individual security, et cetera.*

LIFE-CYCLE INVESTING
Cross-Reference to CFA Institute Assigned Reading #16

Determining Investment Policy

In general, the younger the investor, the longer the investment horizon and the more aggressive the appropriate investment policy.

An investor's **wealth class** is based on the relationship between assets and liabilities. When assets exceed liabilities, the individual has *discretionary wealth*. In general, the greater the level of discretionary wealth, the more aggressive the investment policy.

When individuals outlive their assets, this is known as **superannuation**.

Excerpts from "Lifestyle, Wealth Transfer, and Asset Classes" and "Techniques for Improving After-Tax Investment Performance"

Cross-Reference to CFA Institute Assigned Reading #17

Life Expectancy and Life Span

The relevant time horizon for an individual is his or her *life span*. Since the life span is unknown, it is common to use *life expectancy* as a proxy for planning purposes.

As individuals age, their life span (investment horizon) shrinks, and for most investors, risk tolerance decreases. However, for investors who are assured of remaining independently wealthy, the focus of the time horizon often shifts to the disposition of assets following the investor's death.

When assets are subject to inheritance taxes, features in the tax code that permit the tax-free transfer of assets between spouses create a period during which these taxes are deferred.

When securities are given as charitable donations, capital gains taxes are completely avoided. Moreover, the donor receives tax deductions based upon the current fair market value of the securities.

Tax Efficiency of Alternative Investments

Hedge funds are often highly tax *inefficient* because their long-short structures can double the number of positions held, and they rely on frequent trading to generate returns. Private equity and venture capital present a more favorable level of tax efficiency, since any gains realized on these types of investments are typically long-term and taxed at lower rates. Hard assets, because of their long-term nature and various provisions in the tax code, are typically tax efficient.

Tax-Lot Management

When a position in a security is accumulated over time, identification of *tax lots* is beneficial. By selling those with the greatest cost basis, capital gains and associated taxes are minimized.

Tax-Loss Harvesting

If an investor holds securities that have depreciated below their cost basis, there is a tax benefit associated with selling them to *harvest the losses* and using the losses to offset gains on other securities sold above their cost basis.

Tax-loss harvesting, if done carefully, can result in a *tax alpha*. Tax alpha is the increase in the size of the portfolio (in percentage terms) by not having to pay capital gains taxes.

Portfolio Turnover

To the extent possible, high-turnover funds should be avoided or held in tax-sheltered accounts.

Rebalancing

The manager should measure the after-tax values of asset allocations in determining rebalancing points.

MULTIPLE ASSET LOCATIONS
Cross-Reference to CFA Institute Assigned Reading #18

The Rationale for Multiple Accounts

The primary motivation for holding assets in multiple accounts is to minimize, postpone, or avoid taxation. Taxation occurs at two levels. First, asset returns are taxed when received, either as income or capital gains. Second, assets are often taxed when they are transferred to another party. Segmenting assets into various accounts allows the investor to minimize current taxes and facilitates a more tax-efficient *transfer* of assets to heirs or recipients of charitable bequests.

Account Structure Effectiveness

The benefits to placing assets into different accounts are best evaluated by analyzing the accounts among five criteria:

1. **Term.** Does the account mature in a defined period of time or with the death of the grantor? Does it provide wealth across multiple generations?

2. **Access.** Does the grantor have access to the assets?

3. **Control.** Can the grantor determine how the assets are invested and/or distributed?

4. **Valuation.** Can discounts be applied to the values of the assets to minimize transfer taxes?

5. **Tax efficiency.** Does the account help provide the desired outcome while minimizing present and/or future taxes?

We can evaluate seven possible account structures along the five criteria:

1. **Personal account.** Personal accounts (e.g., savings accounts) are not specifically designed with tax efficiency or estate planning in mind. They are generally created to earn small returns while retaining an ongoing source of *liquidity*.
   - **Term.** The life of the account is determined by the owner, so it can be tailored to meet the owner's needs.
   - **Access.** The owner has complete access to assets in the account.
   - **Control.** The owner has complete control over the assets in the account.
   - **Valuation.** As deposits are in cash, there is no opportunity to apply valuation discounts.
   - **Tax efficiency.** Tax-inefficient, because deposits are made from after-tax dollars and all gains are taxed.

2. **Grantor-retained annuity trust** (GRAT). In a GRAT, the grantor (a.k.a. donor) receives an annuity and the beneficiaries receive what's left in the trust at maturity. The annuity can be fixed or based upon the value of the annuity at the beginning of each period. When the latter payment structure is used, the GRAT is referred to as a *unitrust*. The grantor can elect to pay taxes on the annuity or have the trust pay them.

   GRATs are *grantor trusts* (a.k.a. *defective trusts*) because they satisfy the tax code provisions with respect to gift/estate taxes, but the grantor retains control and access to the assets and receives a *taxable* annuity from the trust. In other words, the trust does not satisfy all aspects of both estate and income tax codes; there is still a taxable position for the grantor.

   - **Term.** Usually relatively short-term (e.g., ≤ 10 years) to retain tax-efficiency and transfer the assets in a relatively short period of time. Long-term (e.g., 20 years) GRATs are tax-inefficient due to estate taxes if the grantor should die.
   - **Access.** Variable according to terms determined by the grantor, but the grantor can usually substitute assets (i.e., change the assets held in the trust).
   - **Control.** Variable according to terms determined by grantor but usually high.
   - **Valuation.** Subject to discounts if the donated assets are part of a limited liability company (LLC), limited partnership, or other privately held vehicle.
   - **Tax efficiency.** GRATs themselves are not considered tax efficient, because the grantor must pay taxes on investment income generated by trust assets. Alternatively, the grantor may opt to have the trust pay the taxes, because the grantor still legally owns the assets. If the grantor pays the taxes out of separate income or assets, this generates a *tax alpha* for the trust similar to loss-harvesting (see Reading 17), which helps increase the final value of the trust. As a wealth transfer vehicle, GRATs are *tax-efficient*, if the donated assets are part of a limited partnership or other private holding that is subject to *valuation discounts*.

3. **Generation-skipping trust (GST)**. GSTs are used to pass assets to future generations. They are *complete* (i.e., meet tax code provisions) from the standpoint of estate taxes, as the grantor loses access to the assets. They may be *defective* with regard to income taxes, however, by allowing the grantor to pay income taxes on investment income. In most U.S. states, GSTs must dissolve within a set period after the death of the grantor. In some states GSTs are allowed to exist in perpetuity (i.e., *dynasty trusts*), meaning that they can be used to transfer assets to distant generations if necessary.
   - **Term.** At least one generation (e.g., 20 years). Dynasty trusts allowed in some states in the United States.
   - **Access.** Forfeited.
   - **Control.** As established in trust documents.
   - **Valuation.** Subject to discounts if the donated assets are part of an LLC, limited partnership, or other privately held vehicle.
   - **Tax efficiency.** Can be complete or defective. When defective, they allow the grantor to increase the value of the trust by paying income taxes and thus generating a tax alpha.

4. **Charitable trusts.** Usually either a *charitable remainder trust* (CRT) or *charitable lead trust* (CLT). In both cases the grantor retains partial ownership of the assets until they are transferred to the beneficiary. Like a grantor-retained annuity trust, a CRT pays the grantor an annuity and charities receive the balance at the end of a specified time period. With a CLT the annuity goes to a charity and the remainder goes to the grantor's beneficiaries. They are taxed differently, but CLTs can use distributions to charities to offset gains on investments, either income or capital gains.
   - **Term.** Usually not more than 20 years.
   - **Access.** Forfeited.
   - **Control.** As established in trust documents.
   - **Valuation.** Discounts are available but the grantor usually wants to maximize the tax deduction for the gift to charity.
   - **Tax efficiency.** Both are taxable entities. They are an efficient means for a grantor to avoid taxes on low-basis stocks and other highly appreciated investments.

5. **Variable Life Insurance Policies.** These are whole-life insurance policies (i.e., insurance policies that accumulate investment value) that allow the owner to determine how the assets are invested; the policy owner faces the investment risk.
   - **Term.** The life of the policy owner or other individual covered by the policy.
   - **Access.** Some allow policy owners to borrow from accumulated value.
   - **Control.** The policy owner can allocate assets only to investments that have been approved by the insurance company and meet federal diversification guidelines.
   - **Valuation.** No opportunity for valuation discounts.
   - **Tax efficiency.** Investment returns are tax-deferred.

6. **Tax-deferred pensions** include various forms of employer-funded accounts such as 401(k) and 403(b) accounts. These can usually be rolled into individual retirement accounts (IRAs). Contributions are made out of before-tax dollars, thus they provide an income tax shelter. Investments in the account also grow tax-deferred. There typically are limitations to the amount an individual can contribute to his account each year. A Roth IRA also grows tax-deferred but deposits come from after-tax dollars. There may also be income restrictions that prohibit high income individuals from utilizing them.
   - **Term.** Typically the life of the account owner.
   - **Access.** Restricted until age 59.5 except for certain emergency situations.
   - **Control.** The policy owner can allocate assets.
   - **Valuation.** Little or no opportunity for valuation discounts.
   - **Tax efficiency.** Investment income is tax-deferred. Annual contributions may be tax-deductible. Withdrawals are subject to both income and capital gains taxes.

7. **Foundations.** Foundations are (usually) very long-term vehicles that are established with a particular funding goal in mind. For example, a private or public foundation might be established to provide grants to the local community to help fund start-up companies. Public foundations are permitted to accept donations from the public, but family foundations are limited to family members. Since the focus of this topic review is wealth transfer and tax avoidance, this discussion is limited to **private** (i.e., family) **foundations.**
   - **Term.** Indefinite.
   - **Access.** Foundation benefactors (i.e., family members) have no access to assets. They are allowed to receive management fees and reimbursement for foundation-related expenses.
   - **Control.** The benefactors can manage both the investment and the distribution of foundation assets.
   - **Valuation.** Little or no opportunity for valuation discounts, because benefactors usually want a maximum deduction for donated assets.

Tax efficiency. Foundations are generally tax-exempt, as long as they meet regulatory guidelines, such as paying at least 5% of accumulated assets each year. Benefactors get tax-deductions against current income for donated assets.

Intergenerational Transfers

1. **Intergenerational loans.** The idea behind intergenerational loans is putting high earning assets under the control of those who are expected to live the longest. For example, the older generation may "loan" assets to members of the younger generation. Members of the younger generation actually borrow the assets and pay interest (i.e., service the loan), but any returns in excess of the interest on the loan accrue to the younger generation.

Also, to provide members of the younger generation with access to capital that they might not have otherwise or as cheaply, the older generation can guarantee loans for them. To the extent that the older generation pays the loan to the lender, the younger generation has received a tax-free gift.

2. **Defective trusts.** Defective trusts allow the grantor to pay the taxes on trust income. This generate a tax alpha, which leads to a significant effect on the rate of accumulation of assets in the trust. The trust can also be funded with discounted assets, so the combined effect is a significant impact on the value received by the beneficiaries. The grantor might also be able to guarantee loans for the trust (discussed above) or make additional cash or asset gifts.

3. **Family Partnerships** (FP). Since partnership assets are usually subject to significant valuation discounts, family partnerships provide a tax-efficient way of transferring assets among family members. As mentioned before, higher earning assets should always be placed with individuals that are expected to live the longest, and FPs provide the means for sharing (allocating) assets among the family members accordingly.

Low-Basis Stock
Cross-Reference to CFA Institute Assigned Reading #19

Basis or, more correctly, cost basis, refers to the reference point for calculating capital gains or losses for a given asset. This is ordinarily either the gross purchase price or the value of the asset when transferred to the holder. In some cases, the cost basis may be extremely small (i.e., close to zero). In these very low-basis situations, the capital gains taxes that accrue upon sale are large. The problem relating to such so-called "low-basis stock" is that the tax ramifications (and other factors) can serve to inhibit the investor from taking an action that would otherwise be desirable. Specifically, when the investor is unwilling to reduce a large position in a low-basis security—at the cost of holding a concentrated portfolio—the level of portfolio risk can be excessive.

The individual will usually fall into one of three categories: *entrepreneur; executive;* or *investor.* The three categories are differentiated by the manner in which the wealth was accumulated and the individual's psychological attachment to the stock (i.e., the firm).

The Entrepreneur

Source of wealth. An entrepreneur is an individual (or family) who has developed a company, usually from inception. The result is that the entrepreneur's wealth is dominated by that one, privately-held stock. The cost basis for the stock is typically far below the stock's current value.

Psychological Issues. A factor that contributes to entrepreneurs' maintaining concentrated portfolios is their psychological attachment to their firms. They are highly loyal to their firm and don't mind having most or all of their wealth tied to it. In fact, while an entrepreneur is running a firm, she feels no need for diversification. She has confidence in her abilities to run the firm and is not averse to having her entire fortune tied to the future of the firm as long as she is in control. As she transfers control to others, however, the entrepreneur becomes increasingly uncomfortable with a concentrated portfolio and begins to desire a more diversified position. The result for the financial advisor is a need to achieve the desired diversification while respecting the entrepreneur's devotion to the firm (to the extent it exists) and reluctance to sell shares.

Risk Considerations. *Specific risk* refers to the risk of the individual security; the risk that can be reduced or eliminated by holding the security in a diversified portfolio. If held in a well-diversified portfolio, the holder is left with only the security's market risk and residual risk. *Residual risk*, which deals with successfully implementing the desired strategy, can be broken down into counterparty risk and regulatory risk. *Counterparty risk* is the probability that a counterparty will not correctly complete the transaction as expected. *Regulatory risk* is the possibility that tax authorities will not accept the tax treatment applied to a transaction.

The Executive

Source of wealth. Executive compensation packages typically contain significant equity components and the higher in the ranks, the greater the proportion of total compensation received in equity. As with an entrepreneur, the result is a heavily concentrated portfolio. The cost basis for the accumulated stock is usually quite low, so an executive also faces the same diversification problem faced by entrepreneurs.

Psychological Issues. Just like an entrepreneur, a top executive's fortunes are tied directly to the firm. Also like an entrepreneur, the more *control* the executive exerts over the fortunes of the firm, the less he is concerned with diversification and the more *psychologically attached* he becomes to the firm.

Risk Considerations. As long as they maintain the concentrated holding, executives face considerable *specific risk*. The executive does not "feel" the specific risk, if he has sufficient control over the firm's operations.

The Investor

Source of wealth. An investor can accumulate a considerable position in a single stock as the result of a particularly good investment. For example, an investor in a venture capital fund can end up with a considerable position in a single, successful firm when the fund liquidates. The investor is faced with the same concentration in one security and the same resulting level of specific risk as both the entrepreneur and the executive.

Psychological Issues. The investor does not usually feel the same attachment as the entrepreneur or top executive. Also, the investor does not exert significant *control* over the firm's operations, so he is less willing to accept exposure to the specific risk.

Risk Considerations. As long as the investor maintains the concentrated position in the single stock, she faces considerable specific risk. The difference between the investor and the entrepreneur or executive is the lack of attachment and the willingness to take the steps necessary to diversify.

The Equity Holding Life

Figure 1 can be utilized in discussing equity holding life, which consists of three stages: (1) the *entrepreneurial stage*, (2) the *executive stage*, and (3) the *investor stage*. The investor stage is further divided into the diversified investor stage, and the indexing stage.

Figure 1: The Effect on Risk of Increasing the Number of Shares in the Portfolio

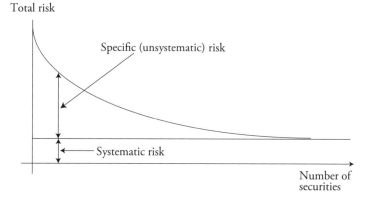

The entrepreneur falls at the extreme left-hand margin of Figure 1. During this **entrepreneurial stage**, all of the individual's wealth is tied to one security (i.e., one firm), so the investor faces the firm's *total risk*.

When the entrepreneur takes the firm public, he ends up with a large position in a now publicly-traded security, and the entrepreneur has entered the **executive stage**. Whether the investor holds a top level position in the firm or not, he or she still has most or all wealth tied to the one firm and thus is faced with considerable specific risk. Remember that the executive's attitude toward risk (i.e., psychological attachment to the firm) varies directly with the amount of control the executive exerts over the firm's operations.

Once the executive advances to the **investor stage**, his primary focus changes from accumulating/generating wealth to protecting and growing the wealth he has. At the investor stage the individual's focus is no longer on owning the firm, per se. Stock in any firm is now just considered a stock investment (i.e., part of an investment portfolio rather than ownership in a firm). Once the individual has entered the investor stage, therefore, he no longer has an emotional tie to the firm.

DIVERSIFICATION TECHNIQUES

There are four principal options for improving the diversification of concentrated portfolios. Figure 2 presents a summary of the advantages and disadvantages of the four techniques.

Figure 2: Effectiveness of Diversification Techniques

Technique	Advantages	Disadvantages
Sale	Simple. Non-systematic risk of position is completely eliminated for shares sold. Proceeds can be reinvested or distributed as desired.	Most costly from a tax standpoint. Requires that shares are publicly traded.
Exchange Funds	By combining funds with those of other investors with concentrated holdings, the investor holds part of a diversified portfolio.	Must pay management fees while funds are commingled. Funds cannot be withdrawn or increased during the period, so this is a diversification tactic only. Cost basis does not change.
Completion Portfolios	Investor builds a diversified portfolio over time, and can avoid capital gains to the extent that the completion portfolio provides the opportunity for harvesting losses.	Requires that investor have investable cash available, or is willing to leverage the concentrated asset to raise funds. May take substantial time to achieve proper diversification.
Hedging	Can be implemented quickly. Can facilitate low risk borrowings that can be used to purchase diversification assets immediately.	Upside potential of hedged position is typically limited after hedge is in place. Potential regulatory risk insofar as investor must adhere to rules regarding constructive sales which may trigger tax consequences.

Goals-Based Investing: Integrating Traditional and Behavioral Finance
Cross-Reference to CFA Institute Assigned Reading #20

Defining portfolio performance relative to the investor's **lifestyle objectives** can help improve the investor's understanding of how investment policy relates to goal achievement.

Objective-Related Risks. Instead of focusing solely on the expected portfolio value given a specific asset allocation, investors would also like to know the associated probability that the portfolio will fall short of funding needs.

Fixed Planning Horizon Insured Strategy (FPH). The investor places the present value of the desired future amount in risk-free bonds and the remainder in risky assets. This differs from a traditional asset allocation strategy in at least three respects. First, there is zero probability that funds will be insufficient to meet objectives. Second, the cost of eliminating the shortfall risk is the reduction in upside potential. Third, the initial allocation will not be held constant through time.

Portfolio Management for Institutional Investors

Topic Weight on Exam	10–20%
Study Note Reference	Book 2, Pages 7–63
Video CD Reference	CD 5
Audio CD Reference	CDs 6 & 7

Study Sessions 4 and 5 are the heart of the Level 3 CFA exam. You *will* see at least one case on an institutional investor in the morning session of the exam. Look for something like 50 to 75 points related to Study Session 5 with a combined total of about 140 points on Study Sessions 4 and 5.

As with Study Session 4, the following contains no scenarios or cases. However, it does contain all the core concepts of Study Session 5, so they'll be fresh when you enter the exam room.

Managing Institutional Investor Portfolios
Cross-Reference to CFA Institute Assigned Reading #21

Types of Pension Plans

In **defined-benefit plan**, the employer promises a retirement pension to plan participants. Benefits relate to years of service, rate of pay, or a combination of both.

In **cash balance plan**, the employer credits the employee's account annually, based on salary and length of employment. The balance only represents a liability to the employer, not a true cash account.

In **defined-contribution plan**, the liability to the sponsor is only the contribution, not the benefit received by the participants.

A **profit sharing plan** is a defined-contribution plan whose contributions are established somewhat by the profitability of the plan sponsor.

Defined-Benefit Plans and Defined-Contribution Plans

The contrasting features between defined-benefit and defined-contribution plans from the perspective of employee and employer are shown in Figure 1.

Figure 1: Features of Defined-Benefit and Defined-Contribution Pension Plans

Plan Type	Employer	Employee
Defined Benefit	• Pension benefits are a liability for the employer. • Benefits are determined by stated criteria usually associated with years of service and salary. • The plan sponsor (the firm) is responsible for managing the plan assets to meet pension obligations.	• Receives periodic payments beginning at retirement or other eligibility date according to a formula. • Subject to "early termination" risk if employee is terminated early. • Does not bear risk/return consequences of investment portfolio performance.
Defined Contribution	• The firm promises to keep all contributions current. • Only financial liability is making contributions to employee's account. • The plan must offer employees a sufficient number of investment vehicles for suitable portfolio construction.	• Owns plan assets and can transport account to other employment situations. • Bears all the risk/return characteristics of investment performance. • Must make all investment decisions given available investment vehicles.

Defined-Benefit Plan (DB) Objectives

The ultimate goal of a DB pension plan is to have pension assets generate returns sufficient to cover pension liabilities. The specific return requirement will depend on the plan's funding status and contributions dictated by accrued benefits. However, a plan's stated desired return may be higher to reflect future pension contributions, and pension plan income.

Plan surpluses exceed the minimum required to meet plan liabilities. The greater the surplus, the greater the ability to take risk. Underfunded plans (i.e., negative surplus) may have a willingness to take greater investment risk, but the underfunded status dictates a *decreased ability* to take risk.

Sponsor Financial Status and Profitability

- Indicated by the sponsor's balance sheet. The debt-to-asset or other leverage ratios often indicate financial condition.
- Lower (higher) debt ratios and higher (lower) current and expected profitability indicate a greater (lower) ability to take risk.

Sponsor and Pension Fund Common Risk Exposure

- Measured by the *correlation* between the firm's and pension's asset returns.
- The higher (lower) the correlation between a firm's operations and pension asset returns, the lower (higher) the risk tolerance.

Plan Features

- Plans that offer early retirement or lump sum payments essentially decrease the time horizon of the retirement liability and increase the liquidity requirements of the plan. Therefore, the ability to assume risk is decreased.

Workforce Characteristics

- In general, the younger the workforce and the greater the ratio of active to retired lives, the greater the ability to take risk when managing pension assets.

DEFINED-BENEFIT PLAN CONSTRAINTS

Liquidity requirements are affected by the number of retired lives, the amount of sponsor contributions, and plan features.

The **time horizon** is determined by whether or not the plan is a going concern, the workforce age, and the ratio of active to retired lives.

Legal and regulatory factors. In the United States, ERISA regulates defined-benefit plans. Pension fund assets must be invested for the sole benefit of plan participants. There are two main classes of **unique circumstances**:

1. ERISA requires plan sponsors to exercise appropriate due diligence when making investment decisions.

2. Pension plans may impose requirements that prohibit investment in some traditional or alternative asset choices.

ESOPs

An **employee stock ownership plan** (ESOP) is a type of DC plan that allows employees to purchase the company stock. Occasionally, an ESOP will purchase a large block of the firm's stock. The block can be purchased through the market or directly from a large stockholder, such as is often the case when a founding proprietor or partner wants to liquidate a holding. The stock is then purchased at regular intervals by plan beneficiaries.

Foundations

Figure 2 contains a summary of the characteristics of the four basic types of foundations.[1]

Figure 2: Types of Foundations and Their Important Characteristics

Type of Foundation	*Description*	*Purpose*	*Source of Funds*	*Annual Spending Requirement*
Independent	Private or family	Grants to charities, educational institutions, social organizations, etc.	Typically an individual or family, but can be a group of interested individuals	5% of assets; expenses cannot be counted in the spending amount
Company-sponsored	Closely tied to the sponsoring corporation	Same as independent; grants can be used to further the corporate sponsor's business interests	Corporate sponsor	Same as independent foundations
Operating	Established for the sole purpose of funding an organization (e.g., a museum, zoo, public library) or some on-going research/medical initiative		Same as independent	Must spend at least 85% of dividend and interest income for its own operations; may also be subject to spending 3.33% of assets
Community	Publicly sponsored grant-awarding organization	Fund social, educational, religious, etc. purposes	General public, including large donors	None

1 Based upon Table 3-2, page 26, "Managing Institutional Investor Portfolios," by R. Charles Tschampion, CFA, Laurence B. Siegel, Dean J. Takahashi, and John L. Maginn, from *Managing Investment Portfolios: A Dynamic Process*, 3rd edition (CFA Institute, forthcoming).

Return. One useful guideline is to set a minimum return equal to the required payout plus expected inflation and fund expenses.

Risk. Since there are no contractually defined liability requirements, foundations are usually more aggressive than pensions.

Time horizon. Except for special foundations required to spend down their portfolio, most foundations have infinite time horizons.

Liquidity. A foundation's anticipated spending requirement is termed its *spending rate*. Other than the minimum spending rate set for private foundations (5% in the United States), most foundations can determine any spending rate desired.

Tax considerations. Unrelated business income is taxable at the regular corporate rate.

Legal and regulatory. In the United States, most states have adopted UMIFA as the prevailing regulatory framework. Otherwise, the prudent investor rule applies.

ENDOWMENTS

Return. A long-term spending rate below the long-term expected portfolio return level is crucial to meeting fund objectives. Spending rates above 5% typically lead to an erosion of principal and should be discouraged.

Risk. The time horizon for endowment funds is typically infinite. This generally equates to an above-average *ability* to tolerate risk, as long as the funded institution does not rely on the endowment to meet a significant portion of its expenses.

The **liquidity requirements** of an endowment depend upon the extent to which the funded institution depends upon funding from the endowment.

Tax considerations. Endowment income is tax-exempt, but some operations of the supported entity may generate *unrelated business income* which is taxed.

Regulatory and legal considerations. Most states have adopted UMIFA as the governing regulation for endowments. If no specific legal considerations are stated in the case you see on the exam, be prepared to write, "Prudent Investor rule applies."

Due to their diversity, endowment funds have many **unique circumstances**. Social issues (e.g., defense policies and racial biases) are typically taken into consideration when deciding upon individual investments.

Life Insurance Companies

Return. Traditional whole life policies have built-in minimum required rates of return. Portfolio returns above the minimum rate generate a *net interest spread*. Multiple return objectives are often found in a life insurance company's IPS.

Risk. Insurance company investment portfolios are considered *quasi-trust funds*. The National Association of Insurance Commissioners (NAIC) directs life insurance companies to maintain an asset valuation reserve (AVR) as a cushion against substantial losses of portfolio value or investment income.

Factors that determine the risk objectives of a life insurance company include asset valuation concerns, cash flow volatility, reinvestment risk, and credit risk.

Liquidity. Life insurance companies need to address three primary concerns: disintermediation, asset-liability mismatch, and asset marketability risk.

Time horizon. Progressively *shorter* as the duration of liabilities has decreased due to increased interest rate volatility and competitive market factors. Individual segments of the overall portfolio have their own time horizons.

Tax considerations. Life insurance companies are taxable entities.

Regulatory and legal constraints. Life insurance companies are heavily regulated, primarily at the state level.

- **Eligible investments.**
- **The prudent investor rule applies.**
- **Valuation methods.**

Unique circumstances. Diversity of product offerings, company size, and level of asset surplus are some of the most common factors impacting the uniqueness of life insurance companies.

Nonlife Insurance Companies

Nonlife companies face greater *uncertainty* than life companies due to the possibility of higher claims frequency. However, they are not as interest rate sensitive since their policies do not typically pay periodic returns.

The main factors impacting nonlife insurance company **return objectives** are competitive pricing, profitability, growth of surplus, after-tax returns, and total return.

Due to the high uncertainty associated with claims, **risk tolerance** must be tempered by their liquidity requirements. Casualty companies generally have average to below average risk tolerance.

Since most nonlife companies offer replacement cost coverage, inflation risk is also a big concern.

Liquidity. Due to the high uncertainty of claims, liquidity requirements for nonlife insurance companies are relatively high.

Time horizon. Due to the shorter duration of their liabilities, nonlife insurance companies have shorter time horizons than life insurance companies.

Tax considerations. Non-life insurance companies are taxable entities.

Regulatory considerations are slightly less onerous for non-life insurance companies than for life insurance companies. An asset valuation reserve (AVR) is not required, but risk-based capital (RBC) requirements have been established. Otherwise, non-life companies are given considerable leeway in choosing investments.

Unique circumstances. The types of policies sold (e.g., focus on auto) is the primary source of unique circumstances.

BANKS

The bank's **security portfolio** is usually a residual use of funds (i.e., excess funds that have not been loaned out).

The **return objective** for the securities portfolio is earning a positive interest spread.

Risk. The allocation of the bank security portfolio is determined in an asset-liability framework, because the most important objective of the portfolio is meeting the costs and liquidity requirements associated with the bank's liabilities. Banks, therefore, usually have a **below average risk tolerance**, since they cannot let losses in the security portfolio interfere with their ability to meet their liabilities.

A bank's **liquidity** needs are driven by deposit withdrawals and demand for loans, as well as regulation. Their securities portfolios typically contain very liquid securities.

Since a bank is an ongoing entity with regular liquidity concerns, the **time horizon** for the securities portfolio is driven by the average maturity of its liabilities (less than ten years).

Banks are taxable entities, so **taxes** must be considered.

Legal and regulatory. Banks in industrialized nations are highly regulated. In addition, risk-based capital guidelines require banks to establish capital reserves of 100% against most loan categories. Banks also have to pledge collateral, usually short-term treasuries, against certain uninsured public deposits.

Unique circumstances vary from bank to bank. Loan concentrations and the inability to sell loans are examples of unique circumstances that would impact the objectives and constraints of the securities portfolio IPS.

Figure 3 contains a summary of asset-liability management concerns of all the institutional investors.

Figure 3: Asset/Liability Management: Pension Funds, Foundations, Endowments, Insurance Companies, and Banks

Pension Funds	Defined Benefit	Surplus management is key. There are typically restrictions on short selling and maximum percentage allocations to asset categories or sectors. In addition, there are typically regulatory and liquidity constraints, such as limitations on private debt. Managers usually attempt to match durations of assets and liabilities to minimize the volatility of the surplus. In addition, managers always minimize the risk (standard deviation) of the asset portfolio while meeting return requirements.
	Defined Contribution	Once annual contributions are met (the sponsor's only financial obligation), the sponsor's only remaining obligations are monitoring the plan and providing sufficient investment alternatives for participants. Beneficiaries manage their own assets.
Foundations		Foundations generally have to meet all funding requirements (grants and operating expenses) through investment earnings. Since they do not have to grow the foundation's assets (can spend all earnings), they can implement aggressive investment policies. That is, generally low spending requirements imply ability to tolerate risk.
Endowments		The overall goal, typically, is to preserve assets while meeting spending requirements. There is usually some sort of spending rule designed to compensate for low/high earnings years to avoid dramatic yearly fluctuations. The ability to tolerate risk is determined by the level of spending and the importance of the spending to recipients' operating budgets.
Insurance Companies		Insurance companies (life and non-life) are taxable entities. They segment their general portfolio into sub-portfolios to match assets to various (liability) product lines according to interest rate risk (duration), return, and credit risk. In this fashion, each sub-portfolio will have its own return and liquidity characteristics, which are dictated by its associated liabilities.
Banks		The most important objective of the bank securities portfolio is meeting the bank's liabilities, so the allocation of the bank securities portfolio is determined using an asset-liability framework. The primary objective is earning a positive interest rate spread.

Figure 4 sums up the factors that determine the investment policies of all the institutional investors.

Figure 4: Factors Affecting Investment Policies of Institutional Investors

IPS Component		Institutional Investor Type					Commercial Banks
		Defined-Benefit Plans	Foundations	Endowment Funds	Life Insurance Companies	Nonlife Insurance Companies	
Objectives	Return	Actuarial rate. A capital gains focus when the fund has low liquidity needs and younger workers. An income focus (duration matching) when there are high liquidity needs and older workers	Private foundations must generate 5% plus management expenses plus inflation. Total return is appropriate.	Total return approach. The return objective must be balanced between a need for high current income and long-term protection of principal.	*Fixed-income segment:* "spread management" and actuarial assumptions. *Surplus segment:* capital gains.	*Fixed income:* maximize the return for meeting claims. *Equity segment:* grow the surplus/supplement funds for liability claims.	Return is determined by the cost of funds. Primarily concerned with earning a positive interest rate spread.
	Risk Tolerance	Depends on surplus, age of workforce, time horizon, and company balance sheet.	Moderate to high, depending on spending rate and time horizon.	Moderate to high, depending on spending needs.	*Fixed-income segment:* conservative. *Surplus segment:* aggressive.	*Fixed-income segment:* conservative. *Surplus segment:* aggressive.	Banks are primarily concerned with meeting their liabilities and other liquidity needs and cannot suffer losses in the securities portfolio. Tend to have below average risk tolerance.

Figure 4: Factors Affecting Investment Policies of Institutional Investors (cont.)

IPS Component		Institutional Investor Type					
		Defined-Benefit Plans	Foundations	Endowment Funds	Life Insurance Companies	Nonlife Insurance Companies	Commercial Banks
Constraints	Liquidity	Depends on age of workforce and retired lives proportion.	Other than 5% requirement for private foundations, spending rate is foundation specific. Spending rules are helpful.	Low, usually only for emergencies and spending.	*Fixed-income portion*: relatively high. *Surplus segment*: nil.	*Fixed-income portion*: relatively high. *Surplus segment*: nil.	Liquidity is also relative to liabilities. Banks need continuing liquidity for liabilities and new loans.
	Time Horizon	Long, if going concern. Short, if terminating plan.	Long, usually infinite.	Long, usually infinite	Getting shorter.	Short, due to the nature of claims.	Time horizon tends to be short to intermediate because of mostly short-term liabilities.
	Legal / Regulatory	ERISA/prudent expert rule.	Few, prudent investor rule applies.	Low, prudent investor rule typically applies.	High, especially on the state level/prudent investor rule.	Moderate, but increasing/prudent investor rule.	Must meet regulatory requirements for liquidity, reserves, and pledging. Usually with short-term Treasuries.
	Taxes	None	Few	None	High	High	Banks are taxable entities, so taxes must be considered.
	Unique Needs	Surplus, age of workforce, time horizon, and company balance sheet policy.	Foundation specific. Moral/ethical concerns may restrict certain securities.	Restrictions on certain securities/asset classes common due to nature of funds.	Must distinguish between strategies for the fixed-income segment and the surplus segment.	The financial status of the firm, the management of investment risk and liquidity requirements	Varies from bank to bank. May use securities portfolio as diversification tool and/or to provide liquidity.

ALLOCATING SHAREHOLDER CAPITAL TO PENSION PLANS
Cross-Reference to CFA Institute Assigned Reading #22

FUNDING SHORTFALL AND ASSET/LIABILITY MISMATCH

Funding shortfall occurs when the market value of the pension plan's assets is less than the market value of its liabilities (i.e., pension obligations). The risk to the participant is that the fund may have insufficient assets to meet pension obligations. The risk to the firm (i.e., plan sponsor) is that the plan is deemed under-funded. If this happens, the sponsor may be required by regulators to increase annual contributions to the plan or even make one or more special contributions to return the plan to fully-funded status.

Asset/liability mismatch occurs when the pension plan's assets and liabilities are exposed to different risk factors or affected differently by the same risk factors. Asset/liability risk is thought to be a bigger risk than funding shortfall for two reasons: (1) the balance sheet doesn't show the types of securities the pension assets are invested in and, therefore, there is no measure of risk, and (2) as of the end of 2001, for the top 20% of U.S. companies pension assets were twice the size of the company's overall market capitalization.

THE WEIGHTED AVERAGE COST OF CAPITAL

The weighted average cost of capital is the discount rate assigned to the firm's overall capital structure, which is usually a combination of equity and debt. The traditional method of determining the WACC in equation form is:

$$\text{weight}_{\text{equity}} \times \text{cost}_{\text{equity}} + \text{weight}_{\text{debt}} \times \text{cost}_{\text{debt}} (1-t)$$

The cost of equity is based on the firm's beta which can be determined from the volatility of the firm's historical share prices. The cost of debt is the interest rate at which the firm can issue new debt. The pension assets can be a large part of the overall assets of the firm, and by not including these assets in the WACC, the overall risk of the asset side of the balance sheet may be understated. Likewise, by not incorporating the pension liabilities into the WACC, the level of the firm's debt is understated, and the leverage ratio is also understated. When the WACC is adjusted to reflect the level of pension assets and liabilities, it will decrease.

The consequence of not incorporating the pension assets and liabilities into the WACC is that the WACC will be overstated, causing too high of a hurdle rate for future projects. Thus, some projects that would have otherwise been accepted are instead being rejected. The result is an underinvestment in the operations of the firm, along with a lower overall firm value.

CHANGING PENSION ASSET ALLOCATIONS

Changing the proportion of pension assets invested in equities will change the overall capital structure of the firm (i.e., operating plus pension assets and liabilities). For example, when the firm's pension assets are weighted more toward equities, the result will be increased risk in its pension assets with an accompanying increased asset beta. This will cause the total (i.e., overall) asset beta to increase and the risk of the firm's equity capital to increase. To keep this from happening, management will need to decrease the amount of debt in the firm's capital structure. To maintain the same *overall* value on the liabilities and equity side of the balance sheet, there must be an increase in equity capital. The associated decrease in debt financing in the capital structure lowers the risk to equity holders and creditors with an accompanying decrease in the firm's debt-to-equity ratio.

If the pension assets were instead shifted toward a greater percentage of debt securities, the result will be less pension asset risk and a lower total asset beta. To maintain the same firm equity beta, there would need to be a shift toward more debt financing in the firm's capital structure. This would increase the risk to stockholders and creditors resulting in an increase in the *firm's* debt-to-equity ratio. To maintain the same value on the liabilities and equity side of the overall balance sheet, the amount of equity financing would have to decrease.

ECONOMIC CONCEPTS FOR ASSET VALUATION IN PORTFOLIO MANAGEMENT

Study Session 6

Topic Weight on Exam	0–10%*
Study Notes Reference	Book 2, Pages 64–141
Video CD Reference	CD 6
Audio CD Reference	CDs 7 & 8

*Tested as part of Portfolio Management

CAPITAL MARKET EXPECTATIONS
Cross-Reference to CFA Institute Assigned Reading #23

Capital market expectations can be referred to as *macro*—expectations regarding classes of assets, and *micro*—relating to individual assets. Formulating capital market expectations is referred to as *beta research* because it is related to systematic risk. *Alpha research* is concerned with earning excess returns through the use of specific strategies within specific asset groups.

PROBLEMS IN FORECASTING

Nine problems encountered in producing forecasts are: (1) limitations to using economic data; (2) data measurement error and bias; (3) limitations of historical estimates; (4) the use of ex post risk and return measures; (5) non-repeating data patterns; (6) failing to account for conditioning information; (7) misinterpretation of correlations; (8) psychological traps; and (9) model and input uncertainty.

FORECASTING TOOLS

Projecting historical data is the most straightforward statistical tool. The analyst projects the historical mean return, standard deviation, and correlations for a data set into the future.

Shrinkage estimators reduce (shrink) the influence of historical outliers through a weighting process.

Assets such as foreign exchange, stocks, and futures have been shown to exhibit **volatility clustering**. A model developed by JP Morgan defines volatility in the current period, σ^2_t, as a weighted average of the previous period volatility, σ^2_{t-1}, and a random error, ε^2_t:

$$\sigma^2_t = \theta\sigma^2_{t-1} + (1-\theta)\varepsilon^2_t$$

Multifactor models can be used to forecast returns and covariances.

The general form of a 2-factor multifactor model is:

$$R_i = \alpha_1 + \beta_{i,1}\, F_1 + \beta_{i,2}\, F_2 + \varepsilon_i$$

Using the factor model, we then formulate the variance of market i, σ_i^2:

$$\sigma^2_i = \beta^2_{i,1}\, \sigma^2_{F_1} + \beta^2_{i,2}\, \sigma^2_{F_2} + 2\beta_{i,1}\beta_{i,2}\mathrm{Cov}(F_1,F_2) + \sigma^2_{\varepsilon,i}$$

The covariance between markets i and j $\mathrm{Cov}(i,j)$:

$$\mathrm{Cov}(i,j) = \beta_{i,1}\beta_{j,1}\sigma^2_{F_1} + \beta_{i,2}\beta_{j,2}\sigma^2_{F_2} + (\beta_{i,1}\beta_{j,2} + \beta_{i,2}\beta_{j,1})\mathrm{Cov}(F_1,F_2)$$

Discounted Cash Flow Models

The Gordon growth model or constant growth model is most commonly used to back out the expected return on equity, resulting in the following:

$$P_0 = \frac{\mathrm{Div}_1}{\hat{R}_i - g} \Rightarrow \hat{R}_i = \frac{\mathrm{Div}_1}{P_0} + g$$

Grinold and Kroner (2002)[1] take this model one step further by including a variable that adjusts for stock repurchases and changes in market valuations as represented by the price-earnings (P/E) ratio.

$$\hat{R}_i = \frac{\mathrm{Div}_1}{P_0} + i + g - \Delta S + \Delta\left(\frac{P}{E}\right) \qquad \text{(know this formula)}$$

---

1   Richard Grinold and Kenneth Kroner, "The Equity Risk Premium," *Investment Insights* (Barclay's Global Investors, July 2002).

Risk Premium Approach

To determine the expected return for equities, the analyst starts with the yield to maturity on a long term government bond and adds an equity risk premium. This approach is referred to as the *bond yield plus risk premium* approach.

Financial Equilibrium Models   (know all these formulas)

The equation for the International CAPM (ICAPM) is:

$$\hat{R}_i = R_F + b_i(\hat{R}_M - R_F)$$

Restating the ICAPM yields the equity risk premium for market *i*:

$$ERP_i = \rho_{i,M}\sigma_i\left(\frac{ERP_M}{\sigma_M}\right)$$

When markets are *segmented*, capital does not flow freely across borders. The opposite of segmented markets are *integrated* markets, where capital flows freely.

Steps for using market risk premiums to calculate expected returns, betas, and covariances of two markets:

1. Calculate the equity risk premium for both markets assuming *full integration*. For an emerging market, a liquidity premium is added.

    $$ERP_i = \rho_{i,M}\sigma_i\left(\frac{ERP_M}{\sigma_M}\right) + LP$$

2. Calculate the equity risk premium for both markets assuming *full segmentation*.

    $$ERP_i = \sigma_i\left(\frac{ERP_M}{\sigma_M}\right) + LP$$

3. Weight the integrated and segmented risk premiums by the degree of integration and segmentation in each market to arrive at the weighted average equity risk premium:

    ERP$_i$ = (degree of integration of i)(ERP assuming full integration)
            + (degree of segmentation of i)(ERP assuming full segmentation)

4. Calculate the betas in each market:

    $$\beta_i = \frac{\rho_{i,M}\sigma_i}{\sigma_M}$$

5. Calculate the covariance of the two markets:

$$Cov(i,j) = \beta_i \beta_j \sigma_M^2$$

Cyclical Analysis

Understanding the business cycle can help the analyst identify *inflection points* (i.e., when the economy changes direction), where the risk and the opportunities for higher return may be heightened. To identify inflection points, the analyst should understand what is driving the current economy and what may cause the end of the current economy.

In general, economic growth can be partitioned into two components: cyclical and trend-growth components. Within cyclical analysis, there are two components: the *inventory cycle* (2 to 4 years) and the *business cycle* (9 to 11 years).

Changes in economic activity delineate cyclical activity. The measures of economic activity are GDP, the **output gap**, and recession. The output gap is the difference between the current GDP and GDP based on a long-term trend line (i.e., potential GDP). When the trend line is higher than the current GDP, the economy has slowed and inflationary pressures have weakened. When it is lower, economic activity is strong as are inflationary pressures. *Recession* is defined as decreases (i.e., negative growth) in GDP over two consecutive quarters.

Inflation

Aggregate inflation is measured most frequently by consumer price indices. Inflation rises in the latter stages of economic expansion and falls during a recession and the initial recovery. *Deflation*, or periods of decreasing prices, reduces the ability of the central bank to stimulate the economy.

Consumer and Business Spending

The primary driver of consumer spending is consumer after-tax income, which in the United States is gauged using non-farm payroll data and new unemployment claims. Savings data are also important for predicting consumer spending.

Business spending is more volatile than consumer spending. A peak in inventory spending is often a bearish signal for the economy.

Monetary Policy

Most central banks strive to balance price stability against economic growth. The ultimate goal is to keep growth near its long-run sustainable rate, since growth faster than the long-run rate usually results in increased inflation. The latter stages of an economic expansion are often characterized by increased inflation. As a result, central banks usually resort to restrictive policies towards the latter parts of an expansion.

To spur growth, a central bank will cut short-term interest rates. Lower interest rates also usually result in a lower value of the domestic currency, which is thought to increase exports. The equilibrium interest rate in a country (the rate at which a balance between growth and inflation is achieved) is referred to as the neutral rate. It is generally thought that the neutral rate is composed of an inflation component and a real growth component.

Fiscal Policy

If the government wants to stimulate the economy, it can decrease taxes and/or increase spending, thereby increasing the budget deficit. If they want to rein in growth, the government does the opposite.

There are two important aspects to fiscal policy. First, it is not the level of the budget deficit that matters, it is the change in the deficit. Second, changes in the deficit that occur naturally over the course of the business cycle are not stimulative or restrictive.

The Yield Curve

When both fiscal and monetary policies are expansive the yield curve is sharply upward sloping (i.e., short-term rates are lower than long-term rates), and the economy is likely to expand in the future. When fiscal and monetary policies are restrictive, the yield curve is downward sloping (i.e., it is *inverted* as short-term rates are higher than long-term rates), and the economy is likely to contract in the future.

When fiscal and monetary policies are in disagreement, the shape of the yield curve is less definitively shaped. Recall that monetary policy controls primarily short-term interest rates. If monetary policy is expansive while fiscal policy is restrictive, the yield curve will be upward sloping, though it will be less steep than when both policies are expansive. If monetary policy is restrictive while fiscal policy is expansive, the yield curve will be more or less flat.

The Business Cycle and Asset Returns

The relationship between the business cycle and assets returns is well documented. Assets with higher returns during business cycle lows (e.g., bonds and defensive stocks) should be favored by investors because the return supplements their income during recessionary periods. These assets should have lower risk premiums. Assets with lower returns during recessions should have higher risk premiums. Understanding the relationship between an asset's return and the business cycle can help the analyst provide better valuations.

Inflation varies over the business cycle, which has five phases: (1) initial recovery, (2) early expansion, (3) late expansion, (4) slowdown, and (5) recession.

Initial Recovery

- Duration of a few months.
- Business confidence is rising.
- Government stimulation is provided by low interest rates and/or budget deficits.
- Falling inflation.
- Low or falling short-term interest rates.
- Bond yields have bottomed out.
- Rising stock prices.

Early Expansion

- Duration of a year to several years.
- Increasing growth with low inflation.
- Increasing confidence.
- Increasing inventories.
- Rising short-term interest rates.
- Flat or rising bond yields.
- Rising stock prices.

Late Expansion

- Confidence and employment are high.
- Inflation increases.
- Central bank limits the growth of the money supply.
- Rising short-term interest rates.
- Rising bond yields.
- Rising stock prices, but risk increases with investor nervousness.

Slowdown

- Duration of a few months to a year or longer.
- Declining confidence.
- Inflation is still rising.
- Falling inventory levels.

- Short-term interest rates are at a peak.
- Bond yields have peaked and may be falling.
- Falling stock prices.

Recession

- Duration of six months to a year.
- Large declines in inventory.
- Declining confidence and profits.
- Inflation tops out.
- Falling short-term interest rates.
- Falling bond yields, rising prices.
- Stock prices increase during the latter stages anticipating the end of the recession.

Inflation and Asset Returns

In a strong expansion, bonds tend to decline in price as inflationary expectations and interest rates rise. Bond prices rise during a recession when inflation and interest rates are declining. This is also true during deflationary times. The exception here is when credit risk for a particular issue or sector increases during a recession.

Low inflation can be positive for equities given that there are prospects for economic growth free of central bank interference. Equities provide an inflation hedge when inflation is moderate and when price increases can be passed along to the consumer. Inflation rates above 3% can be problematic because of increased likelihood that the central bank will restrict economic growth. Declining inflation or deflation is also problematic because this usually results in declining economic growth and asset prices.

Deflation also reduces the value of real assets financed with debt. In the case of real estate, if the property is levered with debt, declines in the property's value lead to steeper declines in the equity position. When inflation is at or below expectations, the cash flows for real estate and other real assets rise slowly, and returns are near their long-run average. When inflation is high, the cash flows and returns for real assets are higher. Real estate thus provides a good inflation hedge.

Low inflation does not affect the return on cash instruments. Higher inflation is a positive for cash, because the returns on cash instruments increase as inflation increases. Deflation is negative for cash because the return falls to almost zero.

The Taylor Rule   (know this formula)

The Taylor rule determines the target interest rate using the neutral rate, expected GDP relative to its long-term trend, and expected inflation relative to its targeted amount. It can be formalized as follows (know this formula):

$$r_{target} = r_{neutral} + [0.5(GDP_{expected} - GDP_{trend}) + 0.5(i_{expected} - i_{target})]$$

where:

r_{target} = the short-term interest rate target
$r_{neutral}$ = the neutral short-term interest rate
$GDP_{expected}$ = the expected GDP growth rate
GDP_{trend} = the long-term trend in the GDP growth rate
$i_{expected}$ = the expected inflation rate
i_{target} = the target inflation rate

ECONOMIC GROWTH TRENDS

Economic *trends* determine long-term economic growth, whereas *cyclical* components are shorter term. Trends are determined in part by demographics, productivity, and structural changes in governmental policies.

The trend growth rate can be decomposed into two main components: **changes in employment levels** and **changes in productivity**. The former component can be further broken down into **population growth** and the **rate of labor force participation.**

Governmental structural policies should enhance or regulate economic growth:

1. Provide the infrastructure needed for growth.
2. Government should have a responsible *fiscal policy.*
3. Government tax policies should be transparent, consistently applied, pulled from a wide base, and not overly burdensome.
4. Government should promote competition in the marketplace.

EMERGING MARKET ECONOMIES

Six questions to ask:

1. Does the country have responsible fiscal and monetary policies?
2. What is the expected growth? Investors should expect at least 4%.
3. Reasonable currency values and current account deficits?
4. Is the country too highly levered?
5. What is the level of foreign exchange reserves relative to short-term debt?
6. What is the government's stance regarding structural reform?

LINKS BETWEEN ECONOMIES

Macroeconomic linkages refer to similarities in business cycles across countries. Economies are linked by both international trade and capital flows.

Another linkage between economies results from **exchange rates. Interest rates** between the two countries will often reflect a risk premium, with the weaker country having higher interest rates. Interest rate differentials between countries can also reflect differences in economic growth, monetary policy, and fiscal policy. Countries with high *real interest rates* should see the value of their currency increase.

ECONOMIC FORECASTING

Econometric analysis utilizes economic theory to formulate the forecasting model.

Advantages:

- Once established, can be reused.
- Can be quite complex and may accurately model real world conditions.
- Can provide precise quantitative forecasts of economic conditions.

Disadvantages:

- May be difficult and time intensive (expensive) to create.
- Proposed model may not be applicable in future time periods.
- Better at forecasting expansions than recessions.
- Requires scrutiny of output to verify validity.

Economic indicators are available from governments, international organizations (e.g., the Organization of Economic Cooperation and Development), and private organizations (e.g., the Conference Board in the United States).

Advantages:

- Available from outside parties.
- Easy to understand and interpret.
- Can be adapted for specific purposes.
- Effectiveness has been verified by academic research.

Disadvantages:

- Not consistently accurate as economic relationships change through time.
- Forecasts from leading indicators can be misleading.

In a **checklist approach**, the analyst "checks off" a list of questions that should indicate the future growth of the economy.

Advantages:

- Simple.
- Allows changes in the model over time.

Disadvantages:

- Requires subjective judgment.
- May be time intensive to create.
- May not be able to model complex relationships.

Economic Conditions and Asset Class Returns

Emerging Market Government Bonds

Most emerging debt is denominated in a non-domestic currency (e.g., dollars, euros, etc.). Thus, the emerging market government must obtain a hard currency to pay back the principal and interest.

Inflation Indexed Bonds

U.S. Treasury Inflation Protected Securities (TIPS) are both credit risk and inflation risk free. If inflation starts rising, the yields for these bonds will fall as the demand for them increases.

Common Stock

Earnings are commonly used to value the stock market. Aggregate earnings depend primarily on the trended rate of growth in an economy, which in turn depends on the growth in the labor force, new capital inputs, and total factor productivity growth.

When the government promotes competition in the marketplace, this increases the efficiency of the economy, which in turn leads to higher long-term growth in the economy and the stock market.

Shorter-term growth is affected by the business cycle. In a recession, sales and earnings decrease. Noncyclical or defensive stocks (e.g., utilities) are less affected by the business cycle and will have lower risk premiums and higher valuations than cyclical stocks (e.g., technology firms). Cyclical stocks are characterized by high business risk (sensitivity to the business cycle) and/or high fixed costs (operating leverage).

In the early expansion phase of the business cycle, stock prices generally increase and firms usually emerge from a recession leaner because they have shed their wasteful projects and excessive spending. Later on in the expansion, earnings growth slows because input costs start to increase. As mentioned earlier, interest rates will also increase during late expansion, which is a further negative for stock valuation.

P/E ratios are higher in an early expansion period when interest rates are low and earnings prospects are high. They decline as earnings prospects decline.

Emerging Market Stocks

Historical returns for emerging market stocks are higher and more variable than those in the developed world, and seem to be positively correlated with business cycles in the developed world. This correlation is due to trade flows and capital flows.

Real Estate

Real estate assets are affected by interest rates, inflation, the shape of the yield curve, and consumption. Interest rates affect both the supply of and demand for properties through mortgage financing rates.

FORECASTING EXCHANGE RATES

Higher interest rates generally attract capital and increase the domestic currency value. At some level though, higher interest rates result in lower currency values, because the high rates (i.e., inflation) may stifle the economy and make it less attractive to invest there.

Four methods of forecasting exchange rates:

The first method is the relative form of **purchasing power parity** (PPP). The country with higher inflation will see their currency value decline. PPP does not hold in the short term or medium term but holds approximately in the long term (five years or more). Its influence on exchange rates may be swamped by other factors such as trade deficits.

The second method of forecasting currency values is the **relative economic strength approach**. Investors may be attracted by short-term interest rates or by the economic growth in a country. High short-term interest rates will attract investors who bid up the currency value over the short term. Low short-term interest rates will result in borrowing in the currency. After the borrowers take out their loan, they sell the currency for another, thereby putting downward pressure on the low interest rate currency.

The third approach to forecasting exchange rates is the **capital flows approach**. This approach focuses primarily on long-term capital flows such as those into equity investments or foreign direct investments. For example, the strength of the U.S.

dollar in the later 1990s was thought to be due to the strength of the U.S. stock market.

The last approach is the **savings-investment imbalances approach**. This approach explains why currencies may diverge from equilibrium values for extended periods. This approach starts with the concept that an economy must fund investment through savings. If investment is greater than domestic savings, capital must flow into the country from abroad to finance the investment.

MACROANALYSIS AND MICROVALUATION OF THE STOCK MARKET
Cross-Reference to CFA Institute Assigned Reading #24

Cyclical indicators are classified as *leading*, *coincident*, and *lagging*. U.S. cyclical indicators are shown in Figure 1.

Figure 1: U.S. Cyclical Indicators

Leading Indices
1. Average weekly hours, manufacturing
2. Average weekly initial claims for unemployment insurance
3. Manufacturers' new orders, consumer goods and materials
4. Vendor performance, slower deliveries diffusion index
5. Manufacturers' new orders, nondefense capital goods
6. Building permits, new private housing units
7. Stock prices, 500 common stocks
8. Money supply, M2
9. Interest rate spread, 10-year Treasury bonds less federal funds
10. Index of consumer expectations

Coincident Indices
1. Employees on nonagricultural payrolls
2. Personal income less transfer payments
3. Industrial production
4. Manufacturing and trade sales

Lagging Indices
1. Average duration of unemployment
2. Inventories to sales ratio, manufacturing and trade
3. Labor cost per unit of output, manufacturing
4. Average prime rate
5. Commercial and industrial loans
6. Consumer installment credit to personal income ratio
7. Consumer price index for services

Macroeconomic Factors and Security Prices

As the money supply increases, the economy generally expands, and stock returns increase. For a fixed coupon bond, higher interest rates result in a lower price, so there is a negative relationship between inflation and bond prices.

The relationship between inflation, interest rates, and stock returns is not as clear-cut as it is for bonds. An increase in inflation and interest rates will increase the required return on equity. For stock prices to be unchanged, firms have to be able to pass inflation on to the consumer.

Microvaluation

To value an entire stock market using the dividend discount model, you must estimate D_1, k_e, and g for the market.

K_e has two components: the nominal risk-free rate and the equity risk premium. Proxies of the **equity risk premium** include the following:

- Average historic stock returns compared to government bond yields.
- The current dividend yield.
- The current credit risk premium defined as the difference between AAA and Baa bond yields.

The most common way to estimate the **growth rate**, g, is to multiply the average retention ratio by the average return on equity (ROE):

$$g = (\text{retention rate})(\text{ROE})$$

The Free Cash Flow Approach

The free cash flow to equity is defined as cash available to stockholders after funding capital requirements, working capital needs, and debt financing requirements. The value of the market, assuming constant growth, is calculated using the constant growth model with estimates of k_e and g.

The value of the market can also be estimated using a 2-stage FCFE model where non-constant growth is assumed for an initial period followed by constant growth thereafter. In the event the required return is not given on the exam, it can be estimated using the constant growth dividend model:

$$P_0 = \frac{D_1}{k_e - \overline{g}} \Rightarrow k_e = \frac{D_1}{P_0} + \overline{g}$$

The Earnings Multiplier Approach

To derive the P/E ratio, we divide both sides of the DDM by E_1:

$$\frac{P_0}{E_1} = \frac{D_1 / E_1}{k_e - g} \qquad \text{(know this formula)}$$

ESTIMATING EARNINGS PER SHARE: SIX STEPS

1. Estimate sales per share.

2. Estimate profits.

3. Estimate depreciation and amortization expenses per share.

4. Estimate interest expense per share.

5. Estimate the corporate tax rate.

6. Putting it all together:

$$\text{EPS} = [(\text{SPS})(\text{EBITDA \%}) - D - A - I](1 - T) \qquad \text{(know this formula)}$$

DIRECTION OF CHANGE APPROACH AND SPECIFIC ESTIMATE APPROACH

We can calculate the P/E for the market using the market's average required return on equity (k_e), the average growth rate in dividends (g), and the average dividend payout ratio (D_1/E_1). The P/E ratio calculated in this fashion is called the *justified* P/E ratio.

To estimate the future dividend payout ratio (D_1/E_1), the analyst should estimate the dividend payment using time-series analysis, and then relate the estimated dividend to estimated earnings.

Direction of change approach. The analyst examines each input's current value and projects whether it will increase, remain the same, or decrease.

Specific estimate approach. The analyst forecasts point estimates for all inputs to the P/E ratio.

Intrinsic Value and Expected Return on the Market Index

We can estimate the index's *intrinsic value* in one year using the formula:

index intrinsic value = (P/E)(EPS_1), where P/E is the intrinsic P/E

ASSET ALLOCATION

Topic Weight on Exam	0–10%
Study Note Reference	Book 2, Pages 142–193
Video CD Reference	CD 7
Audio CD Reference	CD 9

Asset allocation can easily show up as part of a morning case or be tested alone as an item set in the afternoon. Look for asset allocation to comprise 5% or less of the exam.

ASSET ALLOCATION
Cross-Reference to CFA Institute Assigned Reading #25

Strategic asset allocation combines capital market expectations and the investor's IPS and is long term in nature. Studies have shown that portfolio returns can be attributed primarily to the strategic asset allocation.

Tactical asset allocation (TAA) involves short-term deviations from the strategic asset allocation in an attempt to capitalize on capital market disequilibria (mispricing).

ASSET-ONLY AND ASSET/LIABILITY MANAGEMENT (ALM)

ALM strategic asset allocation is determined in conjunction with modeling the liabilities of the investor. Asset allocation is tailored to meet liabilities and to maximize the surplus given an acceptable level of risk.

In *asset-only strategic asset allocation*, the focus is on earning the highest level of return for a given (acceptable) level of risk.

Dynamic asset allocation takes a multi-period view of the investment horizon. **Static asset allocation** ignores the link between optimal asset allocations across different time periods.

Specifying Risk and Return Objectives

The **return objective** for an individual's or institution's portfolio is based upon the size of the portfolio, long-term spending (liquidity) needs, the time horizon, et cetera, and maintenance of the principal.

Investors can be placed into *numerical categories of risk aversion* using a rough approximation or through answers to questionnaires.

We can determine the *utility-adjusted* return the investor will realize from the portfolio:

$$U_p = \hat{R}_P - 0.005(A)(\sigma_P^2) \qquad \text{(know this formula)}$$

Downside Risk

Shortfall risk is the risk of exceeding a maximum acceptable dollar loss. **Semivariance** is the "bottom half" of the variance (i.e., the variance calculated using only the returns below the expected return). **Target semivariance** is the semivariance using some target minimum return, such as zero.

Roy's Safety-First Measure is one of the oldest and most cited measures of downside risk. The measure is stated as a ratio of *excess return* to risk:

$$SF = \frac{\hat{R}_P - R_{Min}}{\sigma_P} \qquad \text{(know this formula)}$$

Specifying Asset Classes

Asset classes are appropriately specified if:

- Assets are similar from a descriptive and statistical perspective.
- They are not highly correlated so they provide the desired diversification.
- Individual assets cannot be classified into more than one class.
- They cover the majority of all possible investable assets.
- They contain a sufficiently large percentage of liquid assets.

MINIMUM VARIANCE FRONTIER AND EFFICIENT FRONTIER

Figure 1 shows an example of a mean-variance frontier and the efficient frontier.

Figure 1: Mean-Variance (Efficient) Frontier

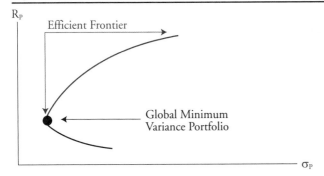

To overcome the uncertainty of estimating the inputs of a mean-variance analysis, the manager uses historical returns, standard deviations, and correlations, assuming they are the true historical values. The manager specifies returns on the efficient frontier and then, using the historical data, has the computer generate a set of mean-variance efficient portfolios; each portfolio (combination of assets) has the minimum standard deviation for the given stated return.

Monte Carlo Simulation

Monte Carlo Simulation overcomes the static (1-period) nature of the typical mean-variance analysis.

Resampled Efficient Frontier

There can be many different combinations (by varying the weights) of a given set of assets that will yield the same expected return and standard deviation, so the program is run many times. Each run generates the same efficient frontier (i.e., same curve on the graph), but each asset has a different weight in each new frontier.

The average weights for each asset are used to represent the weights of the assets in the **resampled efficient frontier.**

The **Black-Litterman process** yields the equilibrium returns implied by existing market prices of assets in a global market index. These returns are used in a mean-variance optimization to determine an efficient frontier. The Black-Litterman method yields portfolios that are much more diversified than those produced in traditional mean-variance analysis.

Asset-Liability Management (ALM) Efficient Frontier

The ALM approach searches for the set of allocations, which maximize the *difference* (the *surplus*) between assets and liabilities at each level of risk. Figure 2 shows an example of an ALM efficient frontier.[1]

Figure 2: The Asset Liability Management (ALM) Efficient Frontier

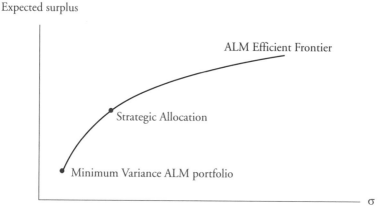

The vertical axis in Figure 2 is the value of the expected surplus, and the horizontal axis represents the associated risk, measured by standard deviation. As with any "efficient" frontier, there is a minimum variance portfolio, which has the minimum expected surplus. As you move to the right on the frontier, both the expected surplus and risk of the allocation increase. In Figure 2, management has selected the allocation labeled "Strategic Allocation."

Experience-based techniques have come about through decades of experience. One accepted guideline is that investors with long-time horizons can tolerate more risk. Another accepted guideline is the 60/40 rule (60% diversified equities and 40% diversified bonds). This long accepted rule is considered a starting point in all individual allocations, because it is considered a *neutral* approach. A guideline that can be applied to adjust this allocation is the "100 – age" rule. You simply subtract the investor's age from 100 to arrive at the preferred allocation to equities, which falls as the investor ages.

Figure 3 contains strengths and weaknesses for the asset allocation approaches discussed.

---

1 The ALM efficient frontier is sometimes referred to as the *surplus* efficient frontier.

©2008 Kaplan Schweser

Figure 3: Strengths and Limitations of Asset Allocation Approaches

Asset Allocation Approach	Strengths	Limitations
Mean variance (MV)	• Optimization programs used to generate the efficient frontier are inexpensive and readily available. • Identifies portfolios with the highest expected return at each level of risk. • Any efficient portfolio (i.e., combination of risk and return) can be created by combining the tangency portfolio with the risk-free rate. • Widely understood and accepted.	• The number and nature of estimates (i.e., expected returns, variances, covariances) can be overwhelming. • Expected returns are subject to estimation bias. • Static (one-period) approach. • Can yield under-diversified (concentrated) portfolios, including the tangency portfolio.
Resampled efficient frontier	• Multiple MV optimization that tends to produce a more stable efficient frontier than the one generated from a single MV optimization. • Tangency portfolio tends to contain all the original assets.	• There is no statistical rationale for this methodology (e.g., no statistical reason that the average weight for each asset in each portfolio should be its most efficient weight in the portfolio). • Relies on historical values (variances and covariances) and estimates (expected returns). • Expected returns are subject to estimation bias. • Static (one-period) approach.
Black-Litterman	• Produces an asset allocation with a higher level of diversification than MV. • Overcomes expected return input bias by incorporating asset class returns implied by a global index.	• Must estimate (i.e., extract) returns from an index. • Can be complex to implement. • Relies on historical values for variance and covariance. • Final product is still a MV optimization. • Static (one-period) approach.

Asset Allocation Approach	Strengths	Limitations
Monte Carlo Simulation	• Overcomes the static nature of the typical MV analysis. • Incorporates the effects of various assumed capital market factors. • Can be used to generate a distribution of probabilities of meeting liabilities (e.g., ALM)	• Can be complex to implement. • Can generate false confidence; the output is only as accurate as the inputs.
ALM	• Considers the allocation of assets with respect to liabilities. • Can generate an ALM frontier that shows the combinations of risk and return and their probability of meeting liabilities.	• Suffers from estimation bias (e.g., expected returns). • Static approach unless combined with Monte Carlo or some other multi-period methodology.
Experience based	• Incorporates decades of asset allocation experience. • Easy to understand. • Inexpensive to implement.	• Not based on sound investment theory. • Allocation rules may be too simple for some investors.

CONSTRAINTS AGAINST SHORT SALES

In the case of a *constrained optimization*, such as no short sales, the minimum variance frontier contains corner portfolios. Figure 4 shows an example of an efficient frontier with six corner portfolios. Portfolio A is the global minimum variance (GMV) portfolio. To create the desired portfolio on the efficient frontier, we only need the characteristics of the two *adjacent* corner portfolios.

Figure 4: Efficient Frontier with Corner Portfolios

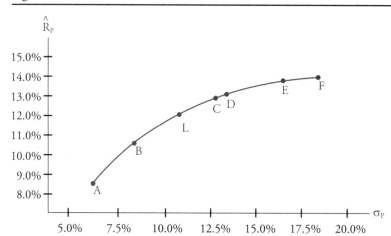

The expected return for the portfolio is the weighted average of the expected returns on the adjacent corner portfolios. The standard deviation of that portfolio is also calculated as a weighted average. Note that this assumes the corner portfolios are perfectly, positively correlated ($\rho = +1$), so the calculated standard deviation is actually the maximum possible standard deviation of the portfolio.

Special Considerations

Sometimes the IPS may specifically provide for some cash flow needs in the short term. For example, an individual investor may consider providing for retirement her primary investment goal, with a secondary goal of taking a vacation in six month. She wants to have $50,000 available towards that planned expense. In such a situation, the *present value* of the projected cash flow should be invested in cash equivalents. The remainder of the portfolio is allocated according to the IPS.

STRATEGIC ASSET ALLOCATION ISSUES

Unlike institutional investors, the typical individual's wealth is accumulated over many years, while the ability to generate income reaches a peak and falls to zero at retirement. The individual's *human capital* is greatest at an early age, while financial capital increases over time and reaches a maximum at retirement.

Another factor that separates individuals from institutions is **longevity risk**. This is the possibility of living longer than planned. The inverse (sort of) of longevity risk is **mortality risk**; the risk of dying younger than expected. Mortality risk is usually mitigated by purchasing life insurance. Note that the individual bears at least part of the longevity risk, but the individual's spouse and other heirs bear the mortality risk.

Defined benefit pension plans are concerned foremost with meeting pension obligations, so an ALM process is generally employed.

The primary goal of an **endowment** is meeting spending requirements while protecting the fund principal. The relevant rate of inflation for an endowment is the rate that affects its institutional beneficiary.

Foundations are formed to provide grants to individuals, communities, and/or organizations. Depending upon their legal status, foundations are required to make minimum annual payouts based upon a percentage of fund assets. The primary goal is to cover the spending requirement while protecting the fund's principal. From a strategic asset allocation standpoint, foundations and endowments are very similar.

The characteristic that distinguishes **insurance companies** from most other institutional investors is the need to *segment* their portfolio. The portfolio is segmented along product lines, as each line has risk and return objectives related to its specific constraints.

The strategic allocation for **banks** is determined by their product mix and the goals of the securities portfolio. The primary goals for a bank's securities portfolio are providing liquidity, managing credit risk, managing duration, and generating income.

LINKING PENSION LIABILITIES TO ASSETS
Cross-Reference to CFA Institute Assigned Reading #26

Under an **asset-only approach**, a pension fund focuses on selecting efficient portfolios. It does not attempt to explicitly hedge the risk of the liabilities. This approach ignores the fact that a future liability is subject to market-related risk.

A more appropriate asset allocation approach would be the **liability-relative approach**, in which the portfolio is chosen for its ability to *mimic* the liability. In the **asset-only approach**, the focus is instead on low-risk investments with a low correlation to firm assets.

Pension Liability Exposures

For most corporations, the future pension obligation is largely unrelated to short-term changes in long-term interest rates, as most corporate pension plans have a long life. An appropriate liability modeling captures the risk of the fund not satisfying short-term obligations, as well as the risk of not satisfying the longer-term liabilities.

Market Exposures due to Accrued Benefits

To decompose the pension liability's risk exposures, the total pension obligation should be separated into that due to *inactive participants* and that due to *active participants*. Active participants are those currently working for the firm. The obligations to these employees can be separated into that owed for past service and that owed for expected future service. As with inactive participants, the obligations for past service are fixed unless there is inflation indexing. The retirement payments owed to inactive participants and the payments for past service to active participants constitute *accrued benefits*.

Market Exposures Due to Future Benefits

In the case where a pension plan is frozen, no future benefits will be paid, and the plan's only liability is that which has accrued. In this case, the liability mimicking portfolio is one consisting of nominal and inflation-indexed bonds.

Future benefits are those from wages to be earned in the future, by existing employees as well as new entrants into the plan. The first component of future benefits is wages to be earned in the future. The growth in future wages can be decomposed into growth from inflation and real growth. In the former case, wages will grow with inflation. Many plans, however, do not index benefits for inflation after the employee retires. Therefore, the liability-mimicking portfolio is a portfolio of inflation-indexed and nominal bonds. The closer the workforce is to retirement, the larger the proportion of nominal bonds in the portfolio. Wage growth arising from real growth is due to increases in labor productivity. This productivity will be reflected in GDP, which is strongly correlated with the stock market.

The *second* component of future benefits is from *future service rendered*. As in the case of future retirement payments, future service benefits are linked to wage growth. This amount, however, is uncertain and not usually funded, so it is not modeled in the investment benchmark. The *third* component of future benefits, from new entrants into the plan, is also excluded from the benchmark portfolio, as it is the most uncertain of plan benefits.

Non-Market Exposures

Pensions are also subject to non-market exposures referred to as *liability noise*. These exposures can be divided into two parts, that due to plan demographics and that due to model uncertainty. Demographics are primarily affected by the number of participants and can be estimated using statistical models. Model uncertainty is less predictable and is different for inactive versus active participants.

Inactive participants can be divided into retirees (i.e., currently receiving benefits) and deferreds (i.e., working for the company but not yet eligible for benefits).

The source of liability noise arising from retirees is the mortality assumption. For deferreds, there is mortality risk (longevity risk) as well as uncertainty arising from when retirement occurs. The sooner the deferreds retire, the smaller the benefit paid for a longer period of time. Thus, for deferreds, there is uncertainty in the timing and amount of liability as well as longevity risk. For these reasons, the liability noise associated with deferreds is larger and less easily hedged than that for retirees. The liability noise arising from active participants is even greater than that from deferreds.

Figure 5 summarizes the exposures of a pension plan and the assets needed to satisfy them, assuming no inflation indexing. For the exam, focus on the top three plan segments.

Figure 5: Pension Liability Exposures

Pension Plan Segment	Market or non-market exposure	Risk Exposure	Liability Mimicking Assets
Inactive-accrued	Market	Term structure	Nominal bonds
Active-accrued	Market	Term structure	Nominal bonds
Active-future wage growth	Market	Term structure	Nominal bonds
	Market	Inflation	Real return bonds
	Market	Economic growth	Equities
Active-future service rendered	Market	Similar to wage growth but more uncertain	Not typically funded
Active-future participants	Market	Very uncertain	Not typically funded
Liability noise-demographics	Non-market	Plan demographics	Not easily hedged
Liability noise-inactive	Non-market	Model uncertainty & longevity risk	Not easily hedged or modeled
Liability noise-active	Non-market	Model uncertainty & longevity risk	Not easily hedged or modeled

Management of Passive and Active Fixed Income Portfolios

Topic Weight on Exam	5–10%
Study Notes Reference	Book 3, Pages 8–64
Video CD Reference	CD 8
Audio CD Reference	CD 10

Fixed-Income Portfolio Management—Part 1[1]
Cross-Reference to CFA Institute Assigned Reading #27

Bond Indexing Strategies

Bond portfolio management strategies form a continuum from an almost do-nothing approach (i.e., pure bond indexing) to a do-almost-anything approach (i.e., full blown active management) as demonstrated graphically in Figure 1.

Figure 1: Increasing Degrees of Active Bond Portfolio Management

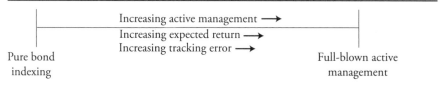

In Figure 1, you will notice the increase of three characteristics as you move from pure bond indexing to full blown active management. The first, *increasing active management*, can be defined as the gradual relaxation of restrictions on the manager's actions to allow him to exploit his superior forecasting/valuation abilities. With pure bond indexing, the manager is restricted to constructing a portfolio with all the securities in the index and in the same weights as the index. This means the portfolio will have exactly the same risk exposures as the index. As you move from left to right, the restrictions on the manager's actions are relaxed and the portfolio risk factor exposures differ more and more from those of the index.

---

1   Much of the terminology utilized throughout this topic review is industry convention as presented in Reading 27 of the 2008 CFA Level 3 curriculum.

The next characteristic, *increasing expected return*, refers to the increase in portfolio expected return from actions taken by the manager. Unless the manager has some superior ability that enables him to identify profitable situations, he should stick with pure bond indexing or at least match primary risk factors.

The third, *increasing tracking error*, refers to the degree to which the portfolio return tracks that of the index. With pure bond indexing, even though management fees and transactions are incurred, the reduced return on the portfolio will track the return on the index almost perfectly. As you move to the right, the composition and factor exposures of the portfolio differ more and more from the index. Each enhancement is intended to increase the portfolio return, but is not guaranteed to do so. Thus, the amount by which the portfolio return exceeds the index return can be quite variable from period to period and even negative. The difference between the portfolio and index returns (i.e., the portfolio excess return) is referred to as *alpha*. The standard deviation of alpha across several periods is referred to as *tracking error*, thus it is the variability of the portfolio excess return that increases as you move towards full blown active management. This increased variability translates into increased uncertainty.

The five classifications of bond portfolio management can be described as (1) *pure bond indexing*, (2) *enhanced indexing by matching primary risk factors*, (3) *enhanced indexing by small risk factor mismatches*, (4) *active management by larger risk factor mismatches*, and (5) *full-blown active management*.

Figure 2 is a summary of the advantages and disadvantages of the bond portfolio strategies.

Figure 2: Advantages and Disadvantages of Bond Portfolio Management Strategies

Strategy	Advantages	Disadvantages
Pure bond indexing (PBI)	• Tracks the index (zero or very low tracking error) • Same risk factor exposures as the index • Low advisory and administrative fees	• Costly and difficult to implement • Lower expected return than the index
Enhanced indexing by matching primary risk factors (sampling)	• Less costly to implement • Increased expected return • Maintains exposure to the index's primary risk factors	• Increased management fees • Lowered ability to track the index (i.e., increased tracking error) • Lower expected return than the index
Enhanced indexing by small risk factor mismatches	• Same duration as index • Increased expected return • Reduced manager restrictions	• Increased risk • Increased tracking error • Increased management fees
Active management by larger risk factor mismatches	• Same duration as index • Increased expected return • Reduced manager restrictions	• Increased risk • Increased tracking error • Increased management fees
Full blown active management	• Increased expected return • Few if any manager restrictions • No limits on duration	• Increased risk • Increased tracking error • Increased management fees

SELECTING A BOND INDEX

A bond portfolio manager should move from a pure indexing position to more active management only when the client's objectives and constraints permit and the manager's abilities justify it.

Regardless of the strategy employed, the manager should be judged against a benchmark, and the benchmark should match the characteristics of the portfolio. Among others, there are four primary considerations when selecting a benchmark: (1) *market value risk*, (2) *income risk*, (3) *credit risk*, and (4) *liability framework risk*.

Here are four points to remember:

1. *Market value risk* varies directly with maturity. The greater the risk aversion, the lower the acceptable market risk, and the shorter the benchmark maturity.

2. *Income risk* varies indirectly with maturity. The more dependent the client is upon a reliable income stream, the longer the maturity of the benchmark.

3. *Credit risk*. The credit risk of the benchmark should closely match the credit risk of the portfolio.

4. *Liability framework risk* is applicable only to portfolios managed according to a liability structure and should always be minimized.

ALIGNING RISK EXPOSURES

To avoid the costs associated with purchasing every bond in the index yet maintain the same risk exposures, the manager will usually hold a sample of the bonds in the index. One sampling technique often utilized is **stratified sampling** (a.k.a. *cell-matching*). Constructing a portfolio with risk exposures identical to the benchmark, however, does not require the composition of the portfolio (i.e., the bonds held) to be representative of the index. A portfolio can be constructed with exactly the same risk factor exposures as the benchmark but with different securities utilizing a **multifactor model**. However, the manager must determine the risk profile of the benchmark. Risk profiling the index requires measuring the index's exposure to factors including duration, key rate duration, cash flow distribution, sector and quality weights, and duration contribution, et cetera.

Duration. Effective duration (a.k.a. option-adjusted or adjusted duration), which is used to estimate the change in the value of a portfolio given a small parallel shift in the yield curve, is probably the most obvious risk factor to be measured. Due to the linear nature of duration, which makes it overestimate the increase or decrease in the value of the portfolio, the convexity effect is also considered.

Key rate duration. Where effective duration measures the portfolio's sensitivity to parallel shifts in the yield curve, key rate duration measures the portfolio's sensitivity to twists in the yield curve.

The manager should also consider the **present value distribution of cash flows (PVD)** of the index used as the portfolio benchmark. PVD measures the proportion of the index's total duration attributable to cash flows falling within selected time periods.

The present value (i.e., the market value) of all cash flows from the index that fall in each period is divided by the present value of all cash flows (i.e., the benchmark market value) to determine the percentage of the total market value that is attributable to cash flows falling in each period.

Next, the manager multiplies the duration of a given period by the percentage of cash flows falling in that period to arrive at the duration contribution for that period. Dividing the duration contribution for each time period by the benchmark duration yields PVD. If the manager duplicates the benchmark PVD, the portfolio and the benchmark will have the same sensitivity to both shifts and twists in the yield curve.

Sector and quality percent. The manager should match the weights of both the sectors and qualities in the index.

Sector duration contributions. The manager should match the proportion of the index duration that is contributed by each sector in the index.

Quality spread duration contribution. The manager should match the proportion of the index duration that is contributed by each quality in the index, where quality refers to categories of bonds by rating.

Sector/coupon/maturity cell weights. Convexity is difficult to measure for callable bonds. To mimic the *callability* of bonds in the index (i.e., the sensitivity of their prices to interest rate changes) the manager is better off matching their sector, coupon, and maturity weights in the index.

Issuer exposure. The final risk factor considered is issuer exposure, which is a measure of the index's *event exposure*. In mimicking the index, the manager should use a sufficient number of securities in the portfolio so that the event risk attributable to any individual issuer is minimized.

SCENARIO ANALYSIS

Potential Performance of a Trade

Estimating expected total return under a single set of assumptions (predictions) only provides a point estimate of the investment's expected return (i.e., a single number). Combining total return analysis with scenario analysis allows the analyst to assess not only the return but also its volatility (distribution) under different scenarios.

CLASSICAL IMMUNIZATION

Interest rate risk has two components: price risk and reinvestment rate risk. *Price risk* refers to the decrease (increase) in bond prices as interest rates rise (fall). *Reinvestment rate risk* refers to the increase (decrease) in investment income as interest rates rise (fall). It is important to note that price risk and reinvestment rate risk cause opposite effects.

Classic Immunization

Classic immunization is the process of structuring a bond portfolio that balances any change in the value of the portfolio with the return from the reinvestment of the coupon and principal payments received throughout the investment period. The goal of classical immunization is to form a portfolio so that:

- If interest rates increase, the gain in reinvestment income ≥ loss in portfolio value.
- If interest rates decrease, the gain in portfolio value ≥ loss in reinvestment income.

Immunizing a Single Obligation

To effectively immunize a single liability:

- *Select* a bond (or bond portfolio) with an effective duration equal to the duration of the liability.
- Set the present value of the bond (or bond portfolio) equal to the present value of the liability.

Adjustments to the Immunized Portfolio

Without rebalancing, classical immunization only works for a 1-time instantaneous change in interest rates. In reality, interest rates fluctuate frequently, changing the duration of the portfolio and necessitating a change in the immunization strategy. Furthermore, the mere passage of time causes the duration of both the portfolio and its target liabilities to change, although not usually at the same rate.

Remember, portfolios cease to be immunized for a single liability when:

- Interest rates fluctuate more than once.
- Time passes.

Rebalancing frequency is a cost-benefit trade-off. Transaction costs associated with rebalancing must be weighed against the possible extent to which the terminal value of the portfolio may fall short of its target liability.

Bond Characteristics to Consider

It is important to consider several characteristics of the individual bonds that are used to construct an immunized portfolio.

- *Credit rating.*
- *Embedded options.*
- *Liquidity.*

Immunization Against Non-Parallel Shifts

Equating the duration of the portfolio with the duration of the liability does not guarantee immunization. *Immunization risk* can be thought of as a measure of the relative extent to which the terminal value of an immunized portfolio falls short of its target value as a result of arbitrary (nonparallel) changes in interest rates. Immunized portfolios with cash flows that are concentrated around the investment horizon have the lowest immunization risk.

ADJUSTING DOLLAR DURATION

Two primary steps:

1. Calculate the new dollar duration of the portfolio.

2. Calculate the **rebalancing ratio** and us it to determine the required percentage change (i.e., cash needed) in the value of the portfolio.

Reestablishing the Portfolio Dollar Duration (know these calculations)

A portfolio with a dollar duration of $162,658 consists of four bonds with the indicated weights, durations, and dollar durations:

	Market Value	×	Duration	× 0.01 =	Dollar Duration
Bond 1	$1,000,000		5.0		$50,000
Bond 2	1,350,000		4.5		60,750
Bond 3	965,000		3.0		28,950
Bond 4	883,000		2.6		22,958
Portfolio	$4,198,000				$162,658

One year later, the yield curve has shifted upward with the following results:

	Market Value	×	Duration	× 0.01 =	Dollar Duration
Bond 1	$958,500		4.1		$39,299
Bond 2	1,100,000		3.6		39,600
Bond 3	725,000		2.2		15,950
Bond 4	683,000		1.8		12,294
Portfolio	$3,466,500				$107,143

$$\text{Rebalancing ratio} = \frac{\text{old DD}}{\text{new DD}} = \frac{162,658}{107,143} = 1.52$$

To readjust back to the original dollar duration as well as maintain the current proportions of each bond in the portfolio, we subtract 1.0 from the rebalancing

---

ratio to arrive at the necessary increase in the value of each bond in the portfolio and, thus, the total increase in the portfolio value (i.e., required additional cash):

$$1.52 - 1 = 0.52; \ 0.52 \times \$3,466,500 = \$1,802,580$$

The increases (in dollars) required for the individual bonds in the portfolio are:

Bond 1:	$958,500	× 0.52	= $498,420
Bond 2:	$1,100,000	× 0.52	= $572,000
Bond 3:	$725,000	× 0.52	= $377,000
Bond 4:	$683,000	× 0.52	= $355,160
			$1,802,580

Alternatively, the manager could select one of the bonds to use as a **controlling position**. Since the dollar duration has fallen dramatically and Bond 1 has the longest duration, the manager could use less additional cash by increasing only the holding in Bond 1 (i.e., using Bond 1 as the controlling position):

Desired increase in DD = $162,658 − $107,143 = $55,515

Increase in Bond 1: New DD of Bond 1 = $39,299 + $55,515 = $94,814

$$\text{Required new value of Bond 1} = \frac{\$94,814}{\$39,299} \times \$958,500 = \$2,312,507$$

Thus, instead of investing $1,802,580 in all the bonds, the manager could purchase another $1,354,007 (= $2,312,507 − $958,500) of Bond 1 and return the portfolio dollar duration back to its original level.

	Market Value	×	Duration	× 0.01 =	Dollar Duration
Bond 1	$2,312,507		4.1		$94,813
Bond 2	1,100,000		3.6		39,600
Bond 3	725,000		2.2		15,950
Bond 4	683,000		1.8		12,294
Portfolio	$4,820,507				$162,657

SPREAD DURATION

Spread duration measures the sensitivity of non-Treasury issues to a change in their spread above Treasuries of the same maturity. (The spread is a function of perceived risk as well as market risk aversion.)

There are three spread duration measures used for fixed-rate bonds:

1. *Nominal spread.*

2. *Zero-volatility spread (or static spread).*

3. *Option-adjusted spread (OAS).*

EXTENSIONS TO CLASSICAL IMMUNIZATION

When the goal is to immunize against a liability we must consider changes in the value of the liability, which in turn could change the amount of assets needed for the immunization. We must also consider the ability to combine indexing (immunization) strategies with active portfolio management strategies. Note that since active management exposes the portfolio to additional risks, immunization strategies are also *risk-minimizing strategies.*

The bottom line is that classical immunization strategies may not be sufficient in managing a portfolio to immunize against a liability. To address the deficiencies in classical immunization, four extensions have been offered: (1) *multifunctional duration,* (2) *multiple liability immunization,* (3) *relaxation of the minimum risk requirement,* and (4) *contingent immunization.*

The first modification or extension to classical immunization theory is the use of **multifunctional duration** (a.k.a. **key rate duration**). The manager focuses on certain key interest rate maturities.

The second extension is **multiple liability immunization**. The goal of multiple liability immunization is ensuring that the portfolio contains sufficient liquid assets to meet all the liabilities as they come due. That is, rather than monitor the value of the portfolio as if the liability is its minimum target value at a single horizon date, there can be numerous certain or even uncertain liabilities with accompanying numerous horizon dates.

The third extension is allowing for **increased risk**, or otherwise relaxing the minimum risk requirement of classical immunization. As long as the manager does not jeopardize meeting the liability structure, he can pursue increased risk strategies that could lead to excess portfolio value (i.e., a terminal portfolio value greater than the liability).

Contingent immunization is the combination of active management strategies and passive management techniques (immunization). As long as the rate of return on the portfolio exceeds a prespecified *safety net return*, the portfolio is managed actively. If the portfolio return declines to the safety net return, the immunization mode is triggered to "lock in" the safety net return. The safety net return is the minimum acceptable return as designated by the client.

Key considerations in implementing a contingent immunization strategy are as follows:

- Determining available target returns.
- Identifying an appropriate safety net return.
- Establishing effective monitoring procedures to ensure adherence to the contingent immunization plan.

IMMUNIZATION RISKS

Interest rate risk is the primary concern when managing a fixed income portfolio, whether against a liability structure or a benchmark.

Contingent claim risk (a.k.a. call risk or prepayment risk). Callable bonds are typically called only after interest rates have fallen. This means that the manager not only loses the higher stream of coupons that were originally incorporated into the immunization strategy, she is faced with reinvesting the principal at a reduced rate of return.

Cap risk. If any of the bonds in the portfolio have floating rates, they may be subject to *cap risk*. As used here, cap risk refers to a cap on the floating rate adjustment to the coupon on a floating rate security. If the bonds are subject to caps when interest rates rise, they might not fully adjust and thus would affect the immunization capability of the portfolio.

IMMUNIZING SINGLE LIABILITIES, MULTIPLE LIABILITIES, AND GENERAL CASH FLOWS

If a manager could invest in a zero-coupon Treasury with a maturity equal to the liability horizon, he has constructed an immunization strategy with no risk. Since this is rarely the case, however, the manager must take steps to *minimize risk*.

To reduce the risk associated with uncertain **reinvestment rates**, the manager should minimize the *distribution* of the maturities of the bonds in the portfolio around the (single) liability date. Concentrating the maturities of the bonds around the liability date is known as a **bullet strategy**. Think of a strategy employing two bonds. One bond matures one year before the liability date and the other matures one year after the liability date. When the first matures, the proceeds must be reinvested for only one year. At the date of the liability, the maturity of the other is only one year off. Thus the reinvestment rate on the first will have a minimal impact on the terminal value of the portfolio and the value of the second is only minimally sensitive to interest rates.

Now consider a **barbell strategy** where the first bond matures several years before the liability date and the other several years after the liability date. The face value of the first must be reinvested when it matures, so the manager must be concerned with both the reinvestment rate and, since the new bond will have several years until maturity, all the other risk factors associated with such a bond. The second bond, since it matures several years after the liability date, is subject to significant interest rate risk. That is, the value of the bond at the liability date is determined by interest rates at that date.

As the maturities of the bullet strategy move away from the liability date and the maturities of the barbell move toward the liability date, the distinction between the two will begin to blur. Rather than base the strategy on subjective judgment, therefore, the manager can minimize M^2 (a.k.a. maturity variance).

Maturity variance is the variance of the differences in the maturities of the bonds used in the immunization strategy and the maturity date of the liability. For example, if all the bonds have the same maturity date as the liability, M^2 is zero. As the dispersion of the maturity dates increases, M^2 increases.

Multiple Liabilities

The key to immunizing multiple liabilities is to decompose the portfolio payment streams in such a way that the component streams separately immunize each of the multiple liabilities. Multiple liability immunization is possible if the following three conditions are satisfied (*assuming parallel rate shifts*):

1. Assets and liabilities have the same present values.

2. Assets and liabilities have the same aggregate durations.

3. The range of the distribution of durations of individual assets in the portfolio exceeds the distribution of liabilities. This is a necessary condition in order to be able to use cash flows generated from our assets (which will include principal payments from maturing bonds) to sufficiently meet each of our cash outflow needs.

Conditions for Cash Flow Matching

Cash flow matching serves as an alternative to immunization for funding a stream of liabilities. The following points describe the process:

- Select a bond with a maturity date equal to that of the last liability payment date.
- Buy enough in par value of this bond such that its principal and final coupon fully fund the last liability.
- Using a recursive procedure (i.e., working backwards), choose another bond that fully funds the second-to-last liability payment and continue until all liability payments have been addressed.

General Cash Flows

General cash flows in this case refers to using cash as part of an immunization strategy even though the cash has not yet been received. For example, expecting a cash flow in six months, the portfolio manager does not put the entire amount required for immunization into the portfolio today. Instead he looks at the expected cash flows as a zero and incorporates its payoff and duration into the immunization strategy.

RISK MINIMIZATION VS. RETURN MAXIMIZATION

Return maximization is the concept behind *contingent immunization*. Consider the manager who has the ability to lock in an immunized rate of return equal to or greater than the required safety net return. As long as that manager feels he can generate even greater returns, he should pursue active management in hopes of generating excess value.

CASH FLOW MATCHING

Cash flow matching is used to construct a portfolio that will fund a stream of liabilities with portfolio coupons and maturity values. To construct the portfolio, the manager first selects a bond with a maturity date and value equal to the last liability. (Maturity value includes the face value and last coupon.) Once that bond has been selected, the manager reduces all earlier liabilities to reflect the other coupons received on that bond. Another bond is then selected to match the maturity of the second to last liability with a maturity value reflecting the remaining value of that liability. The earlier coupons on the second bond are then applied against all remaining liabilities. This progression of matching the maturity value and date of a bond to each successively closer liability is continued until all the liabilities are funded.

Since it is unlikely that the cash flows from a bond portfolio will exactly match the liabilities, reinvestment risk is inherent in cash flow matching. As such, a minimum-risk immunization approach to funding multiple liabilities is at least equal to cash flow matching, and probably better, since it would be less expensive to fund a given stream of liabilities.

The following are the differences between cash flow matching and multi-liability immunization:

- Cash flow matching depends upon all the cash flows of the portfolio, so managers must use conservative reinvestment assumptions for all cash flows. This tends to increase the overall value of the required immunizing portfolio. An immunized portfolio is essentially fully invested at the duration of the remaining horizon, so only the average reinvestment ratio over the entire investment horizon must be considered.

- Owing to the exact matching problem, only asset flows from a cash-flow-matched portfolio that occur prior to the liability may be used to meet the obligation. An immunized portfolio is only required to have sufficient value on the date of each liability because funding is achieved through portfolio rebalancing.

Combination matching, also known as *horizon matching*, is a combination of multiple liability immunization and cash flow matching that can be used to address the asset cash flow/liability matching problem. This strategy creates a portfolio that is *duration* matched. During the first few years, the portfolio would also be cash flow matched in order to make sure that assets were properly dispersed to meet the near-term obligations.

Combination matching offers the following *advantages* over multiple liability immunization:

- Provides liquidity in the initial period.
- Reduces the risk associated with nonparallel shifts in the yield curve which usually take place in the early years.

The primary *disadvantage* of combination matching is that it tends to be more expensive than multiple liability immunization.

RELATIVE-VALUE METHODOLOGIES FOR GLOBAL CREDIT BOND PORTFOLIO MANAGEMENT[2]
Cross-Reference to CFA Institute Assigned Reading #28

In relative value analysis, assets are compared along readily identifiable characteristics and value measures. In comparing firms, for example, we can use measures such as P/E ratios for ranking. With bonds, some of the characteristics used include sector, issue, and structure, which are used to rank the bonds across and within categories by expected performance. You are familiar with two of these methodologies:

- In the **top-down approach**, the manager uses economy-wide projections to first allocate funds to different countries or currencies. The analyst then determines what industries or sectors are expected to outperform and selects individual securities within those industries.
- The **bottom-up approach** starts at the "bottom." The analyst selects undervalued issues.

Any bond analysis should focus on total return. The analyst performs a detailed study of how past total returns for markets or individual securities were affected by macroeconomic events, such as interest rate changes and general economic performance. Any trends detected are used to estimate future total returns, based upon predictions for those same macro-trends.

---

2   The terminology presented in this topic review follows industry convention as presented in Reading 28 of the 2008 CFA Level 3 exam curriculum.

CYCLICAL AND SECULAR CHANGES

Cyclical changes are changes in the number of new bond issues. Increases in the number of new bond issues are sometimes associated with narrower spreads and relatively strong returns. Corporate bonds often perform best during periods of heavy supply.

Secular changes. In all but the high-yield market, intermediate-term bullets dominate the corporate bond market. Bullet maturities are not callable, putable, or sinkable. Callable issues still dominate the high-yield segment.

There are at least three implications associated with these product structures:

1. Securities with embedded options will trade at premium prices due to their scarcity value.

2. Credit managers seeking longer durations will pay a premium price for longer duration securities because of the tendency toward intermediate maturities.

3. Credit-based derivatives will be increasingly used to take advantage of return and/or diversification benefits across sectors, structures, and so forth.

LIQUIDITY

There is generally a positive relationship between liquidity and bond prices. As liquidity decreases, investors are willing to pay less (increasing yields), and as liquidity increases, investors are willing to pay more (decreasing yields).

The corporate debt market has shown variable liquidity over time, influenced to a great extent by macro shocks (i.e., a variety of economic conditions). And while some investors are willing to give up additional return by investing in issues that possess greater liquidity (e.g., larger-sized issues and government issues), other investors are willing to sacrifice liquidity for issues which offer a greater yield (e.g., smaller-sized issues and private placements). The move in debt markets has been toward increased liquidity (i.e., faster and cheaper trading) mainly due to trading innovations and competition among portfolio managers.

RATIONALES FOR SECONDARY BOND TRADES

The following are some of the reasons why managers actively trade in the secondary bond markets, rather than simply hold their portfolios. In all cases, the manager must determine whether trading will produce returns greater than the associated costs or not.

- Yield/spread pickup trades.
- Credit-upside trades.
- Credit-defense trades.

- New issue swaps.
- Sector-rotation trades.
- Yield curve-adjustment trades.
- Structure trades.
- Cash flow reinvestment trades.

Relative-value analysis can be used to identify bonds that will have the greatest price change (and total return) in response to interest rate changes. The following general rules apply:

- If interest rates are expected to rise, buy short-duration bonds and sell long-duration bonds.
- If interest rates are expected to fall, buy long-duration bonds and sell short-duration bonds.

ASSESSING RELATIVE VALUE METHODOLOGIES

Rationales for not trading include:

- Trading constraints.
- Story disagreement.
- Buy and hold.
- Seasonality.

SPREAD ANALYSIS

Mean-reversion analysis. The presumption with mean reversion is that spreads between sectors tend to revert toward their historical means.

- If the current spread is significantly greater than the historic mean, buy the sector or issue.
- If the current spread is significantly less than the historic mean, sell the sector or issue.
- Statistical analysis, using standard deviations and t-scores (for determining significance), can be used to determine if the current spread is significantly different from the mean.

Quality-spread analysis. Quality-spread analysis is based on the spread differential between low and high quality credits.

Percentage yield spread analysis. Percentage yield spread analysis *divides* the yields on corporate bonds by the yields on treasuries with the same duration. If the ratio is higher than justified by the historical ratio, the spread is expected to fall, making corporate bond prices rise.

BOND STRUCTURES

Bullet Structures

Short-term bullets have maturities of one to five years and are used on the short end of a barbell strategy. As opposed to using short-term Treasuries, corporate securities are used at the front end of the yield curve with long-term Treasuries at the long end of the yield curve.

Medium-term bullets (maturities of 5 to 12 years) are the most popular sector in the United States and Europe. When the yield curve is positively sloped, 20-year structures are often attractive, because they offer higher yields than 10- or 15-year structures but lower duration than 30-year securities.

Long-term bullets (30-year maturities) are the most commonly used long-term security in the global corporate bond market. They offer managers and investors additional positive convexity at the cost of increased effective duration.

Early Retirement Provisions

Due to the *negative convexity* caused by the embedded option, *callable* bonds do the following:

- **Underperform** non-callables when interest rates fall (relative to the coupon rate) due to their negative convexity.
- **Outperform** non-callables in bear bond markets with rising rates as the probability of call falls. (When the current rate is lower than the coupon rate, their negative convexity makes callables respond less to increasing rates.)
- When yields are very high, relative to coupon rates, the callable bond will behave much the same as the non-callable (i.e., the call option has little or no value).

Sinking funds. Sinking fund structures priced at a discount to par have historically retained upside price potential during interest rate declines as long as the bonds remain priced at a discount to par (the firm can call the bonds back at par). Furthermore, given that the issuer is usually required to repurchase part of the issue each year, the price of sinking fund structures does not fall as much relative to callable and bullet structures when interest rates rise.

CREDIT ANALYSIS

Credit analysis involves examining financial statements, bond documents, and trends in credit ratings. It provides an analytic framework in assessing key information in sector selection:

- Capacity to pay is the key factor in corporate credit analysis.
- The quality of the collateral and the servicer are important in the analysis of asset-backed securities.

- The ability to assess and collect taxes is the key consideration for municipal bonds.
- Sovereign credit analysis requires an assessment of the country's ability to pay (economic risk) and willingness to pay (political risk).

Figure 3 is a compilation of the primary relative valuation methodologies along with their descriptions.

Figure 3: Relative Value Methodologies

Methodology	Description	Strategy
Total return analysis	Consider coupons (yield) as well as potential price increases or decreases.	Study past bond reactions to macroeconomic changes to project future returns.
Primary market analysis	Supply of and demand for new issues affects returns. Increases (decreases) in new issues tend to decrease (increase) relative yields.	When you expect rates to fall, you expect new issues and refinances to increase.
Liquidity and trading analysis	Liquidity drives bid-ask prices and yields. As liquidity increases, demand increases. As trading increases, prices increase and yields decrease.	Identify issues/sectors that you expect to increase in price from increased liquidity.
Secondary trading rationales	Reasons for trading.	Yield/spread pickup trades. Credit-upside trades. Credit-defense trades. New issue swaps. Sector-rotation trades. Curve-adjustment trades. Structure trades. Cash flow reinvestment.
Secondary trading constraints	Reasons for not trading.	Portfolio constraints. "Story" disagreement. Buy and hold. Seasonality.
Spread analysis	Analyze the various spreads. With increased rate volatility (uncertainty), spreads tend to increase and widen with maturity.	Mean-reversion analysis. Quality-spread analysis. Percentage yield spread analysis.
Structural analysis	Study the structure of bond issues.	Determine which bond structures will perform best given your macro predictions.
Corporate curve analysis	Study credit and yield curves. With increased rate volatility (uncertainty), spreads tend to increase and widen with maturity.	Corporate spread curves tend to change with the economic cycle (i.e., narrow during upturns and widen during downturns).
Credit analysis	Upgrades cause reduced yields and increased prices. Downgrades cause increased yields and decreased prices.	Identify credit upgrade and downgrade candidates.
Asset allocation/ Sector analysis	Macro allocation is across sectors. Micro allocation is within a sector.	Identify sectors/firms expected to outperform.

FIXED-INCOME PORTFOLIO MANAGEMENT—PART II

Topic Weight on Exam	5–10%
Study Note Reference	Book 3, Pages 8–64
Video CD Reference	CDs 9 & 10
Audio CD Reference	CDs 10 & 11

LEVERAGE

The Effect of Leverage on Return

A portfolio manager has a portfolio worth $100 million, $30 million of which is his own funds and $70 million is borrowed. If the return on the invested funds is 6% and the cost of borrowed funds is 5%, **calculate** the return on the portfolio.

Answer:

The gross profit on the portfolio is: $100 million × 6% = $6 million.

The cost of borrowed funds is: $70 million × 5% = $3.5 million.

The net profit on the portfolio is: $6 million − $3.5 million = $2.5 million.

The return on the equity invested (i.e., the portfolio) is thus:

$$\frac{\$2.5}{\$30} = 8.33\%$$

This calculation can also be approached with the following formula:

$$R_p = R_i + [(B / E) \times (R_i - c)] \qquad \text{(know this formula)}$$

where:
R_p = return on portfolio
R_i = return on invested assets
B = amount on leverage
E = amount on equity invested
c = cost of borrowed funds

The formula says to add the return on the investment (the first component) to the net levered return (the second component in brackets).

Using the formula:

$$R_p = 6\% + [(70 / 30) \times (6\% - 5\%)] = 8.33\%$$

In summary:

- As leverage increases, the variability of returns increases.
- As the investment return increases, so does the variability of portfolio returns.

The Effect of Leverage on Duration

Using the original example shown previously, the manager's portfolio was worth $100 million, $30 million of which was his own funds and $70 million was borrowed. If the duration of the invested funds is 5.0 and the duration of borrowed funds is 1.0, **calculate** the duration on the portfolio.

Answer:

The duration can be calculated with the following formula:

$$D_p = \frac{D_i I - D_B B}{E} \qquad \text{(know this formula)}$$

where :
D_p = duration of portfolio
D_i = duration of invested assets
D_B = duration of borrowings
I = amount of invested funds
B = amount of leverage
E = amount of equity invested

Using the provided information:

$$D_p = \frac{(5.0)100 - (1.0)70}{30} = 14.33$$

Note the use of leverage has resulted in the duration of the portfolio (14.33) being greater than the duration of invested assets (5.0).

REPURCHASE AGREEMENTS

In a *repurchase agreement* or repo, the borrower (seller of the security) agrees to repurchase it from the buyer on an agreed upon date at an agreed upon price (repurchase price).

Although it is legally a sale and subsequent purchase of securities, a repurchase agreement is essentially a collateralized loan, where the difference between the sale and repurchase prices is the interest on the loan. The rate of interest on the repo is referred to as the *repo rate*.

As a result of this risk, repos are structured with different delivery scenarios:

1. The borrower is required to physically deliver the collateral to the lender. Physical delivery can be costly however.

2. The collateral is deposited in a custodial account at the borrower's clearing bank. This is a cost-effective way to reduce the fees associated with delivery.

3. The transfer of securities is executed electronically through the parties' banks. This is less expensive than physical delivery but does involve fees and transfer charges.

4. Delivery is sometimes not required if the borrower's credit risk is low, if the parties are familiar with one another, or if the transaction is short term.

The Repo Rate

- The repo rate increases as the **credit risk** of the borrower increases (when delivery is not required).
- As the **quality** of the collateral increases, the repo rate declines.
- As the **term** of the repo increases, the repo rate increases.
- **Delivery.** If collateral is physically delivered, then the repo rate will be lower. If the repo is held by the borrower's bank, the rate will be higher. If no delivery takes place, the rate will be even higher.
- **Collateral.** If the availability of the collateral is limited, the repo rate will be lower.
- The higher the **federal funds rate**, the higher the repo rate.
- As the demand for funds at financial institutions changes due to **seasonal factors**, so will the repo rate.

BOND RISK MEASURES

Standard Deviation

The problems with standard deviation and variance are as follows:

- Bond returns are often not normally distributed around the mean.
- The number of inputs (e.g., variances and covariances) increases significantly with larger portfolios.
- Obtaining estimates for each of these inputs is problematic. Historically calculated risk measures may not represent the risk measures that will be observed in the future. Remember from studying duration that bond prices become less sensitive to interest rate changes as the maturity date nears.

Semivariance

Drawbacks of semivariance include the following:

- It is difficult to compute for a large bond portfolio.
- If investment returns are symmetric, the semivariance yields the same rankings as the variance and the variance is better understood.
- If investment returns are not symmetric, it can be quite difficult to forecast downside risk and the semivariance may not be a good indicator of future risk.
- Because the semivariance is estimated with only half the distribution, it is estimated with less accuracy.

Shortfall Risk

Shortfall risk measures the *probability* that the actual return will be less than the target return.

The primary criticism of the shortfall risk measure is:

- Shortfall risk does not consider the impact of outliers so the magnitude (dollar amount) of the shortfall below the target return is ignored.

Value at Risk

The primary criticism of VAR is:

- As in the shortfall risk measure, VAR does not provide the magnitude of losses that exceed that specified by VAR.

ADVANTAGES OF INTEREST RATE FUTURES

Compared to cash market instruments, futures:

1. Are more liquid.

2. Are less expensive.

3. Make short positions more readily obtainable, because the contracts can be more easily shorted than an actual bond.

DOLLAR DURATION

The **dollar duration** is the dollar change in the price of a bond, portfolio, or futures contract from a given change in the yield. The relationship between duration and dollar duration is straightforward.

For a given bond with an initial "value:"

$$(\%\Delta value) = -(\text{effective duration})(\text{decimal change in interest rates})$$

Multiplying through by the market value of the bond or portfolio, we get dollar duration, represented by DD:

$$DD = (\$\Delta value) = -(\text{effective duration})(\text{decimal change in interest rates})(\text{value})$$

The dollar duration of a futures contract is the change in the dollar value of the futures for a given interest rate change. The dollar duration of a portfolio may be adjusted by taking a position in futures contracts.

To **increase** dollar duration → **buy** futures contracts.

To **decrease** dollar duration → **sell** futures contracts.

Achieving the Target Dollar Duration

The manager of a bond portfolio expects a 40 bp increase in rates so duration should be reduced. For this yield change, the portfolio has a dollar duration of $32,000. The target dollar duration is $20,000. The manager chooses a futures contract with a dollar duration, for the 40 bp change, equal to $1,100. How can the manager achieve the target?

Answer:

$$\text{number of contracts} = \frac{DD_T - DD_P}{DD_f}$$

$$= \frac{\$20,000 - \$32,000}{\$1,100} = -10.91$$

The manager should short (sell) 11 contracts to reduce the dollar duration.

Dollar Duration of a Futures Contract   (know these formulas)

Given this relationship, the dollar duration for a futures contract can be calculated as:

$$DD_f = -(\text{effective dur.})(\text{decimal change in int. rates})(\text{face value})\left(\frac{\text{futures price}}{100}\right)$$

or

$$DD_f = \frac{DD_{CTD}}{\text{CTD conversion factor}}$$

In the previous example, you might have been given that the dollar duration of the CTD is $DD_{CTD} = \$1,375$ and the conversion factor is 1.25. In that case, you would have had to compute $DD_f = \$1,375 / 1.25 = \$1,100$.

From what we have so far, we can write:

$$\text{number of contracts} = \frac{DD_T - DD_P}{DD_f}$$

$$\text{and since } DD_f = \frac{DD_{CTD}}{\text{CTD conversion factor}}$$

$$\text{number of contracts} = \frac{DD_T - DD_P}{DD_{CTD} / \text{conversion factor}} = \frac{\$20,000 - \$32,000}{\dfrac{\$1,375}{1.25}} = -10.91$$

Hedging Issues

Basis Risk and Cross Hedging

Basis risk is the variability of the basis. It is an important consideration for hedges that will be lifted in the intermediate term.

In a *cross hedge*, the underlying security in the futures contract is not identical to the asset being hedged (e.g., using T-bond futures to hedge corporate bonds). A cross hedge can be either long or short.

When implementing a cross hedge, the manager should evaluate the differences in the relevant factor risk exposures of the bond and the futures contract. If the bond has greater risk exposure than the futures contract, more of the futures contract will be needed to effectively hedge the bond position.

The desired hedge ratio is given by:

$$\text{hedge ratio} = \frac{\text{exposure of bond to risk factor}}{\text{exposure of futures to risk factor}}$$

The hedge ratio and hence the number of contracts should be estimated for the time at which the hedge is lifted, because this is when the manager wishes to lock in a value. The manager should also have an estimate of the price, because the effect of changes in risk will vary as price and yield vary.

Given that the pricing of the futures contract depends on the cheapest-to-deliver bond, the hedge ratio can also be expressed as:

$$(1) \quad \text{hedge ratio} = \frac{\text{exposure of bond to risk factor}}{\text{exposure of CTD to risk factor}} \times \frac{\text{exposure of CTD to risk factor}}{\text{exposure of futures to risk factor}}$$

In the formula above, the second term on the right hand side represents the conversion factor for the CTD bond.

We can rewrite the formula for the number of contracts to hedge a bond from the previous numerical example as:

$$(2) \quad \text{hedge ratio} = \frac{DD_P}{DD_{CTD}} \times \text{conversion factor for the CTD}$$

Yield Beta

To adjust for changes in the spread, the yield beta is obtained from a regression equation of the following form:

$$\Delta \text{yield on bond} = \alpha + \beta \, (\Delta \text{yield on CTD}) + e$$

The yield beta, β, measures changes in yield spreads. If the yield spread between the bond being hedged and the CTD issue is assumed to be constant, the yield beta must equal one. In other words, the yield on the hedged bond equals the assumed spread, α, plus one times the yield on the CTD.

To adjust formula (2) above for fully hedging interest rate risk when yield spread is not constant, we must adjust the formula to incorporate the yield beta as follows:

$$\text{hedge ratio} = \frac{DD_P}{DD_{CTD}} \times \text{conversion factor for the CTD} \times \text{yield beta}$$

Evaluating Hedging Effectiveness

There are three basic sources of hedging error.

There can be an error in the:

- Forecast of the basis at the time the hedge is lifted.
- Estimated durations.
- Estimated yield beta.

Managing Default Risk, Credit Spread Risk, and Downgrade Risk With Derivatives

Types of Credit Risk

There are three principal credit-related risks that can be addressed with credit derivative instruments:

1. **Default risk** is the risk that the issuer will not meet the obligations of the issue (i.e., pay interest and/or principal when due). This risk is unique in the sense that it results from a potential action—failure to pay—of the debt issuer.

2. **Credit spread risk** is the risk of an increase in the yield spread on an asset.

3. **Downgrade risk** is the possibility that the credit rating of an asset/issuer is downgraded by a major credit-rating organization, such as Moody's.

Types of Credit Derivative Instruments

Credit options. Credit options provide protection from adverse price movements related to credit events or changes in the underlying reference asset's spread over a risk-free rate. When the payoff is based on the underlying asset's price, the option is known as a binary credit option. When the payoff is based on the underlying asset's yield spread, the option is known as a credit spread option.

Binary credit options. A binary credit put option will provide protection if a specific credit event occurs, and if the value of the underlying asset is less than the option strike price. The option value (OV) or payoff is:

$$OV = \max\,[(\text{strike} - \text{value}), 0]$$

Credit spread options. A credit spread call option will provide protection if the reference asset's spread over the relevant risk-free benchmark increases beyond the strike spread. The increase in the spread beyond the strike spread (i.e., the option being in the money) constitutes an identifiable credit event, in and of itself. The option value (OV) or payoff is:

$$OV = max \: [(actual \: spread - strike \: spread) \times notional \times risk \: factor, \: 0]$$

Credit spread forwards. Credit spread forwards are forward contracts wherein the payment at settlement is a function of the credit spread over the benchmark at the time the contract matures. The value (FV) or payoff to the buyer of a credit spread forward is:

$$FV = (spread \: at \: maturity - contract \: spread) \times notional \times risk \: factor$$

Credit swaps. Credit swaps describe a category of products in the swap family, all of which provide some form of credit risk transfer. Our focus here will be on **credit default swaps** which can be viewed as protection, or insurance, against default on an underlying credit instrument (called the reference asset or reference entity when referring to the issuer).

To obtain the requisite insurance, the protection buyer agrees to pay the protection seller a periodic fee in exchange for a commitment to stand behind an underlying bond or loan should its issuer experience a credit event, such as default. A credit default swap agreement will contain a list of credit events that apply to the agreement.

The terms of a credit swap are custom-designed to meet the needs of the counterparties. They can be cash settled or there can be physical delivery, which generally means the buyer of the swap delivers the reference asset to the counterparty for a cash payment.

INTERNATIONAL BOND EXCESS RETURNS

Six of the potential sources of excess return on international bonds are: (1) market selection; (2) currency selection; (3) duration management; (4) sector selection; (5) credit analysis; and (6) markets outside the benchmark.

Market selection involves selecting appropriate national bond markets.

Currency selection. The manager must determine the amount of active currency management versus the amount of currency hedging he will employ. Due to the complexities and required expertise, currency management is often treated as a separately-managed function.

©2008 Kaplan Schweser

Duration management. Once the manager has determined what sectors (i.e., countries) will be held, she must determine the optimal maturities. Limited maturity offerings in some markets can be overcome by employing fixed income derivatives.

Sector selection. This is directly analogous to domestic bond portfolio management. Due to increasing ranges of maturities, ratings, and bond types (e.g., corporate, government), the international bond portfolio manager is now able to add value through credit analysis of entire sectors.

Credit analysis refers to recognizing value-added opportunities through credit analysis of individual securities.

Markets outside the benchmark. Large foreign bond indices are usually composed of sovereign (government) issues. With the increasing availability of corporate issues, the manager may try to add value through enhanced indexing by adding corporates to an indexed foreign bond portfolio.

INTERNATIONAL BOND DURATIONS

To estimate the sensitivity of the prices of foreign bonds to changes in the domestic interest rate, the manager must measure the *correlations* between changes in their yields and changes in the domestic interest rate.

Assuming there is a relationship (i.e., correlation) between yields on the domestic and foreign bonds, the manager can regress the yield on the foreign bond against the yield on a domestic bond of similar risk and maturity:

$$\Delta yield_{foreign} = \beta(\Delta yield_{domestic}) + e$$

In the regression, β is the *country beta* or *yield beta*, which measures the sensitivity of the yield on the foreign bond to changes in the yield on the domestic bond. Multiplying the country beta times the change in the domestic rate gives the manager the estimated change in the foreign yield.

Duration Contribution of a Foreign Bond

The duration of an Australian bond is 6.0 and the country beta is 1.15. A U.S. portfolio manager has $50,000 in the Australian bond in an otherwise domestic portfolio with a total value of $1,000,000. **Calculate** the Australian bond's duration contribution to the portfolio.

Answer:

First, the bond's "standardized" duration can be estimated as $6 \times 1.15 = 6.90$. Multiplying the bond's "standardized" duration of 6.90 by its weight in the portfolio (5%) gives the bond's contribution to portfolio duration:

$$\text{duration contribution} = \text{weight} \times \text{duration}$$

$$= 0.05 \times 6.90 = 0.35$$

As with a purely domestic portfolio, the duration of a portfolio containing both domestic and foreign bonds can be estimated as the *sum* of the individual bond duration contributions.

THE HEDGING DECISION

Interest Rate Parity

The IRP formula summarizes this arbitrage-free relationship:

$$F = S_0 \left(\frac{1 + c_d}{1 + c_f} \right)$$

where:
F = the forward exchange rate (domestic per foreign)
S_0 = the current spot exchange rate (domestic per foreign)
c_d = the domestic short-term rate
c_f = the foreign short-term rate

If we know the current interest rates and the spot exchange rate, we are able to determine what forward exchange rate must prevail in order to prevent arbitrage.

We can *approximate* the forward premium or discount (i.e., the *currency differential*) as the difference in short-term rates:

$$f_{d,f} = \frac{(F - S_0)}{S_0} \approx c_d - c_f \qquad \text{(know this formula)}$$

COVERED INTEREST ARBITRAGE

Covered interest arbitrage forces interest rates toward *parity*, because risk-free rates must be the same across borders when forward exchange rates exist. If the nominal domestic interest rate is low relative to the nominal foreign interest rate, the foreign currency *must* trade at a forward discount (this relationship is forced by arbitrage).

Alternatively, if the nominal home interest rate is high relative to the nominal foreign interest rate, the foreign currency must trade at a forward premium.

We can check for an arbitrage opportunity by using the covered interest differential. The covered interest differential says that the domestic interest rate should be the same as the *hedged* foreign interest rate. More specifically, the difference between the domestic interest rate and the hedged foreign rate should be zero.

The covered interest differential can be viewed by rewriting IRP in the following way:

$$(1 + c_d) = (1 + c_f)\left(\frac{F}{S_0}\right)$$

The left-hand side of the equation is the domestic interest rate, while the right-hand side is the hedged foreign rate (the foreign rate expressed in domestic terms). Arbitrage will prevent this relationship from getting out of balance. To preclude arbitrage, the left-hand side minus the right-hand side should equal zero. Hence, the covered interest differential can be written as:

$$(1 + c_d) - (1 + c_f)\left(\frac{F}{S_0}\right) = \text{covered interest differential} \quad \text{(know this formula)}$$

Hedging Techniques

The **forward hedge**. The forward hedge is used to eliminate (most of) the currency risk. Utilizing a forward hedge assumes forward contracts are available and actively traded on the foreign currency in terms of the domestic currency. If so, the manager enters a forward contract to sell the foreign currency at the current forward rate.

The **proxy hedge**. In a proxy hedge the manager enters a forward contract between the *domestic currency and a second foreign currency* that is correlated with the first foreign currency (i.e., the currency in which the bond is denominated). Gains or losses on the forward contract are expected to at least partially offset losses or gains in the domestic return on the bond. Proxy hedges are utilized when forward contracts on the first foreign currency are not actively traded or hedging the first foreign currency is relatively expensive.

The **cross hedge**. Notice that in currency hedging the proxy hedge is what we would usually refer to as a cross hedge in other financial transactions. In other words, the manager can't construct a hedge in the long asset, so he hedges using another, correlated asset. In a currency cross hedge, the manager enters into a contract to deliver the original foreign currency (i.e., the currency of the bond) for a third currency. Again it is hoped that gains or losses on the forward contract will at least partially offset losses or gains in the domestic return on the bond. In other words, the manager takes steps to eliminate the currency risk of the bond by replacing it with the risk of another currency. The currency cross hedge, therefore, is a means of changing the risk exposure rather than eliminating it.

Foreign Bond Returns

The return on an investment in a foreign bond can be broken down into its nominal local return and the currency return implied by the forward currency differential:

$$R_b \approx R_l + R_c$$

where:
R_b = the domestic return on the foreign bond
R_l = the local return on the foreign bond (i.e., in its local currency)
R_c = the expected (by the market) currency return; the forward premium or discount

We can decompose the relationship using IRP which demonstrates that the forward premium or discount depends upon the interest rate differential:

$$R_b = R_l + R_c \rightarrow \text{Since } R_c \approx i_d - i_f$$

$$R_b = R_l + R_c \approx R_l + (i_d - i_f) \rightarrow i_d + (R_l - i_f)$$

So, as shown by decomposing the return, as long as the bonds are similar in maturity and other risk characteristics, choosing between them is determined solely by the bond that offers the greatest excess return denominated in its local currency.

The Hedging Decision

We explore the hedging decision by first determining the optimal bond to purchase and then determining whether to hedge or not.

Using only the following data on two foreign bonds with the same risk characteristics (e.g., maturity, credit risk) **determine** which bond should be purchased, if the currency risk of either can be fully hedged with a forward contract.

Country	Nominal Return	Risk-Free Rate
i	4.75%	3.25%
j	5.25%	3.80%

Answer:

Since their maturities and other risk characteristics are similar and an investment in either can be hedged using a forward contract, we can determine the better bond to purchase by calculating their excess returns:

Bond i: 4.75% – 3.25% = 1.50%

Bond j: 5.25% – 3.80% = 1.45%

Bond i offers the higher excess return, so given the ability to fully hedge the manager should select Bond i.

To Hedge or Not to Hedge

A U.S. manager is considering a foreign bond. The U.S. risk-free rate (i.e., the domestic rate) is 4% and the risk-free rate in the foreign country (i.e., the local rate) is 4.8%. The manager expects the dollar to appreciate only 0.4% over the expected holding period. Based on this information and assuming the ability to hedge with forward contracts, **determine** whether the manager should hedge the position or leave it unhedged.

Answer:

We start by calculating the forward differential expected by the market:

$$f \approx i_d - i_f = 4.0\% - 4.8\% = -0.8\%$$

The current nominal risk-free interest rates imply a forward differential of –0.8%; the market expects the foreign currency to depreciate 0.8% relative to the dollar. The manager on the other hand expects the dollar to appreciate only 0.4%. If the manager's expectations are correct, the *forward dollar is too expensive*, or alternatively, the forward price of the foreign currency is too cheap. The manager is better off not hedging the currency risk, as the foreign currency will not fall in value as much as predicted by the market.

BREAKEVEN SPREAD ANALYSIS

Breakeven analysis involves determining the widening in the spread between two bonds that will make their total returns (i.e., coupon plus capital gain or loss) equivalent over a given period. Although it does not address the risk associated with currency movements, breakeven analysis does give the manager an idea of the amount of risk associated with attempting to exploit a yield advantage.

Note that in performing a breakeven analysis, the manager must assume a *set time horizon* and measure the yield change in the bond with the *higher duration*.

Example: Breakeven Analysis

A portfolio manager is performing a breakeven analysis to determine the shift in interest rates that would generate a capital loss sufficient to eliminate the yield advantage of the foreign bond. Determine the breakeven change in the yield of the foreign bond if the intended holding period is three months.

Bond	Nominal Return	Duration
i (domestic)	4.75%	4.5
j (foreign)	5.25%	6.3

Answer:

The foreign bond is currently at an annual yield advantage of 50 bps, which equates to a quarterly advantage of 12.5 bps. Utilizing the duration of the foreign bond, which is the longer of the two, and the fact that its price will change 6.3 times the percentage change in its yield, we can determine the breakeven yield change:

change in price – duration × breakeven yield change

Solving for Δy: (know this formula)

$$\Delta y = \frac{\text{change in price}}{-\text{duration}}$$

$$\Delta y = \frac{-0.125\%}{-6.3} = 0.0198 = 1.98 \text{ bps}$$

The conclusion is that the yield on the foreign bond would have to increase a little under 2 bps over the holding period for the decrease in its price (i.e., the capital loss) to completely wipe out its yield advantage. The manager can compare this breakeven event against her interest rate expectations and currency expectations to assess whether the yield advantage warrants investment in the foreign bond.

Emerging Market Debt

In actively managing a fixed income portfolio, managers often utilize a **core-plus** approach. In a core-plus approach, the manager holds a "core" of investment grade debt and then invests in bonds perceived to add the potential for generating added return. Emerging market debt (EMD) is frequently utilized to add value in a core-plus strategy.

Advantages of investing in EMD include:

- Increasing quality in emerging market sovereign bonds.
- Increased resiliency; the ability to recover from value-siphoning events.
- Lack of diversification in the major EMD index, the Emerging Markets Bond Index Plus (EMBI+). The index is concentrated in Latin American debt (e.g., Brazil, Mexico). The bond investor can diversify the fixed income portfolio, so an undiversified index offers return-enhancing potential.

Risks associated with EMD include:

- Unlike emerging market governments, emerging market corporations do not have the tools available to help offset negative events.
- EMD returns can be highly volatile with negatively skewed distributions.
- A lack of transparency and regulations gives emerging market sovereign debt higher credit risk than sovereign debt in developed markets.
- Under-developed legal systems that do not protect against actions taken by governments.
- A lack of standardized covenants.
- Political risk (a.k.a. geopolitical risk).

Selecting a Fixed Income Manager

Criteria that should be utilized in determining the *optimal mix* of active managers *include style analysis, selection bets, investment processes*, and *alpha correlations*.

Style analysis. The majority of active returns can be explained by the manager's selected style. The primary concerns associated with researching the managers' styles include not only the styles employed but any additional risk exposures due to style.

Selection bets. Selection bets include credit spread analysis (i.e., which sectors or securities will experience spread changes) and the identification of over- and under-valued securities. By decomposing the manager's excess returns, the sponsor can determine the manager's ability to generate superior returns from selection bets.

Investment processes. This step includes investigating the total investment processes of the managers. What type of research is performed? How is alpha attained? Who makes decisions and how are they made (e.g., committee, individual).

Alpha correlations. If the alphas of the various managers are highly correlated, not only will there be significant volatility in the overall alpha, but the alphas will tend to be all positive or negative at the same time.

The process for determining the best mix of fixed income active managers is much the same as that for selecting the best mix of equity portfolio managers. The one consideration that distinguishes the two is the need for a low-fee strategy. That is, fees are an important consideration in selecting any active manager, but the ratio of fees to alpha is usually higher for fixed income managers.

HEDGING MORTGAGE SECURITIES TO CAPTURE RELATIVE VALUE
Cross-Reference to CFA Institute Assigned Reading #30

Convexity refers to the nonlinear relationship between the value of a fixed income instrument and its yield. For a given interest rate increase, the capital loss effect is smaller than the capital gain effect that occurs with an equal interest rate decrease. For **negative** convexity this relationship reverses (i.e., a given decrease in the market interest rate produces a smaller capital gain than the absolute value of the capital loss produced by an equal increase in the market rate).

Figure 1 shows the familiar price-yield curve of a non-callable bond (i.e., bullet).

Figure 1: Positive Convexity in Bond Prices (Bullets)

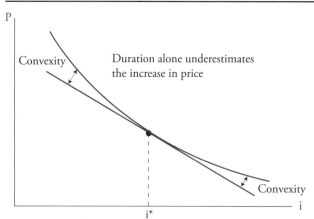

The (positive) convexity in the relationship is indicated by the distance between the price curve and a straight line tangent to the curve, in this case at i^*, which demonstrates the price change predicted using duration alone. Positive convexity means the price of the bond increases at an increasing rate as the interest rate falls below the coupon rate. Positive convexity also means the price of the bond falls at a decreasing rate as the interest rate rises above the coupon rate. Note that the straight line represents the change in price predicted by the bond's duration, when its yield changes from i^*. This demonstrates how duration alone will underestimate the increase in price with falling rates and overestimate the decrease in price with rising rates.

Figure 2 shows the price-yield relationship for the same bond, assuming it is now callable.

Figure 2: Price-Yield of a Callable Bond

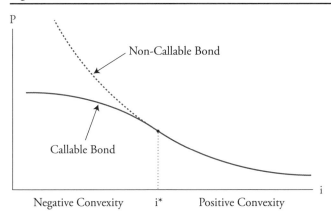

As indicated, when the yield on the bond is below its coupon rate, i^*, the bond exhibits negative convexity; that is, the price of the bond increases at a decreasing rate. Above i^*, the call option on the bond is out-of-the-money, so the bond behaves as if it were non-callable.

From the perspective of the investor, a mortgage security essentially has an embedded short call option because the mortgage payers have a **prepayment option**. When this option is out-of-the-money, the mortgage security will exhibit (positive) convexity. When the option is in-the-money, the mortgage security will tend to exhibit negative convexity, because the price will be compressed from the prepayment option going into the money and reducing the value of the security. In other words, as the yield falls, the increase in the present value of the payments is at least offset by the negative value of the short call position. In contrast, Treasury securities only exhibit positive convexity.

There is a problem with using a hedging instrument that has positive convexity to hedge an asset with negative convexity. If the downside risk from a yield increase is hedged exactly, then the portfolio will likely lose value when interest rates decrease.

MORTGAGE SECURITY RISKS

1. **Spread risk** is the risk of the mortgage security's yield spread over the corresponding T-bond widening, and thus lowering the value of mortgage security relative to the T-bond. Usually the manager focuses on the option-adjusted spread (OAS).

2. **Interest rate risk** is the price fluctuation caused by the volatility of the yield on Treasuries with which the yields on mortgage securities are highly correlated. (It is considered distinct from spread risk, because the interest rate can change without the spread changing.)

3. **Prepayment risk** is the cause of the negative convexity, which means the mortgage security loses more from a given increase in yield than it gains from a corresponding decrease in yield. This is why an unhedged mortgage security is called a "market directional" investment.

4. **Volatility risk** is associated with the embedded prepayment option. As we know from option pricing theory, an increase in volatility increases the value of an option. Since the mortgage security is short the option:

    increased yield volatility → increased value of option → decreased value of mortgage security

5. **Model risk** can be from naively projecting past patterns of interest rates into the future. Another source is not recognizing the effects of technological and institutional innovations, which make prepayment more convenient to the borrower, thus increasing the risk from that source.

YIELD CURVE RISK

Yield curve risk is the risk of nonparallel shifts or "twists" in the yield curve. The usual approach to handling yield curve risk for a portfolio is to focus on a few particular key rate durations.

For a single noncallable bond issue, a manager may generally focus on only one rate, because of the comparatively large bullet in the form of the bond's principal. Even when the yield curve twists, changes in the yield corresponding to the maturity of the bond will explain most of the changes in the price of the bond.

Yield curve risk is much more important for mortgage securities because there is no bullet payment at the end. A manager has to consider hedging against changes in more than a single key rate. Additional complication is added with principal and interest strips. Principal-only (PO) strips have negative key rate durations in the short and intermediate rates, which turn positive for longer (e.g., 10-year) rates. Interest-only (IO) strips start out with positive key rate durations which turn negative. The implication for yield curve twists are fairly obvious.

Hedging Mortgage Securities

Given the complications (i.e., call risk, the need for more key rates and negative convexities), using only a duration-based framework will generally not be adequate for hedging mortgage securities. First, as demonstrated earlier for a security with negative convexity, a duration-based hedge that removes the risk associated with an increase in rates can produce a net loss on the hedged position when rates decrease. Second, a duration-based framework does not effectively deal with two crucial points: (1) observed patterns of yield curve changes over time and (2) the effect yield curve changes have on the propensity for the prepayment by homeowners.

Research has shown that more than 95% of changes in interest rates can be explained by yield curve shifts and twists. Addressing the possibility of *twists* requires more assumptions in forming the hedge. Under a given set of assumptions, managers can form a hedge by using two hedging instruments from two maturity sectors of the yield curve (e.g., a 2-year and a 10-year). Those assumptions are that the manager:

- Incorporates reasonable possible yield curve shifts.
- Uses an adequate model for predicting prepayments given certain changes in yield.
- Includes reliable assumptions in the Monte Carlo simulations of interest rates.
- Knows the security's price change given a small change in yield.
- Knows that the average price change method (a demonstration follows) yields good approximations.

If the previous assumptions are valid, the manager can use a *two-bond hedge* to hedge the risk associated with both an increase and decrease in interest rates as well as a forecasted twist. The following steps summarize how to construct the hedge on a mortgage security, denoted MS, using two hedging instruments with different maturities.

1. Given the assumed positive or negative change in interest rates, Δy, determine the average absolute price change per $100 of MS and the two hedging instruments.

2. Given the assumed twist in the yield curve, determine the average price change for the mortgage security and each of the two hedging instruments.

3. Set up a system of two equations to determine the amount in each hedging instrument.

4. Solve for the amounts of the two securities that should be shorted.

Note: The mathematics are not integral to addressing the LOS. The manager shorts two bonds to construct the hedge; one of the bonds is sensitive to changes in short interest rates and the other to longer interest rates.

EQUITY PORTFOLIO MANAGEMENT

Topic Weight on Exam	5–15%
Study Note Reference	Book 3, Pages 122–200
Video CD Reference	CDs 10 & 11
Audio CD Reference	CDs 11–13

EQUITY PORTFOLIO MANAGEMENT
Cross-Reference to CFA Institute Assigned Reading #31

Historical evidence in the United States and in other countries indicates that **equities** have been a good inflation hedge. There are some important qualifiers, however. First, because corporate tax rates are not indexed to inflation, inflation can reduce the stock investor's return. Second, the greater the competition, the less likely the firm will be able to pass inflation on to its consumers, and its stock will be a less effective hedge.

ACTIVE, PASSIVE, AND SEMIACTIVE STRATEGIES

Passive equity managers do not use forecasts to influence their investment strategies. The most common implementation of passive management is indexing.

Active equity managers buy, sell, and hold securities in an attempt to outperform their benchmark.

Active return is excess return relative to the benchmark. *Tracking risk* is the standard deviation of active return and is a measurement of *active risk*. The more actively (passively) managed the equity portfolio, the greater (less) the potential for active return and tracking risk.

The **information ratio** is the active return divided by the tracking risk, so it shows the manager's active return per unit of tracking risk.

The IPS, Market Efficiency, and Equity Strategies

If the investor is **taxable**, the asset allocation is more likely to favor passive management, because active management requires higher portfolio turnover and taxes are realized more frequently.

- If an investor believes markets are **efficient**, he does not believe the returns of active management will justify the costs of research and trading.
- Passive strategies are appropriate in a wide variety of markets. When investing in *large-cap* stocks, indexing is suitable because these markets are usually informationally efficient. In *small-cap* markets, there may be more mispriced stocks, but the transactions costs of high turnover can be high. In *international* equity markets, the foreign investor may lack information that local investors have. In this case, the manager would be wise to follow a passive strategy.

Equity Index Weighting Schemes

A **price-weighted index** is an arithmetic average of the prices of the securities included in the index.

A **market capitalization-weighted index** (or "value-weighted") is calculated by summing the total market value of all the stocks in the index.

A subtype of a value-weighted index is the **free float-adjusted market capitalization index**.

In an **equal-weighted index**, all stock *returns* are given the same weight.

Biases in the Weighting Schemes

Price-weighted index. Higher priced stocks have a greater impact on the index's value than lower priced stocks. The price of a stock changes through time as a firm splits its stock, repurchases stock, or issues stock dividends. Assumes the investor purchases one share of each stock represented in the index, which is rarely followed by any investor.

Value-weighted index and free float-adjusted market capitalization index. Firms with greater market capitalization have a greater impact on the index. Biased towards large firms that may be mature and/or overvalued. May be less diversified, if they are over represented by large-cap firms. Institutional investors may not be able to mimic a value-weighted index if they are subject to maximum holdings and the index holds concentrated positions.

Equal-weighted index. Biased towards small-cap companies because they have the same weight as large-cap firms. May contain more small firms than large firms. Required rebalancing of this index creates higher transactions costs for index investors. Emphasis on small-cap stocks means that index investors may not be able to find liquidity in many of the index issues.

Index reconstitution refers to the process of adding and deleting securities from an index. Indices that are reconstituted by a committee will have lower turnover, and hence, lower transactions costs and taxes for the index investor. These indices may drift from their intended purpose, though, if they are reconstituted too infrequently. In contrast, an index regularly reconstituted by a mechanical rule will have more turnover and less drifting. Another difference in index methodologies concerns minimum liquidity requirements. The presence of small-cap stocks may create liquidity problems but also offers the index investor a potential liquidity risk premium.

Passive Investing

Index Mutual Funds and Exchange-Traded Funds

There are five main differences between **index mutual funds** and **exchange-traded funds** (ETFs):

1. In the United States, a mutual fund's value is typically only provided once a day, at the end of the day, when trades are executed. An ETF trades throughout the day.

2. ETFs do not have to maintain records for shareholders whereas mutual funds do, and related expenses can be significant. There are trading expenses associated with ETFs, because they trade through brokers like ordinary shares.

3. Index mutual funds usually pay lower license fees to Standard & Poor's and other index providers than ETFs do.

4. ETFs are generally more tax efficient than index mutual funds.

5. Although ETFs carry brokerage commissions, the costs of holding an ETF long-term is typically lower than that for an index mutual fund.

Separate or Pooled Accounts

In a pooled account, the indexed portfolios of several investors are combined under one manager. Pooling is advantageous to smaller funds, which cannot afford a dedicated manager, but it is difficult to differentiate the performances of the separate, pooled funds, and the pool manager may have to hold excess cash to provide liquidity for all the pooled funds.

Equity Futures vs. ETFs

Compared to ETFs, equity futures have two *disadvantages*. First, equity futures contracts have a finite life and must be periodically rolled over. Second, using basket trades and futures contracts in combination for risk management may be problematic, because a basket may not be shorted if one of the components violates the uptick rule.

APPROACHES TO CREATING AN INDEXED PORTFOLIO

Full Replication. All the stocks in the index are purchased according to the weighting scheme used in the index. The *advantage* of replication is that there is low tracking risk and the portfolio only needs to be rebalanced when the index stocks change or pay dividends. The return on a replicated fund should be the index returns minus the administrative fees, cash drag, and transactions costs of tracking the index. A replicating fund will underperform the index to a greater extent when the underlying stocks are illiquid, and the index does not bear the trading costs that the replicating fund does.

Stratified Sampling. The portfolio manager separates the stocks in an index using a structure of two or more dimensions and places the stocks accordingly into cells of the resulting matrix. Within each cell, the manager picks a few representative stocks. The primary *advantage* of stratified sampling is that the manager does not have to purchase all the stocks in an index.

Optimization. A factor model is used to match the factor exposures of the fund to those of the index. The advantage of an optimization is that the factor model accounts for the covariances between risk factors. In a stratified sampling procedure, it is implicitly assumed that the factors (e.g., industry, size, price-earnings ratios) are uncorrelated.

There are three main *disadvantages*. First, the risk sensitivities measured in the factor model are based on historical data. Second, optimization may provide a misleading model. Third, the optimization must be updated to reflect changes in risk sensitivities. Regardless of its limitations, an optimization approach leads to lower tracking risk than a stratified sampling approach.

EQUITY STYLES

Value investors focus on the *numerator* in the P/E or P/B ratio. There are three main *substyles* of value investing: high dividend yield, low price multiple, and contrarian.

Growth investors focus on the *denominator* in the P/E ratio, searching for firms and industries where high expected earnings growth will drive the stock price higher. There are two main *substyles* of growth investing: consistent earnings growth and momentum.

Market-oriented investing is neither value nor growth. Market-oriented investors sometimes focus on stock prices and other times focus on earnings. The *substyles* of market-oriented investing are market-oriented with a value tilt, market-oriented with a growth tilt, growth at a reasonable price (GARP), and style rotation.

Market Capitalization Based Investing

Small-cap investors believe smaller firms are more likely to be underpriced than well-covered, larger cap stocks. *Micro-cap* investors focus on the smallest of the small-cap stocks. *Mid-cap* investors believe that stocks of this size may have less coverage than large-cap stocks but are less risky than small-cap stocks. *Large-cap* investors believe that they can add value using their analysis of these less risky companies. All categories can be further classified as value, growth, or market-oriented.

IDENTIFYING STYLE

In **returns-based style analysis**, the returns on a manager's fund are regressed against the returns for various security indices. The regression coefficients represent the portfolio's exposure to asset classes. The coefficient of determination (R^2) shows the amount (%) of the investor's return explained by the regression's style indices. One minus this amount indicates the amount unexplained by style and due to the manager's security selection.

A single regression in a returns-based style analysis provides the average fund exposures during the time period under analysis. A series of regressions can be used to check the style consistency of a manager over time.

Holdings-Based Style Analysis

Value or growth: Does the manager invest in low P/E, low P/B, and high dividend yield stocks? If so, the manager would be characterized as a value manager. A manager with high P/E, high P/B, and low dividend yield stocks would be characterized as a growth manager. A manager with average ratios would be characterized as market-oriented.

Expected earnings per share growth rate: Does the manager have a heavy concentration in firms with high expected earnings growth? If so, the manager would be characterized as a growth manager.

Earnings volatility: Does the manager hold firms with high earnings volatility? If so, the manager would be characterized as a value manager, because value managers are willing to take positions in cyclical firms.

Industry representation: Value (i.e., price-focused) managers tend to have greater representation in the utility and financial industries, because these industries typically have higher dividend yields and lower valuations. Growth (i.e., earnings-focused) managers tend to have higher weights in the technology and healthcare industries, because these industries often have higher growth. Individual firms within industries do not always fit the industry mold, and the value/growth classification of an industry will vary as the business cycle varies.

Returns-based style analysis is compared to holdings-based style analysis in Figure 1.

Figure 1: Advantages/Disadvantages of Returns-Based Analysis and Holdings-Based Style Analysis

Advantages of Returns-Based Analysis	*Advantages of Holdings-Based Analysis*
Characterizes an entire portfolio	Characterizes each security
Enables comparisons of entire portfolios	Enables comparisons of securities
Summarizes the result of the investment process	Can detect style drift more quickly than returns-based analysis
Methodology backed by theory	
Low information requirements	
Different models usually result in the same conclusions	
Low cost and can be executed rapidly	
Disadvantages of Returns-Based Analysis	*Disadvantages of Holdings-Based Analysis*
May be inaccurate due to style drift	Is not consistent with the method used by many managers to select securities
Misspecified indices can lead to misleading conclusions	Requires subjective judgment to classify securities
	Requires more data than returns-based analysis

EQUITY STYLE INDICES

Viewing style as a category means that there will be no *overlap* when a style index is constructed (i.e., stocks are assigned to only one style). Viewing style as a quantity (i.e., splitting a stock between styles) means that there will be overlap. Another distinguishing characteristic is **buffering**. Buffering means a stock is not immediately moved to a different style when its style changes slightly. This means

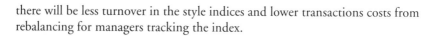

there will be less turnover in the style indices and lower transactions costs from rebalancing for managers tracking the index.

The Equity Style Box and Style Drift

Another method of characterizing a portfolio's style is to use a **style box**. This method is used by Morningstar to characterize mutual funds and stocks. In this approach, a matrix is formed with value/growth characteristics across the top and market cap along the side. Morningstar uses holdings-based style analysis to classify securities.

Categorizing portfolios by size is fairly standard in that market cap is the usual metric for evaluating size. However, different providers use different categorizations of value and growth attributes. For this reason, the categorization of portfolios can differ a great deal depending on the provider. Usually price-multiples are used to define value stocks, whereas earnings or sales growth rates are used to define growth stocks.

Socially Responsible Investing

Socially responsible investing (SRI), also known as ethical investing, is the use of ethical, social, or religious concerns to screen investment decisions. The screens can be negative, where the investor refuses to invest in a company they believe is unethical; or positive, where the investor seeks out firms with ethical practices.

A SRI screen may have an effect on a portfolio's style. For example, some screens exclude basic industries and energy companies, which typically are value stocks. SRI portfolios thus tend to be tilted toward growth stocks. SRI screens have also been found to have a bias toward small-cap stocks. There are two main benefits to monitoring the potential style bias resulting from SRI screens. First, the portfolio manager can take steps to minimize the bias, if it is inconsistent with the investor's risk and return objectives. Second, with knowledge of the portfolio's style bias, the manager can determine the appropriate benchmark for the SRI portfolio. Returns-based style analysis can detect the presence of style bias and monitor the success of its remedy.

Long-Short and Long-Only Investment Strategies

A long-short strategy can earn **two alphas**, where long-only strategy can only earn the long alpha through security selection. Also, while long-only investor is potentially exposed to both systematic and unsystematic risk, the long-short investor can eliminate systematic risk using a *market neutral strategy*.

Four reasons for pricing inefficiencies on the short side:

1. Barriers to short sales that do not exist for long trades.

Application on Adtel

©2008 Kaplan Schweser

2. Stocks are more likely to be overvalued than undervalued.

3. Sell-side is more likely to issue buy recommendations than sell recommendations.

4. Sell-side faces pressure from firm management against issuing sell recommendations.

EQUITIZING A LONG-SHORT PORTFOLIO

An investor can add systematic risk to the market neutral strategy by taking a **long position in an equity futures** contract with a notional principal equal to the cash from the short sales. A market neutral strategy can also be *equitized using ETFs.*

SELLING DISCIPLINES

Substitution is replacing an existing security with another with brighter prospects. This approach is referred to as an *opportunity cost sell discipline.* After careful research, a manager may also conclude that a firm's business will worsen in the future. This is referred to as a *deteriorating fundamentals sell discipline.*

In a *valuation-level sell discipline* a value investor may sell a stock if its P/E or P/B ratio rises to the ratio's historical mean. In a *down-from-cost sell discipline*, the manager may sell a stock if its price declines more than say 20% from the purchase price. In an *up-from-cost sell discipline*, the manager may sell a stock once it has increased, either a percentage or a dollar amount from the purchase price. In a *target price sell discipline*, the manager determines the stock's fundamental value at the time of purchase and later sells the stock when it reaches this level.

ENHANCED INDEXING

Using a **stock-based enhanced indexing strategy**, the manager underweights or overweights index stocks based on beliefs about the stocks' prospects. Risk is controlled by monitoring factor risk and industry exposures. In a **derivatives-based enhanced indexing strategy**, the manager obtains an equity exposure through derivatives.

There are two *limitations* to enhanced indexing: successful managers will be copied and their alpha will disappear, and models obtained from historical data may not be applicable to the future.

The **fundamental law of active management** states that an investor's information ratio (IR) is a function of his depth of knowledge about individual securities (the information coefficient—IC) and the number of investment decisions (the investor's breadth—IB).[1] Investor breadth measures the number of *independent* decisions an investor makes.

More formally:

$$IR = IC\sqrt{IB}$$

A derivatives-based enhanced indexing strategy will have less breadth than a stock-based enhanced indexing strategy, because the investor uses a derivatives contract to gain exposure to equity.

ALLOCATING TO MANAGERS

In a **core-satellite approach**, the investor has a core manager holding a passive index and/or an enhanced index that is complemented by a satellite of active manager holdings. Active risk is mitigated by the core, while active return is added by the satellites. The core is benchmarked to the asset class benchmark, whereas the satellites are benchmarked to more specific benchmarks.

To minimize differences in risk exposures between the portfolio and the benchmark, the investor can use a **completeness fund**. The completeness fund complements the active portfolio, so that the combined portfolios have a risk exposure similar to the benchmark.

COMPONENTS OF TOTAL ACTIVE RETURN

A manager's *normal portfolio* reflects the securities she normally chooses for her portfolio. It is a good benchmark for the manager, because it reflects her style. In contrast, an investor who hires a manager may use a broad-based benchmark for the manager's asset class that does not reflect the manager's style. This portfolio would be referred to as the **investor's benchmark**.

Using these two benchmarks, we decompose the manager's total active return into two parts:

true active return = total active return − normal portfolio return

misfit active return = normal portfolio return − investor's benchmark return

The **true active return** is "true" in the sense that it measures what the manager earned relative to the correct benchmark. The **misfit active return** is "misfit" in the

---

1   Richard C. Grinold and Ronald N. Kahn. *Active Portfolio Management*. (McGraw Hill, 1995).

sense that it measures that part of the manager's return from using a benchmark that is not suited to the manager's style.

Using these components of return, we decompose the manager's total active risk into the true risk and misfit risk:

$$\text{total active risk} = \sqrt{(\text{true active risk})^2 + (\text{misfit active risk})^2}$$

An information ratio that better represents the manager's skills:

$$\text{true information ratio} = \frac{\text{true active return}}{\text{true active risk}} \qquad \text{(know this formula)}$$

Alpha and Beta Separation

In an **alpha and beta separation approach**, the investor gains a systematic risk exposure (beta) through a low-cost index fund or ETF, while adding an alpha through a long-short strategy. An *advantage* of this approach is gaining access to equity styles and asset classes outside of a systematic risk class. A *limitation* of the approach is that it may be difficult or costly to implement short positions, some long-short strategies are not truly market neutral, and long-short investing may not be allowed. These investors, however, could create an alpha and beta separation approach using equity futures. For example, the investor can take a long position in the S&P 500 index futures contract and invest with a European equity manager to generate the alpha. To become market neutral in the European equity market, the investor would then short a futures contract based on European equities. In this case, the investor has generated a (portable) alpha with the European manager that is "transported" to the futures (market) portfolio.

SELECTING EQUITY MANAGERS

Past performance is often no guarantee of future performance, but a manager who achieves superior performance with a consistent staff and investment philosophy is more likely to be hired.

A **manager questionnaire** is used to screen potential managers. There are five sections:

1. The manager's staff and organizational structure.

2. Investment philosophy and procedures.

3. Resources and how research is conducted and used.

4. Performance: the manager's benchmark, expected alpha, sources of risk, and portfolio holdings.

5. Details on the fee schedule.

Fee Schedules

Fees can be charged on an *ad valorem* basis or based on performance. Ad valorem fees are also referred to as asset under management fees (AUM). A *performance-based fee* is often charged as a base fee plus some percentage of the alpha and includes *fee caps* and *high water marks*.

The *advantage* of ad valorem fees is that they are straightforward and known in advance, while their *disadvantage* is that they do not align the interests of managers and investors.

Performance-based fees have two *disadvantages*: they can be complicated and require detailed specifications, and they increase the volatility of the manager's compensation.

The advantage of performance-based fees is that they align the interests of the manager and the investor, especially if they are *symmetric* (i.e., contain penalties for poor performance and rewards for good performance).

INTERNATIONAL EQUITY BENCHMARKS
Cross-Reference to CFA Institute Assigned Reading #32

The portion of the outstanding shares of a firm that are actually available for purchase is known as the *float* or *free float*. When calculating the capitalization of the firm in a market cap-weighted index, only those shares that are freely traded should be included.

INTERNATIONAL INDICES: TRADE-OFFS

Breadth vs. Investability

The **breadth** of an index is a measure of its coverage (i.e., the percentage of all firms in the market or sector that are included in the index). Managers prefer greater breadth, because the greater the breadth, the better the index represents the market.

Investability is a liquidity measure. Managers also prefer greater liquidity due to the costs associated with trading to construct and rebalance a portfolio.

With international indices, liquidity can be a concern, because the shares of small-cap firms and firms with a large proportion of closely held shares can be illiquid. This means international indices can increase breadth only by reducing investability.

Liquidity and Crossing Opportunities vs. Reconstitution Effects

Index reconstitution refers to the process of adding and deleting securities from an index. Popular indices are most liquid and generate correspondingly lower transaction costs for portfolio managers following them. Crossing refers to the process where a money manager matches buy and sell orders of different customers without using a broker and without incurring the resulting transaction cost.

When indices add a security, they generate upward price pressure on that security. Similarly, deleted securities suffer from downward price pressure. Both of these actions result in a real cost (**reconstitution effect**) for portfolios tracking the indices, as they have to sell deleted securities at reduced prices and buy added securities at increased prices.

Precise Float Adjustment vs. Transaction Costs From Rebalancing

Some *index managers* continually adjust the float and resulting market cap of firms in their indices. This "precise float adjustment" results in frequent rebalancing with accompanying high transaction costs for portfolios tracking those indices. Instead of making precise float adjustments, other indices use a band adjustment. As long as the firm's estimated free float stays within that band, they do not adjust the firm's weight in the index.

Objectivity and Transparency vs. Judgment

Objectivity refers to the use of a fixed set of criteria to determine what securities should be included in an index. **Transparency** refers to the availability of those criteria to interested portfolio managers. Objectively (and transparently) constructing an index makes predicting the contents of the index easier and allows for more efficient trading, with lower associated costs.

COUNTRY CLASSIFICATION: EMERGING VS. DEVELOPED

For a country "at the margin," classification as *emerging* or *developed* can have significant consequences for both the country and the index of which it is a member. When an emerging country (economy) has reached a considerable size, for example, it becomes a major component in the emerging markets index. The overall index, therefore, is unduly affected by this country.

When the country is moved to a developed market index, it becomes a "small frog in a large pond." Its affect on the index is more in keeping with its economic size and growth and, since developed countries' equities are more widely traded, its stock becomes more readily available for international trading. Thus, the move to a developed index can actually mean the inflow of more international currency, which in turn helps the country develop further.

CORPORATE GOVERNANCE
Cross-Reference to CFA Institute Assigned Reading #33

A **moral hazard** can occur whenever there is the opportunity for someone to engage in wrongdoing. The first moral hazard problem is that of **insufficient effort**. Behavior is worsened when corporate governance systems fail to monitor or curb the behavior. This can lead to **lack of transparency** regarding management compensation, exploding **managerial compensation, managerial compensation independent of management performance**, and **accounting manipulations that benefit managers** at the expense of shareholders.

MANAGERIAL INCENTIVES

Explicit managerial incentives include executive compensation, which comes in three forms: base salary, bonus, and stock-based (e.g., stock options). The bonus and the stock-based portion are considered incentives. For stock-based pay to remain an incentive, managers cannot be allowed to sell their positions in the firm's equity. Accordingly, managers are often required to hold a minimum amount of the firm's stock and are legally liable, if they use their private information when trading in the firm's stock. The effectiveness of bonuses as an incentive is also limited by the fact that they are usually tied to accounting figures.

Bonuses and stock-based compensation serve different purposes. Bonuses are based on accounting figures, which tend to reflect the executive's short-term success. Stock-based compensation, especially stock options, are affected more by the manager's longer-term successes.

When designing a compensation package, the board must decide on whether stock or stock options should be paid. The advantage of using stock options is that their value depends on the stock price being greater than the exercise price. In contrast, shares of stock provide managers compensation even when the firm is performing poorly. Thus, stock options should provide a greater incentive.

The disadvantage of stock options is that when they are out of the money, managers have an incentive to take greater risks. Alternatively, management may just leave the firm if they believe that the chance of the options coming into the money is low.

Implicit incentives should also motivate managers to work on behalf of the shareholders and include the possibility of:

- Being fired by the board.
- Losing the job due to hostile takeover, et cetera.
- Losing managerial freedom.
- Losing outside financing sources.

The Shortcomings of Boards of Directors

Boards are thought to be ineffective for several reasons:

- Boards typically lack independence.
- Board members pay insufficient attention to board matters.
- Board compensation has traditionally not been connected to firm performance.
- Boards are often ineffective because board members prefer to avoid conflict.

Prescriptions for Improving Director Behavior

- The board should have an independent chairman.
- The majority of the board should be independent.
- The audit, compensation, ethics, and nominating committees should be dominated by independent directors.
- Some board and/or committee meetings should be held without management present.
- The board should be able to seek outside advice at the firm's expense.
- Directors should be required to hold a minimum amount of equity.
- Director compensation should be equity-based.
- Directors should have a mandatory retirement age.
- Self-evaluations of boards should be done.

Investor Activism

An **active investor** must have control, and to have control, the shareholder must have either a majority of the firm's shares (*formal control*) or be able to persuade other minority shareholders of their position (*real control*).

In a proxy fight, an active investor attempts to get elected to the board of directors to get a specific resolution adopted by the board.

Takeovers and leveraged buyouts of firms represent another form of investor activism and are thought to increase corporate and macroeconomic efficiency. A change of ownership is not always optimal, however, and may even encourage managers to focus too much attention on short-term performance.

The Limitations of Investor Activism

- Active investors themselves are often unmonitored.
- Active investors do not always have the same goals as the rest of the shareholders.
- Institutional investors need not be long-term investors, so they don't have a strong incentive to push for change.
- There may be negative side effects from monitoring if corporate managers become too focused on short-term performance.
- There may be regulations discouraging large holdings of stock and, thus, active investors.

DEBT AND CORPORATE GOVERNANCE

Debt as a Management Motivator

- Debt takes excess cash out of management's hands.
- To ensure that the firm has cash flow for future investments after repaying its debt, the managers must assure the firm's liquidity.
- If the firm lacks liquidity to the degree where debtholders force the firm into bankruptcy, the managers lose control of the firm and possibly their jobs. This occurrence, and the threat of it occurring, provides the debtholders with some influence over manager behavior.
- If managers hold the majority of the firm's equity, the issuance of debt, rather than equity, means they don't have to share their residual claim on profits.

Limitations of Debt

- External shocks may be the cause of temporary illiquidity that also reduces the ability to borrow (i.e., sell securities).
- Increased debt increases the probability of bankruptcy.

STAKEHOLDERS VS. STOCKHOLDERS

The current and long-standing goal of managing the modern corporation is the maximization of *shareholder wealth*. Shareholders in this case are narrowly defined as the firm's stockholders, so the goal translates into maximizing the firm's stock price. From a socially responsible view, however, proponents suggest the maximization of *stakeholder wealth*. The definition of "stakeholder" can be very loosely defined as anyone who in any way depends upon the firm, and includes employees, creditors, suppliers, and the surrounding communities.

To advance and secure the relationships among the stakeholder groups, contracts that define the goals and responsibilities of each are required. In addition, representatives of all classes of stakeholders should sit on the firms' boards. One problem with this is that government regulations frequently restrict the ability of the stakeholders to form contracts. Another is the need for each group to thoroughly understand its role as well as the contracts that define it.

Stakeholder Structure: Disadvantages

There are four primary disadvantages to stakeholder maximization as the goal for the firm:

1. *Limited ability to raise capital.* Giving operating control of the firm to all the firm's stakeholders could discourage investment.

2. *Inefficient decision-making.* Having all concerned parties provide input into decisions may lead to natural impasses.

3. *Lack of managerial control.* A single goal, such as maximizing stock price, is fairly easily understood and monitored. The set of goals associated with stakeholder wealth maximization, however, is far less concrete (i.e., it can be quite vague) and very hard to monitor.

4. *Inefficient redistribution of taxes.* Taxes are by their very nature a means of redistributing wealth. To realize the best and most efficient redistribution, the funds are typically handled by elected officials who must answer to their constituents for their decision-making. Stakeholder wealth maximization imposes a de facto tax on investors. The proceeds are then redistributed by the firms' managements and boards to their constituents. The argument against this is a lack of evidence that they can do a better job than elected government officials (i.e., that this represents a more efficient redistribution of wealth).

   Under shareholder wealth maximization, redistribution of taxes (i.e., redistribution of wealth) is done by elected government officials.

Shareholder Wealth Maximization

- Proponents of shareholder wealth maximization do not necessarily disagree with advocates of stakeholder wealth maximization. Rather, they tend to feel that the rights of the stakeholders are better managed through regulations and contracts than through the actions of management.
- In order to insulate themselves against potentially adverse shareholder actions, creditors usually structure contracts with flat claims and exit options. Flat claim refers to the fixed amount of the creditor's claim, which is often supported through a claim on collateral. Exit options provide creditors with exit strategies.

THE CADBURY REPORT[2]

The Cadbury Report was prepared by the Committee on the Financial Aspects of Corporate Governance. The committee was established in the United Kingdom in 1991 by the Financial Reporting Council, the London Stock Exchange (LSE), and

---

2   From a summary of the Cadbury Report as found in the 2008 Level 3 Curriculum, Appendix 33-A, Vol. 4, pp. 241–245.

the Accountancy profession. The report includes recommendations, as well as a Code of Best Practices with accompanying notes.

The Code of Best Practices

1. The board should meet regularly, have complete control of the company, and monitor executive management.

2. Top management should be separated so that no one individual has total control. When one person is both president and chairman of the board, the board should be as strong and independent as possible, and the independent element of the board should contain at least one senior member.

3. The board should contain a sufficient number of non-executive members to provide significant influence.

4. The board should maintain a regular schedule containing a list of regular matters, such that control of the company is maintained.

5. Directors should be able, at the company's expense, to seek outside professional guidance.

6. The company secretary should be responsible for assuring that board procedures are followed. All directors should have necessary access to the secretary, and the secretary should be removed only by a vote of the board.

Non-Executive Directors

1. Non-executive directors should apply independent judgment.

2. The majority of non-executive directors should be independent from management's influence and have no conflicts of interest.

3. Appointment should be for a specified term without automatic renewal.

4. The full board should follow a formal policy when appointing non-executive directors.

Executive Directors

1. The shareholders must approve any executive director's contracts in excess of three years.

2. Total remuneration, including a breakdown of the types of remuneration, should be disclosed for every executive director.

3. Remuneration should be recommended by a remuneration committee comprised mainly of non-executive directors.

Reporting and Controls

1. The board is to provide a full and understandable assessment of the company.

2. An objective and professional relationship with the auditors is to be maintained.

3. An audit committee consisting of *at least three non-executive* directors should be formed, and its authority and duties should be clearly written.

4. Directors should explain their responsibilities immediately before the auditor's statement in the annual report.

5. The directors should file a report on the effectiveness of the internal control system.

6. The directors should file a report that the firm is a going concern and any expectations for change.

Recommendations

*   All companies should follow the Code.
*   Any listed company registered in the United Kingdom *must* follow it.
*   Reviewed compliance statements are necessary for continued listing on the London Stock Exchange.
*   In annual reports after June 1993, listed companies should provide a discussion of how they have complied with the Code as well as cases where they did not.
*   Auditors should verify the compliance statements.
*   The Code is to be followed by individuals and boards who should ensure that actions meet the spirit of the Code.
*   Smaller companies without the necessary resources for immediate compliance may list reasons for that non-compliance, but are encouraged to appoint non-executive board members as soon as is feasible.

Alternative Investments for Portfolio Management

Topic Weight on Exam	5–15%
Study Notes Reference	Book 4, Pages 9–72
Video CD Reference	CD 12
Audio CD Reference	CD 13 & 14

Alternative Investments Portfolio Management[1]
Cross-Reference to CFA Institute Assigned Reading #34

There are **six basic categories** of alternative investments: *real estate, private equity, commodities, hedge funds, managed futures,* and *distressed securities.*

Common Features of Alternative Investments

1. Low liquidity.
2. Diversification benefits.
3. High due diligence costs.
4. Difficult to value.
5. Limited access to information.

Due diligence checkpoints for investing in alternative investments include:

1. Assess the market opportunity offered.
2. Assess the investment process.
3. Assess the organization of the manager.
4. Assess the people.
5. Assess the terms and structure of the investment.
6. Assess the service providers (i.e., lawyers, brokers, ancillary staff, etc.).
7. Review documents such as the prospectus and other memoranda.

---

[1] The terminology used throughout this section is industry convention as presented in Managing Investment Portfolios: A Dynamic Process, 3rd edition, Ch. 8, "Alternative Investments Portfolio Management," Jot K. Yau et al. In addition, facts, figures, and returns presented are from Managing Investment Portfolios: A Dynamic Process, 3rd edition, Ch. 8, "Alternative Investments Portfolio Management," Jot K. Yau et al.

ISSUES FOR PRIVATE WEALTH CLIENTS

1. **Tax issues** can be unique to the individual.
2. Determining the **suitability** of investments varies across individuals.
3. **Communication** with the client is important because the client may not be knowledgeable enough to effectively communicate his/her needs.
4. **Decision risk** is the risk of irrationally changing a strategy.
5. Wealthy individuals frequently hold **concentrated portfolios**.

ALTERNATIVE INVESTMENT GROUPS

Real Estate

Indirect real estate investments include:

- Companies that develop and manage real estate.
- REITS.
- CREFs.
- Separately managed accounts by managers such as CREFs.
- Infrastructure funds, which provide private investment in public projects.

Direct investments in real estate generally have low liquidity, large size, high transactions costs, and asymmetric information in transactions (low transparency).

Real estate provides diversification to a stock/bond portfolio, but real estate as an asset class and each individual real estate asset can have a large idiosyncratic risk component.

Private Equity

Private equity subgroups include *start-up companies, middle-market private companies,* and *private investment in public entities.* The distinguishing feature of the subgroups is the stage of development of the company receiving the invested dollars. Investments in start-up and middle-market private companies have more risk and lower returns than investments in established companies via buyout funds. They also suffer from the risks associated with asymmetric information. All the categories have low liquidity.

A *direct* investment in private equity is when the investor purchases a claim directly from the firm.

Indirect investment is usually done through private equity funds, which include venture capital (VC) and buyout funds.

Commodities

Direct investment is either the purchase of the physical commodity or the derivatives on those assets. *Indirect* investment in commodities is usually done through investment in companies whose principal business is associated with a commodity.

Investments in both commodity futures and publicly traded commodity companies are fairly liquid. Investments in commodities have *low correlation with stocks and bonds*, and most have a *positive correlation with inflation*.

Managed Futures

Managed futures funds share many characteristics with hedge funds. The primary legal structure of most managed futures in the U.S. is the limited partnership. Managed futures funds also utilize much the same compensation scheme for managers. Like hedge funds, they are usually classified as absolute return strategies.

The primary feature that distinguishes managed futures from hedge funds is managed futures funds tend to trade only in derivatives markets. Also, managed futures funds generally take positions based on indices, while hedge funds tend to focus more on individual asset price anomalies.

Buyout Funds

Buyout funds are the largest segment of the private equity market and can be divided into *middle market buyout funds* and *mega-cap buyout funds*. The primary difference between the two is the size of the target.

Middle-market buyout funds concentrate on divisions spun off from larger, publicly-traded corporations and private companies that, due to their relatively small size, cannot efficiently obtain capital. **Mega-cap buyout funds** concentrate on taking publicly-traded firms private.

Buyout funds usually capture value for their investors by selling the acquisitions through private placements or IPOs or through *dividend recapitalization*. In a dividend recapitalization, the buyout fund issues debt through an acquired firm and pays a special dividend to itself and other equity investors. *Recapitalization* in this case refers to reducing the firm's equity and increasing its leverage, sometimes to critical levels. Notice, however, that the buyout fund retains control.

Infrastructure Funds

Infrastructure funds specialize in purchasing public infrastructure assets (e.g., airports, toll roads) from cities, states, and municipalities. Since infrastructure assets typically provide a public service, they tend to produce relatively stable, long-term real returns.

They tend to be regulated by local governments, which only adds to the predictability of cash flows. Their low correlation with equity markets means infrastructure assets provide diversification, and their long-term natures provide a good match for institutions with long-term liabilities (e.g., pension funds). Their relatively low risk, however, means that infrastructure returns are low.

Distressed Securities

Analysts often consider distressed securities to be part of the hedge fund class of alternative investments. It may also be part of the private equity class. One way to construct subgroups in distressed securities is by structure, which determines the level of liquidity. The hedge-fund structure for distressed security investment is more liquid. The private equity fund structure describes funds that are less liquid, because they have a fixed term and are closed ended.

Figure 1 presents a summary of alternative investment characteristics.

Figure 1: Alternative Investment Characteristics

	Types of Investments	*Risk/Return Features*	*Liquidity*
Real estate	Residences; commercial real estate; agricultural land.	Large idiosyncratic risk component; provides good diversification.	Low.
Private equity	Preferred shares of stock; venture capital; buyout funds.	Start-up and middle market private companies have more risk and lower returns than investments in established companies via buyout funds.	Low.
Buyout funds	Well established private firms and corporate spin-offs.	Less risk than venture capital funds; good diversification.	Low.
Infrastructure funds	Public infrastructure assets.	Low risk, low return; good diversification.	Low.
Commodities	Agricultural products; crude oil; metals.	Low correlation with stocks/bonds. Positive correlation with inflation.	Fairly liquid.
Managed futures	Tend to trade only in derivatives market. Private commodity pools; publicly traded commodity futures funds.	Risk is between that of equities and bonds. Negative and low correlations with equities and low to moderate correlations with bonds.	Lower for private funds than for publicly traded commodity futures funds.
Distressed securities	May be part of hedge fund class or private equity class. Investments can be in debt and/or equity.	Depends on skill-based strategies. Can earn higher returns due to legal complications and the fact that some investors cannot invest in them.	Hedge fund structure more liquid; private equity structure less liquid.

ALTERNATIVE INVESTMENT BENCHMARKS

Figure 2 presents a summary of alternative investment benchmarks, their construction, and their associated biases.

Figure 2: Alternative Investment Benchmarks

	Benchmarks	Construction	Biases
Real estate	NCREIF; NAREIT.	NCREIF is value-weighted; NAREIT is cap-weighted.	Measured volatility is downward biased. The values are obtained periodically (annually).
Private equity	Provided by Cambridge Associates and Thomson Venture Economics.	Constructed for buyout and venture capital. Value depends upon events. Often construct custom benchmarks.	Repricing occurs infrequently which results in dated values.
Commodities	Dow Jones-AIG Commodity Index; S&P Commodity Index.	Assume a futures-based strategy. Most types considered investable.	Indices vary widely with respect to purpose, composition, and method of weighting.
Managed futures	MLMI; CTA Indices.	MLMI replicates the return to a trend-following strategy. CTA Indices use dollar-weighted or equal-weighted returns.	Requires special weighting scheme.
Distressed securities	Characteristics similar to long-only hedge fund benchmarks.	Weighting either equally-weighted or based upon assets under management. Selection criteria can vary.	Self-reporting; backfill or inclusion bias; popularity bias; survivorship bias.

Hedge Fund Benchmarks

Hedge fund benchmarks vary a great deal in composition and even frequency of reporting. Also, there is no consensus as to what defines hedge fund strategies, and this leads to many differences in the indices as style classifications vary from company to company.

The following list is of providers of *monthly indices* with a few of their general characteristics:

- *CISDM of the University of Massachusetts*: several indices that cover both hedge funds and managed futures (equally-weighted).
- *Credit Suisse/Tremont*: provides various benchmarks for different strategies and uses a weighting scheme based upon assets under management.
- *EACM Advisors*: provides the EACM100® Index, an equally-weighted index of 100 funds that span many categories.
- *Hedge Fund Intelligence, Ltd.*: provides an equally-weighted index of over 50 funds.
- *HedgeFund.net*: provides an equally-weighted index that covers more than 30 strategies.

Biases often exist in these indices because of the *self-reporting* of fund returns. This can apply to returns as they are earned or when filling in gaps in the historical data. *Backfill* or *inclusion bias* is the potential bias when a hedge fund joins an index and the manager adds historical data to complete the series. Also, the methods for selecting and weighting funds included in the index can cause a wide range of return differences among indices in the same class.

- **Popularity bias** can result if one of the funds in a value-weighted index increases in value and then attracts a great deal of capital.
- **Survivorship bias**. Indices may drop funds with poor track records or that fail, causing an upward bias in reported values.

RETURN ENHANCEMENT AND DIVERSIFICATION

Real estate. High risk-adjusted performance is possible because of the low liquidity, large sizes, high transactions costs, and low information transparency that usually means the seller knows more than the buyer. Real estate provides great *diversification* potential.

Private equity is less of a diversifier and more a long-term return enhancer.

Commodities offer *diversification* to a portfolio of stocks and bonds. The returns on commodities are generally lower than stocks and bonds.

Hedge funds generated higher returns than stocks and bonds over the period 1990–2004 and generally provide moderate to good *diversification* benefits.

Managed futures provide returns similar to that of hedge funds and can provide *diversification*.

Distressed securities have generally beaten stocks and bonds but have a large negative skew and are uncorrelated with the overall stock market.

DIRECT REAL ESTATE EQUITY INVESTING

Advantages:

- Many expenses are tax deductible.
- Ability to use more leverage than most other investments.
- More control than stock investing.
- Ability to diversify geographically.
- Lower volatility of returns than stocks.

Disadvantages:

- Lack of divisibility.
- High information commission, operating and maintenance, and management costs.
- Special geographical risks.

VENTURE CAPITAL INVESTING

Issuers of venture capital include *formative-stage companies* and *expansion-stage companies.* **Buyers** of venture capital include: *angel investors, venture capitalists,* and *large companies,* who are also called *strategic partners.*

The **stages** through which private companies pass are: early stage, later stage, and exit stage.

In contrast to venture capital funds, **buyout funds** usually have:

- A higher level of leverage.
- Earlier and steadier cash flows.
- Less error in the measurement of returns.
- Less frequent losses.
- Less upside potential.

Convertible preferred stock is a good vehicle for direct venture capital investment, because preferred stockholders must be paid a specified amount, before common stockholders receive distributions.

PRIVATE EQUITY INVESTING

Private equity funds usually take the form of **limited partnerships** or **limited liability companies** (LLC).

The sponsor (i.e., general partner) typically gets a *management fee* and *incentive fee.* The **management fee** is usually 1.5% to 2.5% and is based upon the *committed funds.* The **incentive fee** is also called the carried interest. It is the share of the profits that are paid to the manager after the fund has returned the outside investors' capital. A *claw-back* provision may be in place that requires the manager to give back money, if the expected profits are not realized.

Any strategy for private equity investment must address:

- Low liquidity.
- Diversification through a number of positions.
- Plans for meeting capital calls.

THE TERM STRUCTURE OF FUTURES PRICES

Direct commodity investment entails either purchasing the actual commodities or gaining exposure via derivatives. **Indirect commodity investment** is the purchase of indirect claims like shares in a corporation that deals in the commodity.

Direct investment gives more exposure, but cash investment in commodities can incur carrying costs. Indirect investment may be more convenient, but it may provide very little exposure to the commodity, especially if the company is hedging the risk itself.

The components of the return to a commodity futures contract are the *spot return*, the *collateral return*, and the *roll return*.

total return = spot return + collateral return + roll return

The *spot return* (a.k.a. *price return*) is the return on the futures caused by the change in the underlying commodity's price.

The *collateral return* (a.k.a. *collateral yield*) is approximately the risk-free rate.

Roll return (a.k.a. *roll yield*) is usually the result of *normal backwardation*.

The returns of many types of commodities have a **positive correlation with inflation**.

Agricultural commodities can have a **negative correlation with inflation**, because they are not storable.

HEDGE FUND CLASSIFICATIONS

Hedge funds have been classified in various ways by different sources. Since hedge funds are a "style-based" asset class, strategies can determine the subgroups. Within the strategies, there can be even more precise subgroups such as long/short and long-only strategies. The following is a list of nine of the more familiar hedge fund strategies.

1. *Convertible arbitrage* commonly involves buying undervalued convertible bonds, preferred stock, or warrants, while shorting the underlying stock to create a hedge.

2. *Distressed securities* investments can be made in both debt and equity. Since the securities are already distressed, shorting can be difficult or impossible.

3. *Emerging markets* generally only permit long positions, and often there are no derivatives to hedge the investments.

4. *Equity market neutral* (pairs trading) combines long and short positions in undervalued and overvalued securities, respectively, to eliminate systematic risk while capitalizing on mispricing.

5. *Fixed-income arbitrage* involves taking long and short positions in fixed-income instruments based upon expected changes in the yield curve and/or credit spreads.

6. *Fund of funds* describes a hedge fund that invests in many hedge funds. They tend to be more correlated with equities than with individual hedge fund strategies.

7. *Global macro strategies* take positions in major financial and non-financial markets through various means (e.g., derivatives and currencies). They tend to focus on an entire group or area of investment instead of individual securities or classes of securities.

8. *Hedged equity strategies* (a.k.a. *equity long-short*) represent the largest hedge fund classification in terms of assets under management. They take long and short positions in under- and overvalued securities, respectively, similar to equity market neutral strategies. The difference is that hedged equity strategies do not focus on balancing the positions to eliminate systematic risk and can range from net long to net short.

9. *Merger arbitrage* (a.k.a. *deal arbitrage*) focuses on returns from mergers, spin-offs, takeovers, etc.

Another classification scheme divides hedge funds strategies into five general segments: *relative value, event driven, hedged equity, global asset allocators*, and *short selling*.

1. *Relative value* strategies attempt to exploit price discrepancies.

2. *Event-driven* strategies invest with a short-term focus on an event like a merger (merger arbitrage) or the turnaround of a distressed company (distressed securities).

3. *Equity hedge* entails taking long and short equity positions with varying overall net long or short positions and can include leverage.

4. *Global asset allocators* take long and short positions in a variety of both financial and non-financial assets.

5. *Short selling* takes short-only positions.

Styles that are mainly long-only tend to offer less potential for diversification than long/short styles, and liquidity can vary from fund to fund or even within subgroups. A hedge fund within any of the classes can have a lock-up period, for example.

Hedge Fund Structure

The most common **compensation structure** of a hedge fund consists of an assets-under-management fee, or *AUM fee*, and an *incentive fee*. **High water marks** are typically employed to avoid incentive fee double-dipping.

A **lock-up period** is a common provision in hedge funds that limits withdrawals by requiring a minimum investment period (e.g., one to three years), and designating exit windows. The rationale is to prevent sudden withdrawals that could force the manager to have to unwind positions.

Hedge Fund Incentive Fees

Incentive fees are paid to encourage the manager to earn even higher profits. There is some controversy concerning incentive fees, because the manager should have goals other than simply earning a gross return. For example, the manager may be providing limited downside risk and diversification. An incentive fee based upon returns does not reward this service.

Managers with good track records often demand higher incentive fees. The concern for investors is whether the manager with a good historical record can continue to perform well enough to truly earn the higher fees.

Fund of Funds

A **fund of funds** (FOF) is a hedge fund that consists of several, usually 10 to 30, hedge funds. The point is to achieve diversification, but the extra layer of management means an extra layer of fees. Often a FOF offers more liquidity for the investor, but the cost is cash drag caused by the manager keeping extra cash to meet potential withdrawals by other investors.

A FOF may serve as a *better* indicator of aggregate performance of hedge funds (i.e., a better benchmark), because they suffer from less survivorship bias. If a fund of funds includes a fund that dissolves, it includes the effect of that failure in the return of the fund of funds, while an index may simply drop the failed fund.

A FOF can, however, suffer from **style drift** and FOF returns have been more highly correlated with equity markets than those of individual hedge funds. This can produce problems in that the investor may not know what she is getting. Over time, individual hedge fund managers may tilt their respective portfolios in different directions. Also, it is not uncommon for two FOF who claim to be of the same style to have returns with a very low correlation.

HEDGE FUND PERFORMANCE EVALUATION

Some claim that hedge funds **absolute-return vehicles**, which means that no direct benchmark exists. To create comparable portfolios, analysts (1) create single and multi-factor models and (2) use an optimization technique to create a tracking portfolio.

Conventions to consider in hedge fund performance evaluation are the impact of performance fees and lock-up periods, the age of funds, and the size of funds. Empirical studies have found that:

*   Funds with longer lock-up periods tend to produce higher returns than those with shorter lock-up periods.
*   Younger funds tend to outperform older funds.
*   Large funds underperform small funds.

Returns. By convention, hedge funds report *monthly* returns which are then compounded to arrive at annual returns. Note that returns are often biased by entry into and exit from the fund, which are allowed on a quarterly or less frequent basis, and by the frequency of the manager's trading (i.e., cash flows). To smooth out variability in hedge fund returns, investors often compute a *rolling return*, such as a 12-month moving average.

Leverage. The convention for dealing with **leverage** is to treat an asset as if it were fully paid for (i.e., effectively "look through" the leverage). When derivatives are included, the same principle of *de-leveraging* is applied.

Risk. Hedge fund returns are usually skewed with significant leptokurtosis (fat tails), so standard deviation fails to measure the true risk of the distribution.

Downside deviation is a popular hedge-fund risk measure, as it measures only the dispersion of returns below some specified threshold return.

$$\text{downside deviation} = \sqrt{\frac{\sum_{1}^{n}[\min(\text{Return}_t - \text{threshold}, 0)^2]}{n-1}}$$

The threshold return is usually either zero or the risk-free rate of return. If the threshold is a recent average return, then we call the downside deviation the **semivariance.** The point of these measures is to focus on the negative returns and not penalize a fund for high positive returns, which increase measured standard deviation.

The Sharpe Ratio

Annual hedge fund Sharpe ratios are calculated using *annualized* measures:

$$\text{Sharpe}_{HF} = \frac{\text{annualized return } - \text{annualized risk-free rate}}{\text{annualized standard deviation}}$$

In addition to concerns associated with the way returns are calculated, the Sharpe ratio has the following *limitations* with respect to hedge fund evaluation:

- *Time dependency.* The Sharpe ratio is higher for longer holding periods (e.g., monthly versus weekly returns) by a scale of the square root of time, because monthly or quarterly returns and standard deviations are annualized. For example, quarterly returns are multiplied by 4, but the quarterly standard deviation is multiplied by $\sqrt{4}$.
- *Assumes normality.*
- *Assumes liquidity.*
- *Assumes uncorrelated returns:* Returns correlated across time will artificially lower the standard deviation. For example, if returns are trending for a period of time, the measured standard deviation will be lower than what may occur in the future. Serially correlated returns also result when the asset is illiquid and current prices are not available (e.g., private equity investments).
- *Stand-alone measure:* Does not automatically consider diversification effects.

DERIVATIVE MARKETS

Derivatives are a **zero-sum game.** This means the gross long-term return on passively managed and unlevered portfolios should be the risk-free rate. To earn more than the risk-free rate would imply that parties in the market are willing to sacrifice return. This may be the case when hedgers effectively pay a risk-premium to have "insurance" on their cash positions (e.g., protective put).

Since not all market participants can use derivatives, investors in derivatives may be able to capture returns not available to all investors.

DISTRESSED SECURITIES INVESTING

Long-only value investing tries to find opportunities where the prospects will improve. *High-yield investing* is buying publicly-traded, below investment grade debt. *Orphan equities investing* is the purchase of the equities of firms emerging from reorganization.

Distressed debt arbitrage is the purchasing of a company's distressed debt while short selling the company's equity. **Private equity** is an "active" approach where the investor acquires positions in the distressed company, and the investment gives some measure of control. Distressed securities can have event risk, market liquidity risk, market risk, and J-factor risk.

SWAPS
Cross-Reference to CFA Institute Assigned Reading #35

Commodity Swaps vs. Interest Rate Swaps

The financial **settlements** of interest rate swaps and commodity swaps are very similar:

settlement = (difference between fixed and market values) × (notional principal)

With respect to swap **valuation**, memorize the following main points:

1. Value is the present value of the settlement.
2. Values at inception are zero (ignoring fees).
3. Values change as interest rates change. In addition, the value of a commodity swap changes as commodity prices change.
4. Values change as time passes.

Forward contracts can lock in the cash flows, but the changes in the interest rates can change the present value of the cash flows and, hence, the market value of the swap.

Swap Hedging Strategies

From the perspective of the buyer of a **prepaid swap**, there is *credit risk, market risk,* and *financial risk*. For **financially settled swaps**, there is risk from the changes in forward prices and in interest rates, but the credit risk is considerably less.

COMMODITY FORWARDS AND FUTURES
Cross-Reference to CFA Institute Assigned Reading #36

(Know these relationships.)

The forward price (F_T) of a *financial asset* is the future value of the spot price at the risk free rate reduced by the dividend yield:

$$F_{t,0} = S_0 e^{(r - \delta)T}$$
S_0 = current spot price
$F_{T,0}$ = forward price at time 0 for an asset to be delivered at time T
r = risk free rate
δ = dividend yield

The **lease rate** on a commodity is the interest rate (i.e., return) the holder of a commodity would require to lend it out, and it is analogous to the dividend yield on a stock that has been loaned out for a short sale. If we denote the lease rate as δ, the equation also applies to commodities.

$$F_{t,0} = S_0 e^{(r - \delta)T}$$
δ = lease rate

When there are **storage costs** associated with holding the commodity, the forward price can be stated as:

$$F_{t,0} = S_0 e^{(r + \lambda)T}$$
r = risk free rate
λ = storage costs as percentage of commodity value

Note that storage costs act like a *negative lease rate*. If the owner of a storable commodity *lends* the commodity, he is relieved of paying the storage costs.

The non-monetary gain from holding a commodity is referred to as **convenience yield**. Think of the storage costs as being *reduced* by the convenience yield, so the formula for calculating the forward price with storage costs becomes:

$$F_{t,0} = S_0 e^{(r + \lambda - c)T}$$
r = risk free rate
λ = storage costs as percentage of commodity value
c = convenience yield as a percentage of commodity value

Contango and Backwardation

An upward-sloping forward curve indicates that forward prices increase as their maturity increases. The market is described as being in **contango**, which occurs when the lease rate is *less than* the risk-free rate. The market is in **backwardation** when the forward curve is downward-sloping. Backwardation occurs when the lease rate is *greater than* the risk-free rate.

Commodity Spreads

A *commodity spread* results from a commodity that is an input in the production process of other commodities. A trader creates a *crush spread* by holding a long (short) position in soybeans and a short (long) position in soybean meal and soybean oil.

Similarly, petroleum can be refined to produce heating oil, kerosene, or gasoline. This process is known as "cracking" and thus, the difference in prices of crude oil, heating oil, and gasoline is known as a *crack spread*. Thus, an oil refiner could lock in the price of the crude oil input and the finished good outputs by an appropriate crack spread reflecting the refining process. However, this is not a perfect hedge because there are other outputs that can be produced (such as jet fuel and kerosene).

Basis Risk

In order to minimize basis risk, it is ideal to find a futures contract that is highly correlated with the hedged asset. In addition, the timing of the delivery should match the expiration of the hedge in both financial and commodity futures. Minimizing basis risk in commodity futures will, however, depend on more than just timing. Differences due to timing, grade, storage costs, and/or transportation costs can create basis risk.

RISK MANAGEMENT

Topic Weight on Exam	< 5%
Study Notes Reference	Book 4, Pages 73–109
Video CD Reference	CD 12
Audio CD Reference	CD 14 & 15

Risk management will probably be incorporated into morning cases and/or afternoon item sets and total less than 5% of the exam.

RISK MANAGEMENT
Cross-Reference to CFA Institute Assigned Reading #37

The **risk management process** is a *continual* process of:

- Identifying and measuring specific risk exposures.
- Setting specific tolerance levels.
- Reporting risk exposures (deemed appropriate) to stakeholders.
- Monitoring the process and taking any necessary corrective actions.

Risk governance, a part of the overall corporate governance system, is the name given to the overall process of developing and putting a risk management system into use.

- A *decentralized* risk governance system puts risk management in the hands of the individuals (i.e., managers) closest to everyday operations.
- A *centralized* system (also called ERM) provides a better view of how the risk of each unit affects the overall risk borne by the firm.

Some of the specific risks that must be monitored include:

- Market risk (financial risk).
- Liquidity risk (financial risk).
- Settlement risk (non-financial risk).
- Credit risk (financial risk).
- Operations risk (non-financial risk).
- Model risk (non-financial risk).
- Sovereign risk (financial and non-financial risk components).
- Regulatory risk (non-financial).
- Political risk, tax risk, accounting risk, and legal risk (all non-financial).

EVALUATING A RISK MANAGEMENT SYSTEM

The analyst should determine whether:

- Senior management allocates capital on a risk-adjusted basis.
- The ERM system properly identifies all relevant risk factors.
- The ERM system utilizes an appropriate model.
- Risks are properly managed.
- There is a committee in place to oversee the entire system.
- The ERM system has built-in checks and balances.

EVALUATING FINANCIAL (MARKET) RISK

Market risk in this context refers to the response in the value of an asset to changes in interest rates, exchange rates, equity prices, and/or commodity prices.

The measure you are no doubt most familiar with is **standard deviation**. When measured relative to a benchmark, the volatility (standard deviation) of the asset's excess returns is called **active risk, tracking risk, tracking error volatility**, or **tracking error**.

The manager's excess return over the benchmark, called **active return**, is typically compared to the historical volatility of excess returns, measured by **active risk**. The ratio of the active return to the active risk is known as the **information ratio** (IR):

$$IR_P = \frac{\text{active return}}{\text{active risk}} = \frac{R_P - R_B}{\sigma_{(R_P - R_B)}} \qquad \text{(know this formula)}$$

It is very important to recognize that the market risk of an asset has two dimensions: (1) the sensitivity of the asset to movements in a given market factor and (2) changes in the asset's sensitivity to the factor.

EVALUATING NONFINANCIAL RISK

Because most nonfinancial risk (e.g., tax, legal and regulatory, sovereign) are difficult if not impossible to measure, managers will often not even attempt to assign an associated VAR value. Although regulators and managers have made advances in measuring the losses associated with these risk factors, the lack of relevant historical data leads managers to buy *insurance*, which protects against these losses.

VALUE AT RISK

VAR is used as an estimate of the minimum expected loss (alternatively, the maximum loss):

- Over a set time period.
- At a desired level of *significance*.

When estimating VAR for a portfolio, the correlations of the returns on the individual assets must be considered, because the overall VAR is not just the simple sum of individual VARs. Methods for estimating VAR include:

- The **analytical method** (a.k.a. the **variance-covariance** or **delta normal method**).
- The **historical method**.
- **Monte Carlo method**.

For the exam, if you are given the standard deviation of annual returns and need to calculate a daily VAR, the daily standard deviation can be estimated as the annual standard deviation divided by the square root of the number of (trading) days in a year, and so forth:

$$\sigma_{daily} \cong \frac{\sigma_{annual}}{\sqrt{250}}; \; \sigma_{monthly} \cong \frac{\sigma_{annual}}{\sqrt{12}}; \; \sigma_{daily} \cong \frac{\sigma_{monthly}}{\sqrt{22}}$$

Analytical VAR

The expected 1-day return for a $100,000,000 portfolio is 0.00085 and the historical standard deviation of daily returns is 0.0011. **Calculate** daily value at risk (VAR) at 5% significance.

$$VAR = \left[\hat{R}_p - (z)(\sigma)\right]V_p \qquad \text{(know this formula)}$$

$$= \left[0.00085 - 1.65(0.0011)\right]($100,000,000)$$

$$= -0.000965($100,000,000)$$

$$= -$96,500$$

ADVANTAGES AND LIMITATIONS OF VAR

One primary **benefit of VAR** is that it is interpreted the same, regardless of the assets in question. A primary disadvantage is that VAR does not give the magnitude of potential extreme losses (i.e., losses in the lower tail of the distribution).

Incremental VAR (IVAR) is the effect of an individual asset on the overall risk of the portfolio. **Cash flow at risk** (CFAR) measures the risk of the company's cash flows. **Earnings at risk** (EAR) is analogous to CFAR only from an accounting earnings standpoint. **Tail value at risk** (TVAR) is VAR plus the expected value in the lower tail of the distribution, which could be estimated by averaging the possible losses in the tail.

We do not directly consider **liquidity** in measuring VAR, so VAR can give an inaccurate estimate of the true potential for loss.

Stress testing measures the impacts of unusual events that might not be reflected in the typical VAR calculation. **Scenario analysis** is used to measure the effect on the portfolio of simultaneous movements in several factors or to measure the effects of unusually large movements in individual factors.

Stressing Models

In **factor push analysis**, the analyst deliberately pushes a factor or factors to the extreme and measures the impact on the portfolio. **Maximum loss optimization** involves identifying risk factors that have the greatest potential for impacting the value of the portfolio. **Worst-case scenario** is exactly that; the analyst simultaneously pushes all risk factors to their worst cases.

EVALUATING CREDIT RISK

The monetary exposure to credit risk is a function of the probability of a default event and the amount of money lost if the default event occurs.

Current credit risk (also called **jump-to-default risk**) is associated with payments that are currently due, while potential credit risk is associated with payments due in the future. In measuring potential credit risk, creditors must consider cross-default-provisions.

Credit VAR

Credit VAR is also called **credit at risk** or **default VAR**. Unlike traditional VAR, credit managers focus on the *upper tail* of possible returns. An increase in the value of these assets (e.g., a positive return from falling interest rates), for example, accrues to the debtor in the form of the option to refinance.

Forward Contracts

The value of a forward contract:

$$\text{value} = PV_{\text{inflows}} - PV_{\text{outflows}} \qquad \text{(know this formula)}$$

where:
PV_{inflows} = the present value of cash flows to be received under the contract (discounted at the long position's interest rate).

PV_{outflows} = the present value of cash flows given up (i.e., the amount that would be received

---

Swaps

The credit risk of the typical *interest rate swap* is highest somewhere around the middle of its life. As some time passes and interest rates change, one or both of the parties begins to experience credit risk. As the swap nears its maturity and the number of remaining settlement payments decreases, the credit risk decreases.

In a *currency swap*, both parties can be simultaneously exposed to credit risk. Also, due to the exchange of principals at inception and the return of principals on the maturity date, the credit risk of a currency swap is highest between the middle and maturity of the agreement.

Options

The credit risk to an option is only borne by the long position. The credit risk to a *European option* can only be potential until the date it matures.

The credit risk of an *American option* will be at least as great as a similar European option. Also, the potential credit risk of an American option becomes current if the long decides to exercise early.

MANAGING MARKET RISK

Risk budgeting is the process of determining which risks are acceptable and how total enterprise risk is allocated across business units or portfolio managers. Through an ERM system, upper management allocates different amounts of capital across portfolio managers, each with an associated VAR.

An ERM system affords the ability to continuously monitor the risk budget so that any deviations are immediately reported to upper management. Another benefit of a risk budgeting system is the ability to compare manager performance in relationship to the amount of capital and risk allocated (i.e., measure risk-adjusted performance with **return on VAR**).

- **Position limits** place a nominal dollar cap on positions.
- **Liquidity limits** are related to position limits. Risk managers set dollar position limits according to frequency of trading.
- A **performance stopout** sets an absolute dollar limit for losses over a certain period.

MANAGING CREDIT RISK

- **Limit exposure** to any individual debtor.
- **Marking to market.**
- **Collateral** for transactions that generate credit risk.

- **Payment netting** is frequently employed to determine which side faces the credit risk.
- Create **special purpose vehicles** (SPV) and **enhanced derivatives products companies** (EDPC).
- Transfer risk to somebody else:
  - Total return swaps.
  - Credit spread options.
  - Credit spread forwards.
  - Credit default swaps.

MEASURING RISK-ADJUSTED PERFORMANCE

- **Sharpe ratio.**
- **Information ratio** (IR).
- **Risk-adjusted return on invested capital** (RAROC).
- **Return over maximum drawdown:**

$$\text{RoMAD} = \frac{\overline{R}_p}{\text{maximum drawdown}}$$

- **Sortino ratio:**

$$\text{Sortino} = \frac{\overline{R}_p - \text{MAR}}{\text{downside deviation}}$$

SETTING CAPITAL REQUIREMENTS

Nominal position limits, also called **notional** or **monetary position limits**, are specified in terms of the amount of money allocated across portfolio managers based upon upper management's desire for return and exposure to risk.

Problems associated with nominal position limits stem from the ability of the individual portfolio manager to exceed the limit by combining assets (usually derivatives) to replicate the payoffs of other assets, and from management's inability to capture the effects of correlation among the nominal positions.

VAR-based position limits are sometimes used in lieu of nominal position limits. The benefit is a clear VAR picture. The drawback is the failure to consider the correlation of the different positions (i.e., different VARs).

A **maximum loss limit** is the maximum allowable loss. The sum of the individual maximum loss limit is the theoretical maximum the firm will have to endure. The benefit to setting maximum loss limits is the ability to allocate capital so the maximum loss never exceeds the firm's capital. The drawback is the possibility of all units simultaneously exceeding their limits.

Internal and regulatory capital requirements are set by regulation (e.g., banks). The ERM system must recognize the potential for incentive conflicts between management, which allocates the risk and the portfolio managers.

Derivatives Risk Management Strategy

Topic Weight on Exam	5–15%
Study Notes Reference	Book 4, Pages 110–210
Video CD Reference	CDs 13 & 14
Audio CD Reference	CDs 15 & 16

Derivatives are typically well represented on the exam. Look for an afternoon item set with associated calculations. The qualitative concepts are likely to show up in an essay question. Look for total derivatives coverage to amount to about 15% of the exam (~50 points)

Risk Management Applications of Forward and Futures Strategies
Cross-Reference to CFA Institute Assigned Reading #38

Duration of a Futures Contract; Yield of a Futures Contract

The value of a futures contract is sensitive to changes in interest rates; therefore, a futures contract has a duration. This is usually referred to as *implied duration*, and it is a function of the cheapest-to-deliver bond for the futures contract. The reference rate is called an *implied yield*, and it is indicative of the yield of the underlying bond implied by pricing it as though it were delivered at the expiration of the futures contract.

We can write:

change in the futures price = $-(MD_F)$(futures price)(change in implied yield)

where:
MD_F is the modified duration of the futures contract

Yield Beta

The relationship between the yield on a bond and the implied yield of a futures contract is usually assumed to be:

$$\Delta y = (\text{yield beta})\ (\Delta \text{implied yield of futures})$$

or

$$\text{yield beta} = \frac{\Delta y}{\Delta \text{implied yield of futures}}$$

ADJUSTING THE PORTFOLIO BETA

Having selected a *target beta*, we can find the appropriate number of contracts to sell or buy to hedge or leverage the position (reduce or increase beta), respectively:

$$\text{number of contracts} = \left(\frac{\beta_T - \beta_P}{\beta_f}\right)\left(\frac{V_P}{P_f(\text{multiplier})}\right) \quad \text{(know this formula)}$$

INDEX MULTIPLIERS AND SYNTHETIC POSITIONS

The futures price of an equity index is usually the value of the index multiplied by a fixed *multiplier* for that index:

- S&P 500 Index futures trade at 250 times the index value per contract.
- Nasdaq 100 Index futures trade at 100 times the index value per contract.
- DJIA Index futures trade at 10 times the index value per contract.

The basic strategies for creating synthetic cash or equity are as follows:

1. synthetic risk-free asset = long stock − stock index futures (i.e., short position)

2. synthetic equity = long risk-free asset + stock index futures (i.e., long position)

SYNTHETIC STOCK INDEX FUND

Creating a synthetic equity index from a portfolio in T-bills:

Step 1: $\text{number of contracts}_{\text{UNrounded}} = \dfrac{(T_{\text{held}})(1 + R_F)^t}{(P_f)(\text{multiplier})}$

Step 2: $\text{number of contracts}_{\text{rounded}} = \dfrac{(T_{\text{equitized}})(1 + R_F)^t}{(P_f)(\text{multiplier})}$

SYNTHETIC CASH

The required number of equity futures to sell can be determined using:

$$\text{number of equity contracts} = -\frac{V_P(1+R_F)^T}{P_f} \qquad \text{(know this formula)}$$

ADJUSTING THE PORTFOLIO ALLOCATION $\qquad$ (know these formulas)

The basic equation for altering the beta of the portfolio:

$$\text{number of equity index contracts} = \left(\frac{\beta_T - \beta_P}{\beta_f}\right)\left(\frac{V_P}{P_f(\text{multiplier})}\right)$$

The basic equation for altering the duration of the portfolio:

$$\text{number of contracts} = (\text{yield beta})\left(\frac{MD_T - MD_P}{MD_F}\right)\left(\frac{V_P}{P_f(\text{multiplier})}\right)$$

Figure 1: Steps for Synthetically Altering Debt and Equity Allocations

To reallocate an amount $V from *equity to bonds*:

1. Reduce its *beta to zero* (turn it into synthetic cash) by shorting stock index futures.

2. Increase the duration of the synthetic cash created in step (1) to the portfolio duration by taking a long position in bond futures.

To reallocate an amount $V from *bonds to equity*:

1. Reduce its duration to the duration of the cash portion of the portfolio by shorting bond futures (create synthetic cash).

2. Increase the equity exposure by buying equity index futures.

Adjusting the Equity Allocation

To transfer $V from class A to class B, use futures to first transfer $V in class A to cash and then transfer $V in cash to class B using index futures.

Pre-investing is the practice of taking long positions in futures contracts to create an exposure that converts a yet-to-be-received cash position into a synthetic equity and/or bond position.

Exchange Rate Risk

Three types of foreign exchange rate risk.

1. *Economic exposure* is the loss of sales that a domestic exporter might experience if the domestic currency appreciates relative to a foreign currency.

2. *Translation exposure* refers to the decline in the value of assets that are denominated in foreign currencies when those foreign currencies depreciate.

3. *Transaction exposure* is the risk that exchange rate fluctuations will make contracted future cash flows from foreign trade partners decrease in domestic currency value or make planned purchases of foreign goods more expensive.

Derivatives are used most often to hedge *transactions exposure*. Being *long the currency* (in this context) means you have contracted to *receive* the foreign currency. Being *short the currency* means you have contracted to *pay* the foreign currency, and the concern is that the currency will appreciate.

RISK MANAGEMENT APPLICATIONS OF OPTIONS STRATEGIES

Cross-Reference to CFA Institute Assigned Reading #39

 Professor's Note: If you have the time, you can memorize the formulas associated with all the option strategies. But do not take any significant time away from studying other, more valuable areas.

COVERED CALLS AND PROTECTIVE PUTS

Covered Call

An investor creates a *covered call* position by buying the underlying security and selling a call option. Covered call writing strategies are used to generate additional portfolio income when the investor believes that the underlying stock price will remain unchanged over the short-term.

Figure 2: Profit Profile for a Covered Call

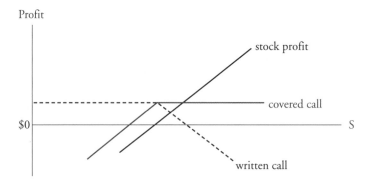

At expiration, the following relationships hold for the investor that both buys the stock and sells the call:

$$\text{profit} = -\max(0, S_T - X) + S_T - S_0 + C_0$$
$$\text{maximum profit} = X + C_0 - S_0$$
$$\text{maximum loss} = S_0 - C_0$$
$$\text{breakeven price} = S_0 - C_0$$
$$S_0 = \text{initial stock price paid}$$

Protective Put

A *protective put* (also called *portfolio insurance* or a *hedged portfolio*) is constructed by holding a long position in the underlying security and buying a put option.

Figure 3: Protect Put

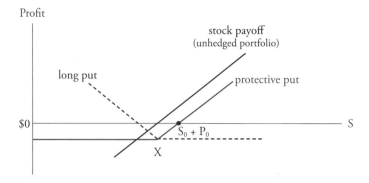

At expiration, the following relationships hold:

$$\text{profit} = \max(0, X - S_T) + S_T - S_0 - P_0$$
$$\text{maximum profit} = S_T - S_0 - P_0 \text{ (no upside limit)}$$
$$\text{maximum loss} = S_0 - X + P_0$$
$$\text{breakeven price} = S_0 + P_0$$

OPTION SPREAD STRATEGIES

Bull Call Spread

In a bull call spread, the buyer of the spread purchases a call option with a low exercise price, X_L, and subsidizes the purchase price of that call by selling a call with a higher exercise price, X_H. The prices are C_{L0} and C_{H0} respectively. At inception, the following relationships hold:

$$X_L < X_H$$
$$C_{L0} > C_{H0}$$

It is usually the case that $S_0 < X_L$ and almost always that $S_0 < X_H$. The investor who buys a bull call spread expects the stock price to rise and the purchased call to finish in-the-money such that $X_L < S_T$. However, the investor does not believe that the price of the stock will rise above the exercise price for the out-of-the-money written call.

Figure 4: Bull Call Spread

Profit

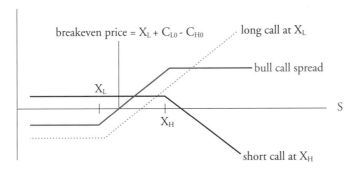

$$\text{profit} = \max(0, S_T - X_L) - \max(0, S_T - X_H) - C_{L0} + C_{H0}$$
$$\text{maximum profit} = X_H - X_L - C_{L0} + C_{H0}$$
$$\text{maximum loss} = C_{L0} - C_{H0}$$
$$\text{breakeven price} = X_L + C_{L0} - C_{H0}$$

Bear Call Spread

The bear call spread is a *short bull spread*. That is, the bear spread trader will purchase the call with the higher exercise price and sell the call with the lower exercise price. This strategy is designed to profit from falling stock prices (which is why it's called a *bear* strategy). As stock prices fall, you keep the premium from the written call, net of the long call premium. The purpose of the long call is to protect you from sharp increases in stock prices.

Figure 5: Bear Call Spread

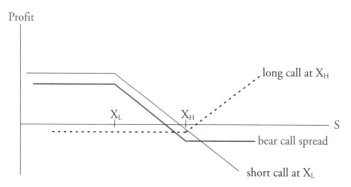

Bear Put Spread

In a bear put spread the investor buys a put with the higher exercise price and sells a put with a lower exercise price. The important relationships are:

$$\text{profit} = \max(0, X_H - S_T) - \max(0, X_L - S_T) - P_{H0} + P_{L0}$$
$$\text{maximum profit} = X_H - X_L - P_{H0} + P_{L0}$$
$$\text{maximum loss} = P_{H0} - P_{L0}$$
$$\text{breakeven price} = X_H + P_{L0} - P_{H0}$$

Butterfly Spread With Calls

A butterfly spread with calls involves the purchase or sale of four call options of three different types:

1. Buy one call with a low exercise price.

2. Buy another call with a high exercise price.

3. Write *two* calls with an exercise price in between.

The buyer of a butterfly spread is essentially betting that the stock price will stay near the strike price of the written calls. However, the loss that the butterfly spread buyer sustains if the stock price strays from this level is not large.

Figure 6: Butterfly Spread Construction and Behavior

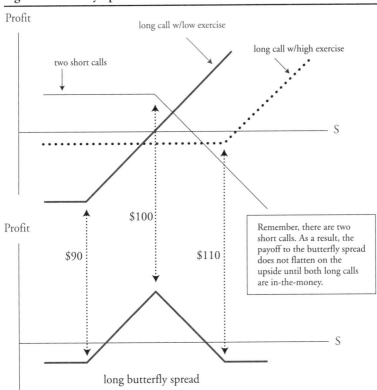

long butterfly spread

$$\text{profit} = \max(0, S_T - X_L) - 2\max(0, S_T - X_M) + \max(0, S_T - X_H) - C_{L0} + 2C_{M0} - C_{H0}$$

$$\text{maximum profit} = X_M - X_L - C_{L0} + 2C_{M0} - C_{H0}$$

$$\text{maximum loss} = C_{L0} - 2C_{M0} + C_{H0}$$

$$\text{breakeven price} = X_L + C_{L0} - 2C_{M0} + C_{H0} \text{ and } 2X_M - X_L - C_{L0} + 2C_{M0} - C_{H0}$$

Butterfly Spread With Puts

A long butterfly spread with puts is constructed by buying one put with a low exercise price, buying a second put with a higher exercise price, and selling two puts with an intermediate exercise price. The profit function is very similar to that of the butterfly spread with calls. You will notice that in each of the max() functions the S_T and X_i have switched, but otherwise it is basically the same format:

$$\text{profit} = \max(0, X_L - S_T) - 2\max(0, X_M - S_T) + \max(0, X_H - S_T) - P_{L0} + 2P_{M0} - P_{H0}$$

As with the butterfly spread with calls, the long-put butterfly spread will have its highest terminal value if the stock finishes at the exercise price for the written puts.

Straddle

A *long straddle* consists of the purchase of both a put option and a call option with the same exercise price and expiration on the same asset. In a long straddle, you expect a large stock price move, but you are unsure of the direction. You lose if the stock price remains unchanged.

Figure 7: Long Straddle

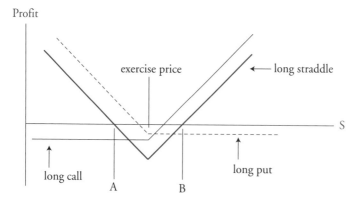

A *short straddle* is the sale of a put and call on the same underlying asset at the same exercise price and the same maturity. The straddle seller is betting that the stock price will not move much over the horizon of the strategy (i.e., vertically flip the graph for the long straddle in your mind). If the stock price remains unchanged, the options expire out-of-the-money, and the straddle seller keeps the put and call premiums.

For the *long straddle*, the important relationships are:

$$\text{profit} = \max(0, S_T - X) + \max(0, X - S_T) - C_0 - P_0$$
$$\text{maximum profit} = S_T - X - C_0 - P_0 \text{ (unlimited upside as } S_T \text{ increases)}$$
$$\text{maximum loss} = C_0 + P_0$$
$$\text{breakeven price} = X - C_0 - P_0 \text{ and } X + C_0 + P_0$$

Collar

A collar is the combination of a protective put and covered call. The usual goal is for the owner of the underlying asset to buy a protective put and then sell a call to pay for the put. If the premiums of the two are equal, it is called a *zero-cost collar*.

Figure 8: Payoff Graph for a Collar

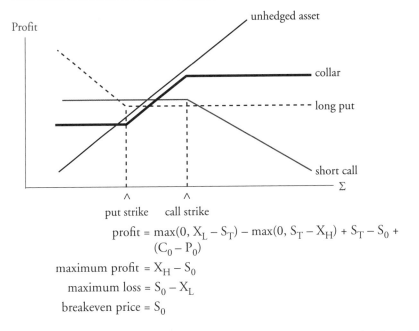

$$\text{profit} = \max(0, X_L - S_T) - \max(0, S_T - X_H) + S_T - S_0 + (C_0 - P_0)$$
$$\text{maximum profit} = X_H - S_0$$
$$\text{maximum loss} = S_0 - X_L$$
$$\text{breakeven price} = S_0$$

For a *zero-cost collar,* the profit is $\max(0, X_L - S_T) - \max(0, S_T - X_H) + S_T - S_0$; that is, the premium paid for the put, P_0, is exactly offset by the premium received for the call, C_0. That is, $C_0 - P_0 = 0$.

Box Spread Strategy

The *box spread* is a combination of a bull call spread and a bear put spread on the same asset.

Note that by combining a bull call spread and a bear put spread on the same asset you have:

- A long call and a short put with the same lower exercise price (X_L).
- A short call and a long put with the same higher strike price (X_H).

The payoff (i.e., profit) to the box spread is always the same, so if the options are priced correctly, the payoff must be the risk-free rate. If the options are not priced correctly, however, there is an arbitrage opportunity.

Figure 9: Payoff to the Box Spread

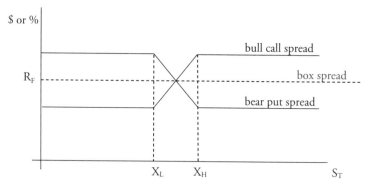

INTEREST RATE OPTIONS   (know these formulas)

An interest rate **call option** can be purchased to protect the rate on future borrowing. It makes a payment to the owner when the reference rate (a.k.a the "underlying") exceeds the strike rate (i.e., the exercise rate). Since LIBOR is the usual reference rate, we will put that in the formula. The formula for the payment is:

$$\text{payoff} = (NP)[\max(0, \text{LIBOR} - \text{strike rate})](D / 360)$$

An interest rate **put option** has a payoff to the owner when the reference rate, usually LIBOR, is *below* a certain strike rate at the maturity of the option:

$$\text{payoff} = (NP)[\max(0, \text{strike rate} - \text{LIBOR})(D / 360)]$$

A lender can combine a long position in an interest rate put with a specific floating-rate loan to place a lower limit on the income to be earned on the position.

INTEREST RATE CAPS, FLOORS, AND COLLARS

An interest rate cap is an agreement in which the cap seller agrees to make a payment to the cap buyer when the reference rate exceeds a predetermined level called the *cap strike* or *cap rate*. An interest rate floor is an agreement in which the seller agrees to pay the buyer when the reference rate falls below a predetermined interest rate called the *floor strike* or *floor rate*.

Interest Rate Caps

Caps and floors are usually paid in arrears meaning that, for example, the 3-month rate today would be used to calculate the payment three months from today. Since

©2008 Kaplan Schweser

the first quarterly cash flow over the next year is already predetermined by the current rate, there is no time value for the first of the four options or *caplets*.

At each settlement date the payoff is based upon the value of the reference rate, usually LIBOR, at the *beginning* of the period.

$$\text{payoff} = NP[\max(0, LIBOR_{t-1} - \text{strike rate}_t)(91 / 360)]$$

When a long position in a cap is combined with a floating-rate loan, the payoffs can offset interest costs when the floating rate increases. Since caps trade over the counter, the terms of the cap are very flexible, so the cap buyer/borrower can align the settlements of the cap with the interest rate payments.

Interest Rate Floors

A bank or other lender can combine a floor (a series of interest rate puts) with a floating rate loan to fix a lower bound on the interest income to be received each period.

Interest Rate Collar

An interest rate collar is a combination of a cap and a floor where the agent is long in one position and short in the other. It would be attractive to a bank that has among its liabilities large deposits with floating interest rates. When the rates start to rise, the bank's increasing costs can be offset by the payments from the collar. By selling the floor, the bank may have to make payments if the interest rates on the deposits fall too much, but the bank earned a premium for exposing itself to this risk.

A special interest rate collar occurs when the initial premiums on the cap and the floor are equal and offset each other. The combination of the two would be called a *zero-cost collar* (a.k.a. a *zero-premium collar*).

DELTA HEDGING

Delta hedging a derivative position means combining the option position with a position in the underlying asset to form a portfolio, such that its value does not change in reaction to changes in the price of the underlying over a short period of time. The value of that portfolio should grow at the risk-free rate over time, as it is dynamically managed.

Delta (Δ) is the change in the price of an option for a one-unit change in the price of the underlying security. For a call:

$$\Delta_{call} = \frac{C_1 - C_0}{S_1 - S_0} = \frac{\Delta C}{\Delta S}$$

Unfortunately:

- Delta is only an *approximation* of the relative price changes of the stock and call and is less accurate for larger changes in stock price, ΔS.
- Delta changes as market conditions change, including changes in S.
- Delta changes over time without any other changes.

Gamma is just the change in the value of delta given a change in the value of the underlying stock:

gamma = (change in delta) / (change in S)

RISK MANAGEMENT APPLICATIONS OF SWAP STRATEGIES
Cross-Reference to CFA Institute Assigned Reading #40

USING SWAPS TO CONVERT LOANS FROM FIXED (FLOATING) TO FLOATING (FIXED)

The most common interest rate swap is the *plain vanilla* interest rate swap. In this swap, Company X agrees to pay Company Y a periodic fixed rate on a notional principal over the tenor of the swap. In return, Company Y agrees to pay Company X a periodic floating rate on the same notional principal. Payments are in the same currency, so only the net payment is exchanged.

Most interest rate swaps use the London Interbank Offered Rate (LIBOR) as the reference rate for the floating leg of the swap. Finally, since the payments are based in the same currency there is no need for the exchange of principal at the inception of the swap.

DURATION OF AN INTEREST RATE SWAP

Each counterparty in a swap is essentially either of the following:

- Long a fixed cash flow and short a floating cash flow.
- Short a fixed cash flow and long a floating cash flow.

Two important points with respect to fixed and floating-rate instruments:

1. For fixed-rate instruments, duration will be higher, since the change in interest rates will change the present value of the fixed cash flows.

©2008 Kaplan Schweser

2. For floating-rate instruments, duration is close to zero because the future cash flows vary with interest rates, and the present value is fairly stable with respect to changes in interest rates.

For a **pay-floating** counterparty in a swap, the duration can be expressed as:

$$D_{pay\ floating} = D_{fixed} - D_{floating} > 0$$

For the **pay-fixed** counterparty:

$$D_{pay\ fixed} = D_{floating} - D_{fixed} < 0$$

CONVERSION OF A FIXED-RATE LOAN TO A FLOATING-RATE LOAN

Cash flow risk is a concern with floating-rate instruments. Since their cash flows are reset each period according to the prevailing rate at the beginning of the period, however, their market values are subject to only minor changes. For example, the maximum duration of a floating rate instrument is the length of its reset period and its minimum duration is 0.

Market value risk is a concern with fixed-rate instruments. The cash flows to fixed rate instruments are set at inception, so there is no uncertainty associated with the amount of each cash flow. The duration of a fixed instrument, however, is considerably greater than the duration of a comparable floating rate instrument.

USING SWAPS TO CHANGE DURATION   (know these formulas)

The dollar duration of the portfolio plus a swap position is calculated as:

$$V_p(MD_T) = V_p(MD_p) + NP(MD_{swap})$$

Usually, the portfolio manager selects a swap of a certain maturity which determines the modified duration of the swap, MD_{swap}. He then selects the NP that will achieve the desired MD_T.

$$NP = \left(V_p\right)\left(\frac{MD_T - MD_p}{MD_{swap}}\right)$$

CURRENCY SWAPS

A *currency swap* is different from an interest rate swap in two very important ways:

1. There are two notional principals, one in each currency, and the counterparties generally exchange the principals on the effective date and return them at the maturity date.

2. Since the cash flows in a currency swap are denominated in different currencies, the periodic interest payments are not usually settled on a net basis, so each counterparty makes a payment to the other in the appropriate currency.

    A *plain vanilla currency swap* is one in which the floating-rate cash flows (usually based on LIBOR) are in one currency, while the other cash flows (in another currency) are based on a fixed rate.

Figure 10: Cash Flows for a Plain Vanilla Currency Swap Example

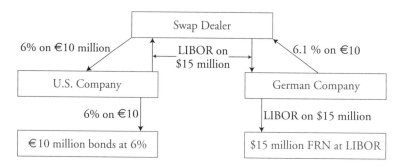

A counterparty may use a currency swap to gain access to a foreign currency at a lower cost. Borrowing in a foreign country via a foreign bank may be difficult, and the interest rates may be high. A U.S. firm that wishes to initiate a project in a foreign country, say Korea, might not have the contacts necessary to borrow Korean currency (the won) cheaply. A Korean counterparty may exist that would like to borrow dollars to invest in the United States.

The U.S. firm borrows in the United States because it has established relationships with banks in the United States. It swaps the principal (borrowed dollars) with the Korean counterparty for the won, which the Korean firm borrowed in Korea.

Currency Swaps Without Exchanging Notional Principals

Consider a U.S. firm that wishes to convert its quarterly cash flows of €6 million each to dollars upon receipt. The exchange rate is currently €0.8/$, and the swap rates in the United States and Europe are 4.8% and 5%, respectively. To obtain the swapped dollar cash flow, we first back out the notional principal in euros, translate this to a dollar notional principal, and then calculate the interest in dollars:

$$\text{NP}\left(\frac{0.05}{4}\right) = \text{€}6,000,000$$

$$\text{NP} = \frac{\text{€}6,000,000}{0.05 / 4} = \text{€}480,000,000$$

The corresponding dollar amount is €480,000,000 / (€0.8/$) = $600,000,000. The quarterly interest payments on this amount would be $600,000,000(0.048 / 4) = $7,200,000.

The swap would then allow the firm to exchange its €6,000,000 quarterly inflow for $7,200,000 per period. The maturity of the swap would be negotiated to meet the needs of the firm. You should note that no exchange of principals was required.

EQUITY SWAPS

An equity swap is a contract where at least one counterparty makes payments based upon an equity position. The other counterparty may make payments based upon another equity position, a bond, or just fixed payments. We will begin with that example.

Figure 11: Quarterly Cash Flows to an Equity Swap: Example

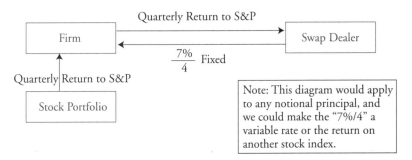

With respect to the international diversification, it may be the case that the firm trying to diversify its domestic position has a portfolio of stocks and not the S&P 500. The firm could approach the dealer about a swap based on the returns of that portfolio, but the firm would probably get a better deal (lower spread) for a swap based on the S&P 500. This can introduce additional risk in that the portfolio will not be perfectly correlated with the S&P 500; therefore, there will be tracking error.

Changing Allocations of Stock and Bonds

Another type of swapping of index returns can occur between, for example, large and small cap stocks. A firm with an equity portfolio that is 60% in large-cap stocks, 30% in mid-cap stocks, and 10% small-cap stocks can use a swap to synthetically adjust this position.

This concept can also be applied to the synthetic adjustment of a *bond portfolio*. A firm with a given portfolio of high-grade and low-grade bonds can enter into a swap that pays the return on an index of one type (e.g., the high-grade) and receives the return on the index of another type (e.g., the low-grade). *Do not confuse this with an interest rate swap!* In the swap based on bond returns, there is an interest component and a capital gain component just as there is in an equity swap.

INTEREST RATE SWAPTIONS

An *interest rate swaption* is an option on a swap where one counterparty (buyer) has paid a premium to the other counterparty (seller) for an option to choose whether the swap will actually go into effect on some future date.

There are two types of swaptions:

1. *Payer swaption* (or *put swaption*): a payer swaption gives the buyer the right to be the fixed-rate payer (and floating-rate receiver) in a prespecified swap at a prespecified date.

2. *Receiver swaption* (or *call swaption*): a receiver swaption gives the buyer the right to be the fixed-rate receiver (and floating-rate payer) at some future date.

A corporate manager may wish to purchase a fixed-rate payer swaption to synthetically "lock in" a maximum fixed rate to be paid on an FRN to be issued in the future. The timeline is illustrated in Figure 12. Today the manager enters into a swaption by paying a premium. The option expires at the time the loan will be taken out.

- The payer swaption would convert a future floating-rate loan to a fixed-rate loan.
- The receiver swaption would convert a future fixed-rate loan to a floating-rate loan.

Figure 12: Swaption and Future Loan

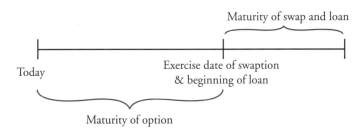

A manager who is under contract in an existing swap can enter into a swaption with the exact characteristics of the existing swap, but take the other counterparty's positi Figure 13 has the same general form as Figure 12, but it has been relabeled to depict "cancellation" of an existing swap with a swaption.

Figure 13: Swaption Cancels Swap

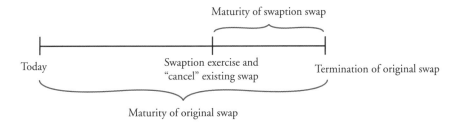

EXECUTION OF PORTFOLIO DECISIONS

Approximate Weight on Exam	≤ 3%
Study Note Reference	Book 4, Pages 211–239
Video CD Reference	CD 14
Audio CD Reference	CD 16

EXECUTION OF PORTFOLIO DECISIONS[1]
Cross-Reference to CFA Institute Assigned Reading #41

A **market order** is an order to immediately execute the trade at the best possible price. If the order cannot be completely filled in one trade which offers the best price, it is filled by other trades at the next best possible prices. The emphasis is *speed*. The disadvantage is **price uncertainty**.

A **limit order** is an order to trade at the limit price or better. If not filled on or before the specified date, limit orders expire. The emphasis is price. A limit has **execution uncertainty**.

THE EFFECTIVE SPREAD

From a trader's perspective, the best bid price is referred to as the **inside bid** or **market bid**. The best ask price is referred to as the **inside ask** or **market ask**. The best bid price and the best ask price in the market constitute the **inside** or **market quote**. Subtracting the best bid price from the best ask price results in the **inside bid-ask spread** or **market bid-ask spread**. The average of the inside bid and ask is the **midquote**.

---

1   The terminology utilized in this section follows industry convention as presented in Ananth Madhaven, Jack L. Treynor, and Wayne H. Wagner, "Execution of Portfolio Decisions," Ch. 10, Managing Investment Portfolios: A Dynamic Process, 3rd edition (CFA Institute, forthcoming).

The **effective spread** compares the transacted price against the midquote of the market bid and ask prices. This difference is then doubled. More formally:

effective spread for a buy order = 2 × (execution price – midquote)

effective spread for a sell order = 2 × (midquote – execution price)

(know these calculations)

Suppose a trader is quoted a market bid price of $11.50 and an ask of $11.56. **Calculate** and **interpret** the effective spread for a buy order, given an executed price of $11.55.

The *midquote* of the quoted bid and ask prices is $11.53 [= (11.50 + 11.56)/2]. The *effective spread* for this buy order is: 2 × ($11.55 – $11.53) = $0.04, which is two cents better than the quoted spread of $0.06 (= $11.56 – $11.50). A dealer's willingness to offer a better price has resulted in a price improvement for the trader.

Effective spreads are often averaged over all transactions during a period in order to calculate an average effective spread. Lower average effective spreads indicate better liquidity for a security.

MARKET STRUCTURES

Securities markets provide **liquidity, transparency,** and **assurity of completion.**

There are three types of securities markets:

1. Quote-driven markets: investors trade with dealers.

2. Order-driven markets: investors trade with each other without the use of intermediaries.

3. Brokered markets: investors use brokers to locate the counterparty to a trade.

A fourth market, a hybrid market, is a combination of the other three markets. Additionally, new trading venues have evolved, and the electronic processing of trades has become more common.

QUOTE-DRIVEN MARKETS

In **quote-driven** markets, traders transact with dealers (a.k.a. *market makers*) who post buy and sell prices, so quote-driven markets are sometimes called **dealer markets**.

In an **order-driven** market, traders transact with other traders.

In an **auction market,** traders post their orders to compete against other orders for execution. An auction market can be periodic (a.k.a. batch) or continuous.

Automated auctions are also known as electronic limit-order markets.

In **brokered markets**, brokers act as traders' agents to find counterparties to their trades, and **hybrid markets** combine features of quote-driven, order-driven, and broker markets.

MARKET QUALITY

A **liquid** market has small bid-ask spreads, market depth, and resilience. Market *depth* allows larger orders to trade without largely affecting security prices. A market is *resilient* if asset prices stay close to their intrinsic values, and any deviations from intrinsic value are minimized quickly.

In a **transparent** market, investors can obtain both pre-trade information (regarding quotes and spreads) and post-trade information (regarding completed trades). If a market does not have transparency, investors lose faith in the market and decrease their trading activities.

When markets have **assurity of completion**, investors can be confident that the counterparty will uphold their side of the trade agreement. To facilitate this, brokers and clearing bodies may provide guarantees to both sides of the trade.

EXECUTION COSTS

The **explicit costs** in a trade include commissions, taxes, stamp duties, and fees. **Implicit costs** include the bid-ask spread, market or price impact costs, opportunity costs, and delay costs (a.k.a. slippage costs).

Volume weighted average price (VWAP) is a weighted average of execution prices during a day.

Implementation shortfall has four elements:

1. **Explicit costs**, such as commissions, taxes, fees, etc.

2. **Realized profit/loss** is the difference between the execution price and the closing price on the preceding day divided by the benchmark price and weighted by the portion of the order that is filled.

3. **Delay or slippage costs** are the difference between the closing price on the day the order was not filled and the previous day's closing price. It is weighted by the portion of the order that is filled.

4. **Missed trade opportunity cost** is the difference between the closing price on the day the order is cancelled and the benchmark price. It is weighted by the portion of the order that is not filled.

Decomposition of Implementation Shortfall   (know these calculations)

- On Wednesday the stock price for Megabites closes at $20 a share. (This price will be used as the benchmark price.)
- On Thursday morning before market open, the portfolio manager decides to buy Megabites and submits a limit order for 1,000 shares at $19.95. The price never falls to $19.95 during the day, so the order expires unfilled. The stock closes at $20.05.
- On Friday, the order is revised to a limit of $20.06. The order is partially filled that day as 800 shares are bought at $20.06. The commission is $18. The stock closes at $20.09 and the order for the remaining 200 shares is cancelled.

We first calculate the **gain on the paper portfolio**, which is assumed to include all 1,000 shares purchased at the benchmark price. Its terminal value is based on the cancellation price (i.e., the closing price the day the order is cancelled).

- The investment made by the paper portfolio is 1,000 × $20.00 = $20,000.
- The terminal value of the paper portfolio is 1,000 × $20.09 = $20,090.
- The gain on the paper portfolio is $20,090 − $20,000 = $90.

We next calculate the **gain on the real portfolio**. As might be expected, the investment made in the real portfolio considers the commission, the actual number of shares bought, and the actual execution price. Its terminal value is the actual number of shares times the cancellation price.

- The investment made by the real portfolio is (800 × $20.06) + $18 = $16,066.
- The terminal value of the real portfolio is 800 × $20.09 = $16,072.
- The gain on the real portfolio is $16,072 − $16,066 = $6.

The total implementation shortfall is the gain on the paper portfolio minus the gain on the real portfolio as a percentage of the paper portfolio investment:

$$\text{Implementation shortfall} = \frac{\text{paper portfolio gain} - \text{real portfolio gain}}{\text{paper portfolio investment}}$$

$$= \frac{\$90 - \$6}{\$20,000} = 0.0042 = 0.42\%$$

$$\text{Explicit costs} = \frac{\text{commission}}{\text{paper portfolio investment}} = \frac{\$18}{\$20,000} = 0.0009 = 0.09\%$$

$$\text{Realized loss} = \frac{\text{execution price} - \text{previous day close}}{\text{benchmark price}} \times \frac{\text{shares purchased}}{\text{shares ordered}}$$

$$= \left(\frac{\$20.06 - \$20.05}{\$20.00}\right) \times \left(\frac{800}{1,000}\right) = 0.0004 = 0.04\%$$

$$\text{Delay costs} = \frac{\text{previous day closing price} - \text{benchmark close}}{\text{benchmark price}} \times \frac{\text{shares purchased}}{\text{shares ordered}}$$

$$= \left(\frac{\$20.05 - \$20.00}{\$20.00}\right) \times \left(\frac{800}{1,000}\right) = 0.0020 = 0.20\%$$

$$\text{MTOC} = \frac{\text{cancellation price} - \text{benchmark price}}{\text{benchmark price}} \times \frac{\text{shares not purchased}}{\text{shares ordered}}$$

$$= \left(\frac{\$20.09 - \$20.00}{\$20.00}\right) \times \left(\frac{200}{1,000}\right) = 0.0009 = 0.09\%$$

The sum of the components equals the total implementation cost calculated previously:

total implementation cost = 0.42% = 0.09% + 0.04% + 0.20% + 0.09%

Advantages of VWAP:

- Easily understood.
- Simple to compute.
- Can be applied quickly to enhance trading decisions.
- Most appropriate for comparing small trades in nontrending markets.

Disadvantages of VWAP:

- Not informative for trades that dominate trading volume.
- Can be gamed by traders.
- Does not evaluate delayed or unfilled orders.
- Does not account for market movements or trade volume.

Advantages of implementation shortfall:

- Portfolio managers can see the cost of implementing their ideas.
- Demonstrates the tradeoff between quick execution and market impact.
- Decomposes and identifies costs.

- Can be used to minimize trading costs and maximize performance.
- Not subject to gaming.

Disadvantages of implementation shortfall:

- May be unfamiliar to traders.
- Requires considerable data and analysis.

Econometric models can be used to forecast transaction costs, because trading costs are nonlinearly related to:

- Security liquidity: trading volume, market cap, spread, price.
- Size of the trade relative to liquidity.
- Trading style: more aggressive trading results in higher costs.
- Momentum: trades that require liquidity.
- Risk.

MAJOR TRADER TYPES

Figure 1 contains a summary of the major trader types, including their motivations and order preferences:

Figure 1: Summary of Trader Types and their Motivations and Preference

Trader Types	Motivation	Time or Price Preference	Preferred Order Types
Information-motivated	Time-sensitive information	Time	Market
Value-motivated	Security misvaluations	Price	Limit
Liquidity-motivated	Reallocation & liquidity	Time	Market
Passive	Reallocation & liquidity	Price	Limit

TRADING TACTICS

A summary of trading tactics is presented in Figure 2.

Figure 2: Summary of Trading Tactics

Trading Tactic	Strengths	Weaknesses	Usual Trade Motivation
Liquidity-at-any-cost	Quick, certain execution	High costs & leakage of information	Information
Costs-are-not-important	Quick, certain execution at market price	Loss of control of trade costs	Variety of motivations
Need-trustworthy-agent	Broker uses skill & time to obtain lower price	Higher commission & potential leakage of trade intention	Not information
Advertise-to-draw-liquidity	Market-determined price	Higher administrative costs and possible front running	Not information
Low-cost-whatever-the-liquidity	Low trading costs	Uncertain timing of trade & possibly trading into weakness	Passive and value

ALGORITHMIC TRADING

Algorithmic trading is a form of automated trading that accounts for about one-quarter of all trades. The **motivation for algorithmic trading** is to execute orders with minimal risk and costs.

Algorithmic trading strategies are classified into *logical participation, opportunistic, and specialized strategies*. There are two subtypes of logical participation strategies: simple logical participation strategies and implementation shortfall strategies.

Simple logical participation strategies (SLP) seek to trade with market flow so as to not become overly noticeable to the market and to minimize market impact.

In a VWAP SLP, the order is broken up over the course of a day so as to equal or outperform the day's VWAP.

In a time-weighted average price strategy (TWAP), trading is spread out evenly over the whole day so as to equal a TWAP benchmark.

Implementation shortfall strategies, or arrival price strategies, minimize trading costs as defined by the implementation shortfall measure or total execution costs. Both measures use a weighted average of opportunity costs and market impact costs.

The basis of simple participation strategies is to break up the trade into small pieces so that each trade is a small part of trading volume and market impact costs are minimized. In contrast, an implementation shortfall strategy focuses on trading early to minimize opportunity costs. An implementation shortfall strategy typically executes the order quickly, whereas a simple participation strategy breaks the trade into small pieces and trades throughout the day.

Monitoring, Rebalancing, and Execution of Portfolio Decisions

Topic Weight on Exam	≤ 3%
Study Notes Reference	Book 5, Pages 10–56
Video CD Reference	CD 15
Audio CD Reference	CD 18

Study Session 15 will probably be tested as part of morning cases for Study Sessions 4 and 5 and will comprise no more than 3% of the exam.

Monitoring and Rebalancing
Cross-Reference to CFA Institute Assigned Reading #42

Note: Much of this material repeats Study Sessions 4 and 5, and as such has been omitted.

Monitoring

The manager must regularly monitor the client's circumstances and determine, for example, when to start shifting out of equities and real estate and into bonds and other less risky assets. Remember that changes to any one of the investor's objectives or constraints can potentially affect the others.

Common factors that can lead to changes to the portfolio allocation include the following:

- Change in wealth.
- Changing time horizons.
- Changing liquidity requirements.
- Tax treatment.
- Laws and regulations.
- New asset alternatives.
- Changes in asset class risks.
- Bull versus bear markets.

- The stock market and central bank policy.
- Changes in inflation.
- Changes in asset class expected returns.

REBALANCING

Calendar rebalancing. The primary benefit to calendar rebalancing is that it provides discipline without the requirement for constant monitoring. The *drawback* is that the portfolio could stray considerably between rebalancing dates.

Percentage-of-portfolio rebalancing (PPR) is also referred to as *percent range rebalancing or interval rebalancing*. By not waiting for specified rebalancing dates, PPR provides the benefit of minimizing the degree to which asset classes can violate their allocation corridors. The primary *cost* to PPR is associated with the need to constantly monitor the portfolio.

OPTIMAL CORRIDOR WIDTH

The optimal width of a corridor minimizes transactions costs while simultaneously minimizing the probability of the allocation changing significantly.

Transactions costs. Generally, the more expensive it is to trade (e.g., illiquid assets), the less frequently you should trade, and the corridor for the class should be wide.

Correlations. The more highly correlated the assets, the less frequently the portfolio will require balancing, and the wider the corridors.

Volatility. Generally, the greater the volatility of the individual asset class, the tighter the corridor.

DYNAMIC REBALANCING STRATEGIES

The **buy-and-hold strategy** is illustrated in the payoff diagram in Figure 1.

Figure 1: Buy-and-Hold Strategy

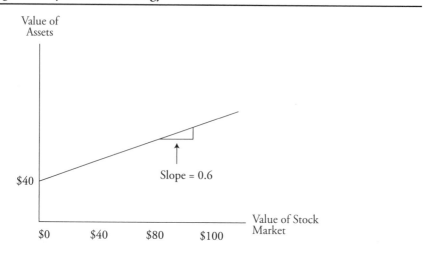

The **constant mix strategy** payoff is illustrated in Figure 2.

Figure 2: Constant Mix Strategy

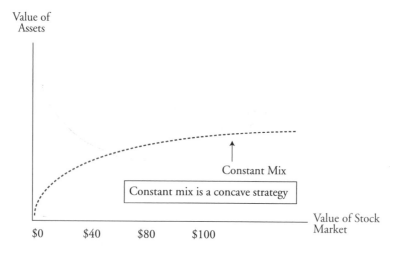

For constant proportion strategies, also known as constant proportion portfolio insurance (CPPI) strategies, the equation used to create the desired dollar amount of stock is the following:

$ in stock = m(TA – F)

REBALANCING IN UP AND DOWN MARKETS

When comparing dynamic strategies for asset allocation, keep the following points in mind:

- The buy-and-hold investor travels up and down a single straight line in the payoff diagram. The constant mix investor rebalances by changing the number of shares of stock held. Therefore, the slope of the payoff line changes. The slope of the line remains constant with CPPI, but the floor value fluctuates as stock prices move.
- Constant mix buys stocks as they fall and sells stocks as they rise (*concave strategy*). CPPI sells stocks as they fall and buys stocks as they rise (*convex strategy*).
- A constant mix strategy will outperform buy-and-hold and CPPI strategies in a *flat* but *oscillating* market (e.g., up-down oscillation). CPPI does poorly in a flat, oscillating market. In a flat, oscillating market, CPPI sells on weakness only to have the market rebound. Alternatively, it buys on strength only to see the market falter.
- A constant mix strategy will *underperform* comparable buy-and-hold and CPPI strategies when there are *no reversals* (e.g., down-down oscillation). CPPI will do at least as well as the floor (i.e., the strategy is protected on the downside). CPPI outperforms the other strategies in a trending market (bull or bear).
- The value of a constant mix investor's assets after several rebalancings will depend on both the final level of the stock market and on the manner in which the stocks moved period by period.
- Cases in which the market ends up near its starting point are likely to favor constant mix strategies, while those in which the market ends up far from its starting point are likely to favor CPPI.

Figure 3 summarizes the **risk and return** consequences of the strategies in up, down, and flat markets:

Figure 3: Impact of Strategies on Risk and Return

	Buy-and-Hold	*Constant Mix*	*CPPI*
Return	Outperforms a constant mix strategy in a trending market; outperforms CPPI in a *flat* but *oscillating* market.	Outperforms a comparable buy-and-hold strategy, which, in turn, outperforms a CPPI strategy in a *flat* but *oscillating* market.	Outperforms a comparable buy-and-hold strategy, which, in turn, outperforms a constant mix strategy in trending markets.
Risk	Passively assumes that risk tolerance is directly related to wealth.	Assumes that risk tolerance is constant regardless of wealth level.	Actively assumes that risk tolerance is directly related to wealth.

CONVEX AND CONCAVE STRATEGIES

- Any procedure that buys when stocks rise or sells when stocks fall (e.g., CPPI) is a convex strategy. The more investors follow convex strategies, the more volatile the markets will become.

- Any procedure that buys when stocks fall or sells when stocks rise (e.g., constant mix) is a concave strategy. If more investors follow concave strategies, the markets will become too stable (i.e., excessive buyers in down markets and excessive sellers in up markets).

- Convex and concave strategies are mirror images. If there is more demand for one strategy, it will be more costly. The more popular strategy will subsidize the other.

Performance Evaluation and Attribution

Approximate Weight on Exam	≤ 3%
Study Note Reference	Book 5, Pages 8–89
Video CD Reference	CD 15
Audio CD Reference	CDs 17 & 18

Study Session 16 will more than likely show up as part of an item set in the afternoon and should comprise about 3% of the exam.

Evaluating Portfolio Performance
Cross-Reference to CFA Institute Assigned Reading #43

The three components of performance evaluation include performance measurement, performance attribution, and performance appraisal.

Return Calculations With External Cash Flows

(know these formulas)

If there is an external cash flow at the *beginning* of the evaluation period:

$$r_t = \frac{MV_1 - (MV_0 + CF)}{MV_0 + CF}$$

When the cash flow is at the *end* of the evaluation period:

$$r_t = \frac{(MV_1 - CF) - MV_0}{MV_0}$$

A portfolio return can be broken up into three components: *market, style,* and *active management.*

$$P = M + S + A$$

The manager's *active management decisions* (A) are assumed to generate the difference between the portfolio and benchmark returns (P – B):

P = B + A

Introducing the market index (M):

P = M + (B – M) + A

The manager's *investment style* is assumed to generate the difference between the benchmark return and the market index (B – M):

P = M + S + A

Properties of a Valid Benchmark

1. Specified in advance.
2. Appropriate.
3. Measurable.
4. Unambiguous.
5. Reflective of current investment opinions.
6. Accountable.
7. Investable.

There are seven primary types of benchmarks in use:

1. Absolute.
2. Manager universes.
3. Broad market indices.
4. Style indices.
5. Factor-model-based.
6. Returns-based.
7. Custom security-based.

The construction of a **custom security-based benchmark** entails the following steps:

1. Identify the manager's investment process, asset selection (including cash), and weighting.

2. Use the same assets and weighting for the benchmark.

3. Assess and rebalance the benchmark on a predetermined schedule.

Tests of Benchmark Quality

- Minimal systematic bias in the benchmark relative to the account.
- A manager's active decision making (A) should be *uncorrelated* with the manager's investment style (S), and the difference between portfolio returns and the market should be positively correlated with the manager's style.
- Tracking error is relatively small.
- An account's systematic risk should be similar to the benchmark's.
- The coverage ratio is the market value of the securities that are in both the portfolio and the benchmark as a percentage of the total market value of the portfolio. The higher the coverage ratio, the more closely the manager is replicating the benchmark.
- Benchmark turnover is the proportion of the benchmark's total market value that is bought or sold during periodic rebalancing. Passively managed portfolios should utilize benchmarks with low turnover.
- For actively managed long-only accounts, you would expect the manager to hold primarily **positive active positions**. If not, an inappropriate benchmark has been selected or constructed.

Macro performance attribution is done at the fund sponsor level. The approach can be carried out in percentage terms and/or monetary terms. **Micro performance attribution** is done at the investment manager level.

There are three main inputs into the **macro attribution** approach:

1. Policy allocations.
2. Benchmark portfolio returns.
3. Fund returns, valuations, and external cash flows.

Macro Attribution Analysis

There are six levels of investment policy decision making, by which the fund's performance can be analyzed:

1. Net contributions.
2. Risk-free asset.
3. Asset categories.
4. Benchmarks.
5. Investment managers.
6. Allocation effects.

Starting at **net contributions**, management determines how much of the fund's assets to allocate to each level and will place assets in the next highest level only if that allocation will produce sufficient incremental return.

At the **asset categories** level, the fund is allocated to different asset category benchmarks. This is a pure benchmarking or benchmark replication strategy.

The incremental return to the asset category level:

$$R_{AC} = \sum_{i=1}^{n}(w_i)(R_i - R_F)$$

At the **benchmark level**, fund assets are still passively managed, but they are assumed to be invested in style portfolio *manager benchmarks* according to policy weights.

The incremental return at the *benchmark level*:

$$R_B = \sum_{i=1}^{n}\sum_{j=1}^{m}(w_i)(w_{i,j})(R_{B,i,j} - R_i)$$

If only one manager per category:

$$R_B = \sum_{i=1}^{n}(w_i)(R_{B,i} - R_i)$$

At the **investment managers** level, funds are allocated according to policy as if invested directly in the managers' portfolios. The return to the *investment managers* level:

$$R_{IM} = \sum_{i=1}^{n}\sum_{j=1}^{m}(w_i)(w_{i,j})(R_{i,j} - R_{B,i})$$

Note: You will probably NOT have to calculate the return at the various levels. Instead, be able to discuss each level.

Micro Performance Attribution (know these formulas)

$$R_V = \sum_{j=1}^{S}(w_{P,j} - w_{B,j})(R_{B,j} - R_B) + \sum_{j=1}^{S}(w_{P,j} - w_{B,j})(R_{P,j} - R_{B,j}) + \sum_{j=1}^{S}w_{B,j}(R_{P,j} - R_{B,j})$$

$$\underbrace{\qquad\qquad\qquad}_{\text{pure sector allocation}}\qquad\underbrace{\qquad\qquad\qquad\qquad}_{\text{allocation/selection interaction}}\qquad\underbrace{\qquad\qquad}_{\text{within-sector selection}}$$

R_V = the value-added return

The **pure sector allocation** return measures the impact on performance attributed only to the *sector weighting* decisions by the manager. It assumes that the manager holds the same securities in each sector and in the same weights as in the benchmark.

The **within-sector selection** return assumes the manager weights each sector in the portfolio in the same proportion as in the overall benchmark, and excess returns are due to security selection.

The **allocation/selection** return involves the joint effect of assigning weights to both sectors and individual securities.

Fundamental Factor Model Micro Attribution

It should be possible to construct multifactor models to conduct micro attribution. This involves combining economic sector factors with other fundamental factors (e.g., a company's size, its growth characteristics, its financial strength). Constructing a suitable factor model would involve the following:

- Identify the fundamental factors that will generate systematic returns.
- The exposures of the portfolio and the benchmark to the fundamental factors of the model must be determined at the start of the evaluation period.
- A benchmark needs to be specified. This could be the risk exposures of a style or custom index, or it could be a set of *normal* factor exposures that are typical of the manager's portfolio.
- Determine the performance of each of the factors.

The results of the fundamental factor micro attribution will indicate the source of portfolio returns, based upon actual factor exposures versus the manager's normal factor exposures (e.g., sector rotation), the manager's ability to time the market (e.g., adjust the portfolio beta and/or duration in response to market expectations), et cetera.

The strengths and limitations of the allocation/selection and fundamental factor model attributions are summarized in Figure 1.

Figure 1: Strengths and Limitations of Allocation/Selection Attribution and Fundamental Factor Model Attribution

	Allocation/Selection Attribution	*Fundamental Factor Model Attribution*
Strengths	Disaggregates performance effects of managers' decisions between sectors and securities. Relatively easy to calculate.	Identifies factors other than just security selection or sector allocation.
Limitations	The need to identify an appropriate benchmark with specified securities and weights at the start of the evaluation period. Security selection decisions will have a knock-on effect on sector weighting decisions. Can cause confusion as it reflects the joint effect of allocating weights to both securities and sectors (i.e., difficult to separate the two factors), so often not worth the time and effort.	Exposures to the factors need to be determined at the start of the evaluation period. Can prove to be quite complex, leading to potential spurious correlations.

Fixed-Income Portfolio Return Attribution

- Interest rate management effect. The ability of the manager to predict changes in relevant interest rates.
- Sector/quality effect. The ability of the manager to select and overweight (underweight) outperforming (underperforming) sectors and qualities.
- Security selection effect. The ability of the manager to select superior securities to represent sectors.
- Trading activity. The residual effect. Assumed to measure the return to active trading (buying and selling) over the period.

Risk-Adjusted Performance Measures   (know these formulas)

Ex post alpha uses the security market line (SML) as a benchmark to appraise performance.

$$\alpha_p = R_p - \left[R_F + \beta_p(R_m - R_F) \right]$$

- A portfolio that generates a *positive alpha* would plot *above* the SML.
- A portfolio that generates a *zero alpha* would plot *on* the SML.
- A portfolio that generates a *negative alpha* would plot *below* the SML.

Similar to alpha, the **Treynor measure** compares an account's excess returns to its systematic risk, using beta.

$$T_P = \frac{\bar{R}_P - \bar{R}_F}{\beta_P}$$

The **Sharpe ratio** calculates excess returns above the risk-free rate, relative to **total** risk measured by standard deviation.

$$S_P = \frac{\bar{R}_P - \bar{R}_F}{\sigma_P}$$

Using the capital market line (CML), **the M^2 measure** compares the account's return to the market return.

$$M_P^2 = \bar{R}_F + \left(\frac{\bar{R}_P - \bar{R}_F}{\sigma_P} \right) \sigma_M$$

Quality Control Charts

To construct a chart, three important assumptions are made about the distribution of the manager's value-added returns:

1. The null hypothesis: the expected value-added return is zero.

2. Value-added returns are independent and normally distributed.

3. More or less constant variability of the value-added returns.

Figure 2 shows an example of a quality control chart.

Figure 2: Example Quality Control Chart

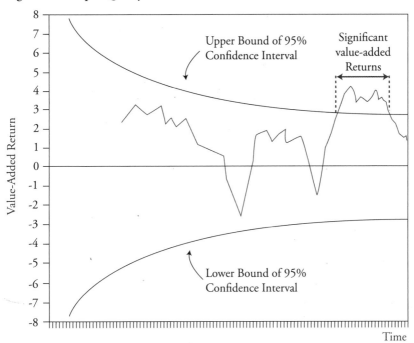

Manager Continuation Policies

Guidelines associated with the management review process:

*   Replace managers only when justified.
*   Develop formal policies and apply them consistently to all managers.
*   Use portfolio performance and other information in evaluating managers.
    *   Appropriate and consistent investment strategies.
    *   Relevant benchmark (style) selections.
    *   Personnel turnover.
    *   Growth of the account.

Type I Errors and Type II Errors

H_0: The manager adds no value.
H_A: The manager adds positive value.

Type I error – Rejecting the null hypothesis when it is true. (Keeping managers who are not adding value.)

Type II error – Failing to reject the null when it is false. (Firing good managers who are adding value.)

GLOBAL PERFORMANCE EVALUATION
Cross-Reference to CFA Institute Assigned Reading #44

Currency Movements and Portfolio Returns   (know these formulas)

For a purely domestic portfolio, the return on the portfolio can be broken down into capital gains and cash flow yield:

$$R_j = CG_j + CF_j$$

where:
R_j = return on asset j
CG_j = capital gain/loss on asset j
CF_j = cash flow yield (dividend or coupon yield) for asset j

For a global portfolio, the equation must be modified to capture the effects of currency value fluctuations:

$$R_{j,d} = CG_j + CF_j + C_j$$

where :
$R_{j,d}$ = return on asset j in the domestic (base) currency
C_j = return due to currency movements = $e_j(1 + CG_j + CF_j)$
e_j = percentage change in the value of currency j

Global Portfolio Returns

We can expand the equation to include all sectors in a global portfolio:

$$R_{p,d} = \sum_{j=1}^{n} w_j \left(CG_j \right) + \sum_{j=1}^{n} w_j \left(CF_j \right) + \sum_{j=1}^{n} w_j \left(C_j \right)$$

©2008 Kaplan Schweser

Global Portfolio Attribution   (know these formulas)

The currency allocation effect is the portion of the excess return $(R_{p,d} - R_{b,d})$ attributable to the movements of the related currencies.

$$\text{current allocation effect} = \sum_{j=1}^{n}(w_{j,p}C_{j,p} - w_{j,b}C_{j,b})$$

where :
$w_{j,b}$ = weight of sector j in the benchmark
$w_{j,p}$ = weight of sector j in the portfolio
$C_{j,p} = R_{j,p,d} - R_{j,p,f}$ = portfolio return in domestic currency − portfolio
$C_{j,b} = R_{j,b,d} - R_{j,b,f}$ = benchmark return in domestic currency −
benchmark return in foreign currency

The **market allocation effect** measures the excess return due to weighting markets (sectors) differently in the portfolio than in the benchmark:

$$\text{market allocation effect} = \sum_{j=1}^{n}(w_{j,p} - w_{j,b})R_{j,b,f}$$

where :
$R_{j,b,f}$ = return on sector j in the benchmark in local (foreign) currency
$W_{j,b}$ = weight of sector j in the benchmark
$W_{j,b}$ = weight of sector j in the portfolio

The security allocation effect measures the manager's ability to select individual securities:

$$\text{security allocation effect} = \sum_{j=1}^{n} w_{j,p}(R_{j,p,f} - R_{j,b,f})$$

where:
$w_{j,p}$ = weight of the sector in the portfolio
$R_{j,p,f}$ = return for sector j in the portfolio
$R_{j,b,f}$ = return for sector j in the benchmark

Benchmark Tracking Error

$$SR_t = R_t - R_{b,t} \text{ and } \sigma_{SR} = \sqrt{\frac{\sum (SR_t - SR_{avg})^2}{n-1}}$$

where :

SR_t = surplus return (also called alpha) for period t

R_t = portfolio return for period t

$R_{b,t}$ = benchmark return for period t

σ_{SR} = standard deviation of surplus returns

SR_{avg} = average surplus return

The **information ratio** is the ratio of the average surplus return to its standard deviation:

$$\text{information ratio} = \frac{\overline{SR}}{\sigma_{SR}} \qquad \text{(know this formula)}$$

Global and International Benchmarks

Custom benchmarks should identify specific weights assigned to individual countries and/or sectors, and specific industries within each country or sector. A currency-hedging component may also be present (if desired by the plan sponsor). The individual country weights may be based on the total market capitalization of the country's publicly traded securities or another macroeconomic measure such as GDP.

Sometimes, benchmarks bypass country weights and assign weights to industries worldwide, irrespective of the companies' countries of registration. This has become more popular with multiple listing of shares of large international corporations and expansion of world trade.

Sometimes, benchmarks are established purely on the basis of style, ignoring countries. For example, a small-cap growth manager may be assigned an international small-cap growth index as benchmark. The key is to have a custom benchmark that accurately reflects the investment objectives of the portfolio.

Portfolio Management in a Global Context

Topic Weight on Exam	5%
Study Notes Reference	Book 5, Pages 90–153
Video CD Reference	CD 16
Audio CD Reference	CDs 18 & 19

As the Level 3 curriculum develops more and more of a global focus, Study Session 17 becomes more likely to show up on every exam. Look for an 18-point item set (5%).

THE CASE FOR INTERNATIONAL DIVERSIFICATION
Cross-Reference to CFA Institute Assigned Reading #45

Factors that cause economies to behave independently and their resulting correlations to be low include the following:

- Government regulations.
- Technological specializations.
- Fiscal policies.
- Monetary policies.
- Cultural and sociological differences.

The Global Efficient Frontier

The benefits from foreign diversification are illustrated in Figure 1.

Figure 1: The Global Efficient Frontier

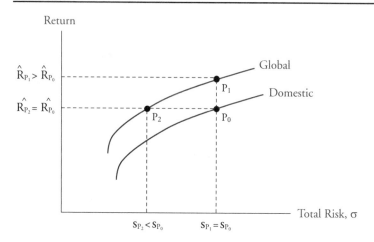

Adding international bonds to a global stock portfolio offers opportunities for lower risk and higher return, as illustrated in Figure 2.

Figure 2: Risk and Returns for International Bond Markets

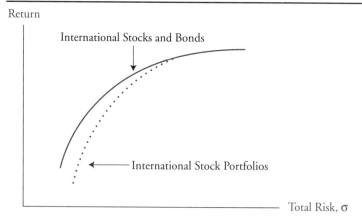

Currency Return

For an investor who invests overseas, the return from a foreign asset is:

$$R_\$ = R_{LC} + S + (R_{LC})(S) \qquad \text{(know this formula)}$$

where:
$R_\$$ = return on the foreign asset in U.S. dollar terms
R_{LC} = return on the foreign asset in local currency terms
S = percentage change in the foreign currency

Currency Effects on Risk

The formula for the risk of a foreign asset is much the same as for portfolio risk, except the weights of both the asset and the currency are 1.0.

$$\sigma_\$^2 = \sigma_{LC}^2 + \sigma_S^2 + 2\sigma_{LC}\sigma_S\rho_{LC,S} \qquad \text{(know this formula)}$$

where:

$\sigma_\$^2$ = variance of the returns on the foreign asset in U.S. dollar terms

$\sigma_{LC}^2, \sigma_{LC}$ = variance and standard deviation of the foreign asset in local currency terms

σ_S^2, σ_S = variance and standard deviation of foreign currency

$\rho_{LC,S}$ = correlation between returns for the foreign asset in local currency terms and movements in the foreign currency

The difference between the risk of the investment in U.S. dollar terms and in local currency terms is referred to as the contribution of currency risk:

$$\text{contribution of currency risk} = \sigma_\$ - \sigma_{LC}$$

Currency risk only slightly magnifies the volatility of foreign investments because:

- Currency risk is about half that of foreign stock risk.
- Foreign asset risk and currency risk are not additive.
- Currency risk can be hedged.
- Currency risk will be diversified away in a portfolio of many foreign assets.

International Diversification Should Not Work

The increasing correlations argument against international diversification states that the benefits of international diversification are generally overstated because:

- Correlations have increased over time.
- Correlations among markets increase during periods of increased volatility.

According to proponents, correlations have been *increasing* over time because:

- Free trade among nations has increased.
- Capital markets are becoming integrated.
- Corporations have increased exports, foreign operations, and foreign mergers and acquisitions.
- The mobility of capital has increased.

Correlation During Crises

Academic research has found that the previously reported increases in correlation during volatile stock markets are manifestations of the higher volatility and not increases in the true correlation. An alternative to the correlation for measuring co-movement of assets during volatile periods would be to examine the *cross-sectional* standard deviation of a portfolio of international stocks. If it is large, then markets are moving independently. If it decreases, then the markets are moving together.

Global Investing

Global investing diversifies across industries as well as countries, in contrast to traditional international diversification that only considers country diversification.

Emerging Markets

Risks unique to emerging markets include the following:

- Unstable political and social environments.
- Undeveloped infrastructure.
- Poor educational systems.
- Corrupt governments.

The return correlation among emerging markets can be high in times of crisis, depending on the cause of the crisis. If the crisis is due to local factors, it does not usually spread to other emerging markets. If it is caused by outside factors, however, the crisis can be contagious, and crises in emerging markets are usually more prolonged than in developed countries. Emerging market crises do not usually spread to developed markets, which accounts for the low correlation between emerging and developed markets.

Although the stand-alone risk of emerging markets can be quite high, the incremental risk from adding emerging markets to a portfolio is reasonable, as the correlations with developed markets are typically low.

In emerging markets, currencies are more volatile than in developed markets and stock returns and currency returns are usually *positively correlated*. Currency devaluations are common and the central banks are usually weak.

Investability

Although the returns from emerging markets can appear quite attractive, the foreign investor may not be able to exploit these returns for several reasons:

- Restrictions on the amount of stock held by foreigners.
- Low float because the government is often the primary owner of stock.
- Repatriation of invested capital is often restricted, especially in times of crisis.
- Discriminatory taxes are sometimes applied to foreign investors.
- Convertibility of foreign currency is often restricted.
- Authorized investors are sometimes the only investors able to invest in local firms.
- Liquidity in emerging markets is often quite low.

CURRENCY RISK MANAGEMENT
Cross-Reference to CFA Institute Assigned Reading #46

In addition to the risk associated with the uncertain future value of the investment, foreign investing also exposes the investor to translation risk—the risk associated with exchanging the foreign currency back into the investor's domestic currency.

Translation risk is the risk associated with translating the value of the asset back into the domestic currency. **Economic risk** is the risk associated with the relationship between exchange rate changes and changes in asset values in the foreign market.

The relationship between the minimum-variance hedge ratio and these two risks, regress unhedged domestic return on the futures return to determine the optimal hedge ratio, h:

$$R_{D,u} = \alpha + h(R_{Fut})$$

Algebraic manipulation accompanied by assumptions about the spot rate, futures rates, and the basis breaks the optimal hedge ratio, h, into its two components:

$$h = \frac{Cov\left(R_{D,u}, R_{Fut}\right)}{\sigma^2_{R_{Fut}}} = h_T + h_E = 1 + \frac{Cov\left(R_L, R_C\right)}{\sigma^2_{R_C}} \Rightarrow h_T = 1$$

$$\text{and } h_E = \frac{Cov\left(R_L, R_C\right)}{\sigma^2_{R_C}}$$

where:

h_T = the portion of the hedge ratio that compensates for translation risk
h_E = the portion of the hedge ratio that compensates for economic risk
R_L = the return in the local currency
R_C = the currency return (i.e., percentage change in the spot rate)
$\sigma^2_{R_C}$ = the variance of the currency return

Professor's Note: The derivation of this relationship is beyond the scope of the curriculum. Only the final result (the descriptions of h_T and h_E) are important for the exam (i.e., the optimal hedge ratio, h, is the sum of h_T and h_E).

Translation risk. The first term in the equation ($h_T = 1$) refers to the optimal hedge ratio to compensate for translation risk, and it says the ratio should be 1.0. This means 100% of the principal should be hedged (i.e., *hedging the principal*). When we hedge the principal using futures, the hedge ratio does not change ($h_T = 1$).

Economic risk. The second term in the equation, $h_E = \frac{Cov\left(R_L, R_C\right)}{\sigma^2_{R_C}}$, is the portion of the optimal hedge ration that compensates for economic risk. It depends upon the covariance of local asset returns and currency movements.

Basis Risk

Basis is the difference between the spot and futures exchange rates at a point in time. The magnitude of the basis depends upon the spot rate and the interest rate differential between the two economies. *Interest rate parity* describes the relationship between spot and futures exchange rates and local interest rates:

$$\frac{F_{D/L}}{S_{D/L}} = \frac{1 + i_D}{1 + i_L}$$

If the ratio of the interest rates should change, the ratio of the futures rate to the spot rate changes accordingly. If, for example, the domestic interest rate increases relative to the local rate, the futures rate also increases (i.e., the domestic currency depreciates relative to the local currency).

Hedging Multiple Currencies

To determine the optimal hedge ratio for a multi-currency portfolio, the manager can perform a sort of returns-based style analysis. Rather than attempt to determine an optimal hedge ratio for each individual currency, the manager can regress the portfolio's historic domestic returns on the futures returns for a few major, actively traded currencies.

$$R_D = \alpha + h_1 F_1 + h_2 F_2 + h_3 F_3 + e$$

where :
h_i = the optimal hedge ratio for currency i
F_i = the return on currency future i

Professor's Note: Futures returns may not be readily available. In that case, since changes in spot rates are the major driver of changes in futures prices, currency (spot) returns can be used in the regression.

Using Currency Options

The primary benefit to using currency options rather than futures to protect against translation losses is the relative nature of their payoffs. The payoff to a futures contract is *symmetric*. A put option, on the other hand, is used like *insurance*, because it gives the holder the right to sell the currency at a specified price over a specified time period.

Currency Delta Hedging

Delta, δ, shows how the value of the option changes in response to *small* changes in the underlying exchange rate. It is calculated as the change in the option premium divided by the change in the exchange rate:

$$\delta = \frac{\Delta P}{\Delta E} = \frac{P_1 - P_0}{E_1 - E_0}$$

Delta indicates the number of options to purchase to hedge translation risk. Specifically, for every unit of currency we should hold $(-1/\delta)$ put options.

Indirect Currency Hedging

Another way to manage currency exposure is buying options or futures on the foreign assets, instead of the assets themselves. For example, assume a manager wishes to purchase a foreign stock index. The manager has two choices: (1) buy all or a representative sample of the stocks in the index, or (2) buy futures or options on the foreign index.

If the manager selects the first alternative and purchases many different stocks denominated in the same currency, the manager has the entire value of the stocks exposed to currency movements. Then, any profits on the stocks are further exposed.

If instead, the manager chooses to purchase foreign equity index futures, the manager has only the initial margin committed (i.e., exposed to translation risk). Further, the investor may find the desired index future traded on an American exchange.

Options on foreign assets work in the same way. That is, only the option premiums are exposed to translation risk. The premium, and the margin on the foreign index futures, can be hedged if so desired. This ability to realize the gains on the underlying foreign assets by purchasing options or futures is sometimes referred to as *indirect currency hedging*, because the investor can enjoy the profits associated with the assets without incurring the currency exposure.

Currency Management

Under a **balanced mandate** approach, the investment manager is given total responsibility for managing the portfolio, including managing the currency exposure.

The **currency overlay** approach still follows the IPS guidelines, but a separate manager is hired to manage the currency exposure.

When currency is considered a **separate asset**, it is managed as if it were a totally separate allocation given to a separate manager and managed under its own, separate guidelines.

Emerging Markets Finance
Cross-Reference to CFA Institute Assigned Reading #47

Market Integration

Financial and Economic Market Integration

Financial liberalization refers primarily to domestic liberalization, which is often characterized by the privatization of firms and bank reform. Financial liberalization and complete market integration occur when there is unrestricted free flow of capital so that domestic investors can invest in foreign markets and foreign investors can invest in domestic markets. From a finance perspective, markets are completely integrated when assets of the same risk offer the same expected return.

Changes Resulting From Market Integration

Equity prices and liquidity increase when the government announces a *liberalization* policy, and the greater the credibility of the government, the greater the price increases. That is, when the announcement is made, investors analyze both the impact of the liberalization policy and the probability that it will be fully implemented. Any increase in prices will initially benefit local investors only, since foreign investors will not be allowed in the market until liberalization has taken place.

Market Liberalization vs. Market Integration

The difference between market liberalization and market integration is that an economy can be liberalized, but not fully integrated with the rest of the world due to various impediments. In other words, the two concepts are related, but not necessarily the same in the real world. The presence of one does not guarantee the presence of the other. Liberalization is a slow and intricate process. Integration is difficult to measure and there are various degrees of integration.

Financial Effects of Liberalization

The financial changes due to liberalization are reflected in the country's financial markets in the form of its *stock market performance, capital flows, political risk,* and *diversification benefits.*

Economic Effects of Liberalization

Liberalization has also been found to have beneficial effects for the economy at large in the form of improved *firm efficiency, GDP growth,* and *other macroeconomic changes.*

ISSUES FOR EMERGING MARKET INVESTORS

Contagion occurs when a crisis spreads to other countries. Contagion in currencies may occur for one of five reasons:

1. A country might devalue its currency to keep its exports competitive with another country who devalued.

2. A country might see its exports decline to countries in crisis.

3. The initial devaluation might serve as a "wake-up call" to investors that other countries' currencies have weaknesses.

4. A crisis in one country creates a credit crunch in others.

5. The initial crisis causes investors to liquidate their investments in other countries.

Market Efficiency and Market Microstructure

A microstructure that facilitates efficient markets is one in which transactions costs are low, liquidity is high, and transactions are executed quickly. These conditions should facilitate security prices that reflect the fundamental value of the security and are immune to manipulation by a large trader. It is usually the case that market reforms will result in a better microstructure.

Market Efficiency and Security Pricing

If a market is efficient, information should be reflected quickly in security prices and differences in expected returns should be solely attributable to risk. In inefficient markets, however, investor reactions to information can seem irrational.

Privatizations and the Cost of Capital

The cost of capital in emerging markets decreases post-liberalization because security prices increase and expected returns decrease. Likewise, when firms that were formerly government owned are privatized, the government signals its intent to reduce its interference in the economy and investors become more willing to invest in risky assets. Hence expected returns and cost of capital fall in the economy.

Privatizations also increase investment opportunities which allows for better performing portfolios. This also increases investors' willingness to hold risky assets and reduces the cost of capital.

Corporate Governance

Corporate governance practices vary widely in emerging markets. In most emerging countries, however, corporate governance practices and the enforcement of shareholder rights have traditionally been weak.

- Management often has greater voting power and this results in the firm's shares selling at a greater discount.
- The frequency of takeovers that could discipline poor management is negligible.
- Firm shares may be owned by another firm, which concentrates control of the firm.
- The government may impose capital controls that benefit favored firms.
- Some countries have strong creditor rights that result in a greater frequency of bankruptcy filings.
- Firms with weaker corporate governance are more likely to suffer during emerging market crises.
- Firms with high degrees of insider control have less CEO turnover after poor performance, so poor management is left in place.

Corporate governance in emerging countries can be improved, however, with the following mechanisms:

- Outside shareholders with a large degree of control who have a strong incentive to monitor management.
- A higher level of debt issued by the firm, especially when it is issued internationally, because debt holders can help monitor management.
- The firm lists its stock as an ADR, which requires stricter adherence to corporate governance standards. This improves firm valuation, especially when the firm is domiciled in a country with weak shareholder rights.
- The firm's analyst coverage increases which improves firm valuation, especially when the firm is controlled by family and management and when the firm is from a country with poor shareholder rights.
- Greater press coverage.

DREAMING WITH BRICs: THE PATH TO 2050
Cross-Reference to CFA Institute Assigned Reading #48

ECONOMIC POTENTIAL OF THE BRICs

Potential Economic Size and Growth

In U.S. dollar terms, the size of the BRIC economies as a whole is currently about 15% of that of the G6. However, by the year 2025, they could be more than half the size of the G6. By 2040, the total size of the BRIC economies may surpass that of the G6.

Individually, China's economy is projected to be the largest of the BRICs and might surpass the U.S. economy in 2039. By the year 2050, the largest economies are

---

projected to be China, followed by the United States, India, Japan, Brazil, Russia, the U.K., Germany, France, and Italy, in that order. So, of the six largest economies in 2050, four are projected to be BRIC economies, and only two are from the current G6.

In terms of economic growth, India is projected to have the strongest growth at 5% annually for the next 30 to 50 years. For other BRIC countries, growth will decline more swiftly over time, so that growth will be in the neighborhood of 3% by 2050.

Demographics and Per Capita Income

In terms of per capita income, all the BRIC countries except Russia are expected to remain below that of G6 countries. China is projected to have per capita income similar to the current levels in the G6. By 2050, U.S. income may climb to $80,000 per person.

Growth in Global Spending

Currently, the annual increase in global spending, measured in U.S. dollar terms, is about the same for the G6 and the BRICs as a whole. But by 2025, annual increases in spending could be more than twice as high in the BRIC countries. By 2050, the annual change in spending should be four times larger in the BRIC countries.

Trends in Real Exchange Rates

Real exchange rates in the BRIC countries could strengthen by 300% by 2050. The Chinese yuan could increase by 100% in value over the next ten years if growth remains healthy and the yuan is allowed to float. Note that about a third of the projected BRIC GDP growth, as measured in U.S. dollar terms, should come from rising exchange rates.

ECONOMIC GROWTH

Potential Returns on Capital and Productivity

Developing economies have the potential to increase returns on capital and productivity, because they are currently operating below the levels of more mature, developed countries. Furthermore, as developing countries adopt technology available in developed countries, their productivity will increase.

Appreciating Currencies

When countries have low per capita income levels, their currencies tend to be weak and below levels predicted by Purchasing Power Parity (PPP). As the developing countries mature and income rises, their currencies appreciate and converge toward the value predicted by PPP.

ELEMENTS OF ECONOMIC GROWTH

Technological Progress

The rate of technological progress in developing countries should eventually catch up to that in developed countries. The wider the income gap between a developing and developed country, the greater the potential for technological progress and the faster the technological growth should be. Stronger technological progress should result in higher economic growth and a stronger currency.

Growth in Capital Stock

The growth in capital stock is less important for economic growth than it is for technological progress, but it does have an impact on economic growth. Reducing the projected growth in capital stock by 5% would reduce GDP levels by 13% in the BRIC countries in 2050.

Employment Growth

The projected growth/decline in working age populations is based on population growth estimates. It will play a more positive role in economic growth in India and Brazil than in the rest of the BRIC countries.

Note that the projections for employment growth do not account for increases in labor force participation or an extension of the retirement age, both of which could offset the negative effects of a graying population in these countries.

THE CONDITIONS FOR SUSTAINED ECONOMIC GROWTH

Macroeconomic Stability

A stable macroeconomic environment promotes economic growth and is characterized by stable inflation, responsible fiscal policies, stable currency values, and accommodating governmental policies. High inflation hampers growth because it discourages investment in the economy by households and businesses. As such, governmental fiscal and monetary policies should focus on controlling inflation.

Institutional Efficiency

The relevant institutions here are the country's financial institutions, markets, legal system, government, health care industry, and educational system. Inefficient institutions are often symptomatic of other chronic problems. BRICs have had trouble in this area, particularly in the case of Russia.

Open Trade

With an open economy, a country gains increased access to technology, inputs, and markets. Research has verified that openness in an economy results in higher growth, with much of the benefit coming at the industry level. BRICs have had varying degrees of success in opening up their economies; India has been particularly slow to do so.

Worker Education

Higher levels of education are associated with increased economic growth in a country. An educated workforce is particularly important for BRICs to enter the next stage of economic growth. Although some BRIC countries have made some progress in this area as demonstrated with increasing school enrollments, the primary and secondary education systems in India are quite poor.

During past periods of **contagion**, emerging market returns were lower, risk was higher, and the correlations with developed markets were higher. This clearly indicates that adding emerging market stocks to a global portfolio during these crises will lower the portfolio's return and increase its risk.

If the tech sector is excluded from correlation calculations, the correlation between emerging markets and developed markets is lower, so financial bubbles diminish diversification benefits.

Allocating Emerging Markets in a Portfolio

The three methods of determining the appropriate asset allocation to emerging markets are using market capitalizations, using mean-variance analysis, and using practical considerations. Once investment restrictions are considered, the first approach would yield an allocation of approximately 4%. Although mean-variance analysis yields an optimal long-term allocation of 18%, it is very sensitive to inputs and not appropriate over short time horizons. Practical considerations imply that investors will often want to hold the same allocations as their benchmarks.

GLOBAL INVESTMENT PERFORMANCE STANDARDS

Study Session 18

Approximate Weight on Exam	About 5%
Study Note Reference	Book 5, Pages 154–230
Video CD Reference	CD 16
Audio CD Reference	CD 19 & 20

You will be required to critique a performance presentation and identify Global Investment Performance Standards (GIPS) violations and requirements. Until 2007, GIPS was tested as a 15- to 18-point constructed response essay question. In 2007, GIPS was tested as an 18-point item set.

GLOBAL INVESTMENT PERFORMANCE STANDARDS
Cross-Reference to CFA Institute Assigned Reading #49

GIPS Definition of the Firm

For a firm to claim compliance with GIPS, the standards must be applied on a *firm-wide basis*. According to the GIPS, firms must be defined as:

> *"An investment firm, subsidiary, or division held out to clients or potential clients as a distinct business entity."*

A result of this definition is that a subsidiary may be GIPS compliant while its parent company is not. Alternatively, one division of an asset management firm may be compliant while another is not. Note that for a division to be considered a "firm," it really must have the appearance of a separate entity. For example, if a company has separate divisions for individual and institutional clients and these two parts of the business use similar investment strategies, processes, and styles, the company would not be able to claim compliance within just one of the divisions.

GIPS Compliance Statement

Once a firm has met all of the required elements of the GIPS, the firm may use the following compliance statement to indicate that the performance presentation is in compliance with the GIPS:

> *(Insert name of firm) has prepared and presented this report in compliance with the Global Investment Performance Standards (GIPS®).*

If the performance presentation does not meet *all* of the requirements of the GIPS, firms **cannot** represent that the performance presentation is "in compliance with the Global Investment Performance Standards *except for...*"

> *Professor's Note: Take care distinguishing requirements from recommendations—if an exam question asks for breaches of GIPS, then noting recommendations will not score you any marks.*

INPUT DATA REQUIREMENTS AND RECOMMENDATIONS

GIPS Input Data Requirements

> *Professor's Note: For the exam, you will need only general knowledge of the standards.*

- **Standard 1.A.1.** All data and information necessary to support a firm's performance presentation and to perform the required calculations must be captured and maintained.
- **Standard 1.A.2.** Portfolio valuations must be based on market values (not cost basis or book values).
- **Standard 1.A.3.** For periods prior to January 1, 2001, portfolios must be valued at least quarterly. For periods between January 1, 2001 and January 1, 2010, portfolios must be valued at least monthly. For periods beginning January 1, 2010, firms must value portfolios on the date of all large external cash flows.
- **Standard 1.A.4.** For periods beginning January 1, 2010, firms must value portfolios as of the calendar month-end or the last business day of the month.
- **Standard 1.A.5.** For periods beginning January 1, 2005, firms must use trade-date accounting.
- **Standard 1.A.6.** Accrual accounting must be used for fixed income securities and all other assets that accrue interest income. Market values of fixed income securities must include accrued income.
- **Standard 1.A.7.** For periods beginning January 1, 2006, composites must have consistent beginning and ending annual valuation dates. Unless the composite is reported on a non-calendar fiscal year, the beginning and ending valuation dates must be at calendar year-end (or on the last business day of the year).

GIPS Input Data Recommendations

- **Standard 1.B.1.** Accrual accounting should be used for dividends (as of the ex-dividend date).
- **Standard 1.B.2.** When presenting net-of-fees returns, firms should accrue investment management fees.
- **Standard 1.B.3.** Calendar month-end valuations or valuations on the last business day of the month are recommended.

Calculation Methodology Requirements and Recommendations

The related LOS this year asks candidates to "**summarize** and **justify** the requirements of the GIPS standards with respect to return calculation methodologies..." These command words suggest you might be asked to explain or compare their calculations, but you will not be asked to perform the calculations.

- **Standard 2.A.1.** Total return, including realized and unrealized gains and losses plus income, must be used.
- **Standard 2.A.2.** Time-weighted rates of return that adjust for external cash flows must be used. Periodic returns must be geometrically linked. External cash flows must be treated in a consistent manner with the firm's documented, composite-specific policy. At a minimum:
  a. For periods beginning January 1, 2005, firms must use approximated rates of return that adjust for daily weighted external cash flows.
  b. For periods beginning January 1, 2010, firms must value portfolios on the date of all large external cash flows.

A total return formula for a portfolio for which no cash flows have occurred is the basic holding period return formula:

$$R_{TR} = \frac{EMV - BMV}{BMV}$$

The GIPS *require* TWRRs that adjust for *daily-weighted* cash flows for periods beginning on or after January 1, 2005 and will *require* the use of TWRRs with valuations at the time of external cash flows by January 1, 2010.

- The **Original Dietz method** (permitted until January 1, 2005) assumes all external cash flows occur at the middle of the measurement period.

$$R_{Dietz} = \frac{EMV - BMV - CF}{BMV + 0.5CF}$$

- TWRR methodologies that adjust for daily cash flows (required for periods after January 1, 2005).

The **modified Dietz method** weights each external cash flow by the proportion of the measurement period the cash flow is held in (or out of) the portfolio.

$$R_{MDietz} = \frac{EMV - BMV - CF}{BMV + \sum_{i=1}^{n} W_i \times CF_i}$$ (know this formula)

The **modified IRR method** (MIRR) considers the timing of each cash flow. This changes the traditional IRR method from a money-weighted calculation method to a time-weighted method.

$$EMV = \sum_{i=0}^{n} F_i (1+R)^{W_i}$$

For example, if there are three cash flows, including the beginning-of-period market value, the MIRR formula will have three terms:

$$EMV = F_0 (1+R)^{W_0} + F_1 (1+R)^{W_1} + F_2 (1+R)^{W_2}$$

- TWRR using revaluation at the time of external cash flows (required beginning January 1, 2010).

  The **daily valuation method** calculates the true TWRR rather than an estimate:

  $$R_i = \frac{EMV - BMV}{BMV}$$

  The subperiod returns are then geometrically linked (chain-linked) to calculate a total return:

  $$R_{TR} = \left[(1+R_1)(1+R_2)...(1+R_n) \right] - 1$$ (know this formula)

Composite Returns and Asset-Weighted Returns

For the exam, know the methods of asset weighting only. You will not be asked to calculate a composite return.

- **Standard 2.A.3.** Composite returns must be calculated by asset weighting the individual portfolio returns using beginning-of-period values or a method that reflects both beginning-of-period values and external cash flows.
  a. The beginning market value-weighted composite return, R_{BMV}, can be calculated using the formula:

  $$R_{BMV} = \frac{\sum_{i=1}^{n} (BMV_i)(R_i)}{BMV_{Total}}$$

b. The beginning market value plus cash flow-weighted method represents a refinement to the asset-weighted approach.

- **Standard 2.A.4.** Returns from cash and cash equivalents held in portfolios must be included in total return calculations.
- **Standard 2.A.5.** All returns must be calculated after the deduction of the actual trading expenses incurred during the period. Estimated trading expenses are not permitted.
- **Standard 2.A.6.** For periods beginning January 1, 2006, firms must calculate composite returns by asset-weighting the individual portfolio returns at least quarterly. For periods beginning January 1, 2010, composite returns must be calculated by asset weighting the individual portfolio returns at least monthly.
- **Standard 2.A.7.** If the actual direct trading expenses cannot be identified and segregated from a bundled fee:
  a. When calculating gross-of-fees returns, returns must be reduced by the entire bundled fee or the portion of the bundled fee that includes the direct trading expenses. The use of estimated trading expenses is not permitted.
  b. When calculating net-of-fees returns, returns must be reduced by the entire bundled fee or the portion of the bundled fee that includes the direct trading expenses and the investment management fee. The use of estimated trading expenses is not permitted.

GIPS Calculation Methodology Recommendations

- **Standard 2.B.1.** Returns should be calculated net of non-reclaimable withholding taxes on dividends, interest, and capital gains. Reclaimable withholding taxes should be accrued.
- **Standard 2.B.2.** Firms should calculate composite returns by asset weighting the member portfolios at least monthly.
- **Standard 2.B.3.** Firms should value portfolios on the date of all large external cash flows.

Composite Construction Requirements and Recommendations

A composite is an aggregation of discretionary portfolios into a single group that represents a particular investment objective or strategy. Composites are the primary vehicle for presenting performance to a prospective client. The composite return is the asset-weighted average of the performance results of all the portfolios in the composite. Creating meaningful, asset-weighted composites is critical to the fair presentation, consistency, and comparability of results over time and among firms.

Discretionary Portfolios

A portfolio is classified as discretionary if the manager is able to successfully implement intended strategies. If client-imposed constraints become too restrictive, placing significant limitations on the manager's ability to implement value-generating strategies, the portfolio may be reclassified as non-discretionary.

- **Standard 3.A.1.** All actual, fee-paying, discretionary portfolios must be included in at least one composite. Although non-fee-paying discretionary portfolios may be included in a composite (with appropriate disclosures), nondiscretionary portfolios are not permitted to be included in a firm's composites.

Constructing Composites: Investment Strategies and Styles

- **Standard 3.A.2.** Composites must be defined according to similar investment objectives and/or strategies. The full composite definition must be made available on request.

Constructing Composites: Adding Portfolios and Terminating Portfolios

- **Standard 3.A.3.** Composites must include new portfolios on a timely and consistent basis after the portfolio comes under management unless specifically mandated by the client.
- **Standard 3.A.4.** Terminated portfolios must be included in the historical returns of the appropriate composites up to the last full measurement period that the portfolio was under management.
- **Standard 3.A.5.** Portfolios are not permitted to be switched from one composite to another unless documented changes in client guidelines or the redefinition of the composite make it appropriate. The historical record of the portfolio must remain with the appropriate composite.
- **Standard 3.A.6.** Convertible and other hybrid securities must be treated consistently across time and within composites.
- **Standard 3.A.7.** Carve-out segments excluding cash are not permitted to be used to represent a discretionary portfolio and, as such, are not permitted to be included in composite returns. When a single asset class is carved out of a multiple asset class portfolio and the returns are presented as part of a single asset composite, cash must be allocated to the carve-out returns in a timely and consistent manner. Beginning January 1, 2010, carve-out returns are not permitted to be included in single asset class composite returns unless the carve-out is actually managed separately with its own cash balance.
- **Standard 3.A.8.** Composites must include only assets under management within the defined firm. Firms are not permitted to link simulated or model portfolios with actual performance.
- **Standard 3.A.9.** If a firm sets a minimum asset level for portfolios to be included in a composite, no portfolios below that asset level can be included in that composite. Any changes to a composite-specific minimum asset level are not permitted to be applied retroactively.

Composite Construction Recommendations

- **Standard 3.B.1.** Carve-out returns should not be included in single asset class composite returns unless the carve-outs are actually managed separately with their own cash balance.

- **Standard 3.B.2.** To remove the effect of a significant external cash flow, the use of a temporary new account is recommended (as opposed to adjusting the composite composition to remove portfolios with significant external cash flows).
- **Standard 3.B.3.** Firms should not market a composite to a prospective client who has assets less than the composite's minimum asset level.

GIPS Required Disclosures

On the exam, you will probably have to critique a performance presentation. A thorough knowledge of the following required disclosures will help you get all the available points. Your GIPS bookmark also contains a complete list. Before you enter the exam room, be sure you know these 26 required disclosures.

- **Standard 4.A.1.** Firms must disclose the definition of "firm" used to determine the total firm assets and firm-wide compliance.
- **Standard 4.A.2.** Firms must disclose the availability of a complete list and description of all of the firm's composites.
- **Standard 4.A.3.** Firms must disclose the minimum asset level, if any, below which portfolios are not included in a composite. Firms must also disclose any changes to the minimum asset level.
- **Standard 4.A.4.** Firms must disclose the currency used to express performance.
- **Standard 4.A.5.** Firms must disclose the presence, use, and extent of leverage or derivatives (if material), including a sufficient description of the use, frequency, and characteristics of the instruments to identify risks.
- **Standard 4.A.6.** Firms must clearly label returns as gross-of-fees or net-of-fees.
- **Standard 4.A.7.** Firms must disclose relevant details of the treatment of withholding tax on dividends, interest income, and capital gains. If using indices that are net-of-taxes, the firm must disclose the tax basis of the benchmark (e.g., Luxembourg-based or U.S.-based) versus that of the composite.
- **Standard 4.A.8.** Firms must disclose and describe any known inconsistencies in the exchange rates used among the portfolios within a composite and between the composite and the benchmark.
- **Standard 4.A.9.** If the presentation conforms with local laws and regulations that differ from the GIPS requirements, firms must disclose this fact and disclose the manner in which the local laws and regulations conflict with the GIPS standards.
- **Standard 4.A.10.** For any performance presented for periods prior to January 1, 2000 that does not comply with the GIPS standards, firms must disclose the period of noncompliance and how the presentation is not in compliance with the GIPS standards.
- **Standard 4.A.11.** For periods prior to January 1, 2010, when a single asset class is carved out of a multiple-asset portfolio and the returns are presented as part of a single-asset composite, firms must disclose the policy used to allocate cash to the carve-out returns.
- **Standard 4.A.12.** Firms must disclose the fee schedule appropriate to the presentation.

- **Standard 4.A.13.** If a composite contains portfolios with bundled fees, firms must disclose for each annual period shown the percentage of composite assets that is bundled fee portfolios.
- **Standard 4.A.14.** If a composite contains portfolios with bundled fees, firms must disclose the various types of fees that are included in the bundled fee.
- **Standard 4.A.15.** When presenting gross-of-fees returns, firms must disclose if any other fees are deducted in addition to the direct trading expenses.
- **Standard 4.A.16.** When presenting net-of-fees returns, firms must disclose if any other fees are deducted in addition to the investment management fee and direct trading expenses.
- **Standard 4.A.17.** Firms must disclose that additional information regarding policies for calculating and reporting returns is available upon request.
- **Standard 4.A.18.** Beginning January 1, 2006, firms must disclose the use of a subadvisor(s) and the periods a subadvisor(s) was used.
- **Standard 4.A.19.** Firms must disclose all significant events that would help a prospective client interpret the performance record.
- **Standard 4.A.20.** Firms must disclose the composite description (e.g., objectives, style, strategy).
- **Standard 4.A.21.** If a firm is redefined, the firm must disclose the date and reason for the redefinition.
- **Standard 4.A.22.** If a firm has redefined a composite, the firm must disclose the date and nature of the change. Changes to composites are not permitted to be applied retroactively.
- **Standard 4.A.23.** Firms must disclose any changes to the name of a composite.
- **Standard 4.A.24.** Firms must disclose the composite creation date.
- **Standard 4.A.25.** Firms must disclose if, prior to January 1, 2010, calendar month-end portfolio valuations or valuations on the last business day of the month are not used.
- **Standard 4.A.26.** Firms must disclose the dispersion of returns of the individual portfolios in the composite and which dispersion measure is used.

GIPS Recommended Disclosures

- **Standard 4.B.1.** If a parent company contains multiple defined firms, each firm within the parent company is encouraged to disclose a list of the other firms contained within the parent company.
- **Standard 4.B.2.** Firms should disclose when a change in a calculation methodology or valuation source results in a material impact on the performance of a composite return.
- **Standard 4.B.3.** Firms that have been verified should add a disclosure to their composite presentation stating that the firm has been verified and clearly indicating the periods the verification covers if the composite presentation includes results for periods that have not been subject to firm-wide verification.

GIPS Presentation and Reporting Requirements

- **Standard 5.A.1.** The following items must be reported for each composite presented:

    a. At least five years of performance (or a record for the period since firm or composite inception if the firm or composite has been in existence less than five years) that meets the requirements of the GIPS standards; after presenting five years of performance, the firm must present additional annual performance up to ten years. (e.g., after a firm presents five years of compliant history, the firm must add an additional year of performance each year so that after five years of claiming compliance, the firm presents a 10-year performance record.)

    b. Annual returns for all years.

    c. The number of portfolios and amount of assets in the composite, and either the percentage of the total firm assets represented by the composite or the amount of total firm assets at the end of each annual period. If the composite contains less than five portfolios, the number of portfolios is not required.

    d. A measure of dispersion of individual portfolio returns for each annual period. If the composite contains less than five portfolios for the full year, a measure of dispersion is not required.

The GIPS Handbook identifies the following acceptable methods for calculating **internal dispersion**:

- The range of annual returns.
- The high and low annual returns.
- Interquartile range.
- The standard deviation of equal-weighted annual return.
- The asset-weighted standard deviation of annual returns.

The **range** of annual returns and the **high and low** annual returns are the simplest and most easily understood measures of dispersion. The advantages of these measures include simplicity, ease of calculation, and ease of interpretation. Disadvantages include the fact that an extreme value can skew the data, and they do not stand alone as adequate risk measures.

The **interquartile range** is the middle 50% of a population, excluding the top 25% and bottom 25%. Hence, it measures the part of the population between the bottom of the first quartile and the bottom of the third quartile.

The **standard deviation** across equally weighted portfolios is the most widely accepted measure of dispersion within a composite.

- **Standard 5.A.2.** Firms may link non-GIPS-compliant returns to their compliant history so long as the firms meet the disclosure requirements for noncompliant performance and only compliant returns are presented for periods after January 1, 2000. (e.g., a firm that has been in existence since 1995 and wants to present its entire performance history and claim compliance beginning

January 1, 2005 must present returns that meet the requirements of the GIPS standards at least from January 1, 2000 and must meet the disclosure requirements for any noncompliant history prior to January 1, 2000.)

- **Standard 5.A.3.** Returns of portfolios and composites for periods of less than one year are not permitted to be annualized.
- **Standard 5.A.4.**
  a. Performance track records of a past firm or affiliation must be linked to or used to represent the historical record of a new firm or new affiliation if:
    i. Substantially all the investment decision makers are employed by the new firm (e.g., research department, portfolio managers, and other relevant staff).
    ii. The staff and decision-making process remain intact and independent within the new firm.
    iii. The new firm has records that document and support the reported performance.
  b. The new firm must disclose that the performance results from the past firm are linked to the performance record of the new firm.
  c. In addition to 5.A.4.a and 5.A.4.b, when one firm joins an existing firm, performance of composites from both firms must be linked to the ongoing returns if substantially all the assets from the past firm's composite transfer to the new firm.
  d. If a compliant firm acquires or is acquired by a noncompliant firm, the firms have one year to bring the noncompliant assets into compliance.
- **Standard 5.A.5.** Beginning January 1, 2006, if a composite includes or is formed using single asset class carve-outs from multiple asset class portfolios, the presentation must include the percentage of the composite that is composed of carve-outs prospectively for each period.
- **Standard 5.A.6.** The total return for the benchmark (or benchmarks) that reflects the investment strategy or mandate represented by the composite must be presented for each annual period. If no benchmark is presented, the presentation must explain why no benchmark is disclosed. If the firm changes the benchmark that is used for a given composite in the performance presentation, the firm must disclose both the date and the reasons for the change. If a custom benchmark or combination of multiple benchmarks is used, the firm must describe the benchmark creation and re-balancing process.
- **Standard 5.A.7.** If a composite contains any non-fee-paying portfolios, the firm must present, as of the end of each annual period, the percentage of the composite assets represented by the non-fee-paying portfolios.

GIPS Presentation and Reporting Recommendations

- **Standard 5.B.1.** It is recommended that firms present the following items:
  a. Composite returns gross of investment management fees and administrative fees and before taxes (except for non-reclaimable withholding taxes).
  b. Cumulative returns for composite and benchmarks for all periods.
  c. Equal-weighted mean and median returns for each composite.

    d. Graphs and charts presenting specific information required or recommended under the GIPS standards.

    e. Returns for quarterly and/or shorter time periods.

    f. Annualized composite and benchmark returns for periods greater than 12 months.

    g. Composite-level country and sector weightings.

- **Standard 5.B.2.** It is recommended that firms present relevant composite-level risk measures, such as beta, tracking error, modified duration, information ratio, Sharpe ratio, Treynor ratio, credit ratings, value at risk (VAR), and volatility, over time of the composite and benchmark returns.

- **Standard 5.B.3.** After presenting the required five years of compliant historical performance, the firm is encouraged to bring any remaining portion of its historical track record into compliance with the GIPS standards. (This does not preclude the requirement that the firm must add annual performance to its track record on an on-going basis to build a 10-year track record.)

Real Estate and Private Equity

For **real estate**, the following investment types would fall under the *general provisions* of the GIPS standards (as opposed to the provisions dealing directly with real estate and private equity):

- Publicly traded real estate securities, including any listed securities issued by public companies.
- Commercial mortgage-backed securities (CMBS).
- Private debt investments, including commercial and residential loans where the expected return is solely related to contractual interest rates without any participation in the economic performance of the underlying real estate.

Note that publicly traded securities include Real Estate Investment Trusts (REITs). If a portfolio consists of real estate plus other investments, the carve-out provisions of GIPS (Standard 3.A.7) would apply.

- **Standard 6.A.1.** Real estate investments must be valued at market value at least once every 12 months. For periods beginning January 1, 2008, real estate investments must be valued at least quarterly.

- **Standard 6.A.3.a.** In addition to the other disclosure requirements of the GIPS standards, performance presentations for real estate investments must disclose the calculation methodology for component returns—that is, component returns are (1) calculated separately using chain-linked, time-weighted rates of return, (2) adjusted such that the sum of the income return and the capital return is equal to the total return, or (3) income cash recognition mode.

- **Standard 6.A.4.** The income and capital appreciation component returns must be presented in addition to total return.

Real Estate Calculations   (know these formulas)

Total return to real estate can be split into **income return** and **capital return**. The measurement of capital return is dependent on having a recent and reliable value of each property, hence the requirement to value investments at least annually (and increasing to quarterly in 2008).

All the return calculations are based upon total **capital employed** (invested). You will notice that capital employed is the weighted average capital invested during the period:

$$C_E = C_0 + \sum_{i=1}^{n}\left(CF_i \times w_i\right)$$

The **capital return** is calculated as the percentage change in the value of the property after consideration of capital improvements and sales proceeds.

$$R_C = \frac{MV_1 - MV_0 - E_C + S}{C_E}$$

The **income return** is calculated as the *net investment income* earned over the period divided by capital employed (C_E). Net investment income is gross investment income less non-recoverable expenses, interest paid on debt, and property taxes (capital employed is as defined previously):

$$R_I = \frac{INC_A - E_{NR} - INT_D - T_P}{C_E}$$

The **total return** for the period is the sum of the capital and income returns:

$$R_T = R_C + R_I$$

GIPS Private Equity Requirements and Recommendations

Requirements

- **Standard 7.A.20.** Firms must present both the net-of-fees and gross-of-fees annualized SI-IRR of the composite for each year since inception.
- **Standard 7.A.21.** For each period presented, firms must report:
  a. Paid-in capital to date (cumulative drawdown).
  b. Total current invested capital.
  c. Cumulative distributions to date.

- **Standard 7.A.22.** For each period presented, firms must report the following multiples:
  a. Total value to paid-in capital (investment multiple or TVPI).
  b. Cumulative distributions to paid-in capital (realization multiple or DPI).
  c. Paid-in capital to committed capital (PIC multiple).
  d. Residual value to paid-in capital (RVPI).
- **Standard 7.A.23.** If a benchmark is shown, the cumulative annualized SI-IRR for the benchmark that reflects the same strategy and vintage year of the composite must be presented for the same periods for which the composite is presented. If no benchmark is shown, the presentation must explain why no benchmark is disclosed.

Recommendations

- **Standard 7.B.2.** Firms should present the average holding period of the investments (portfolio companies) over the life of the composite.

GIPS Verification

A firm may *voluntarily* hire an independent third party to verify its claim of complinace. The *primary purpose of verification* is to increase the level of confidence that a firm claiming GIPS compliance did, indeed, adhere to the Standards of a firm-wide basis.

Upon completion of verification, a verification report is issued that must confirm the following:

- The investment firm has complied with all the composite construction requirements of GIPS on a firm-wide basis.
- The firm's processes and procedures are designed to calculate and present performance results in compliance with the GIPS.

Other noteworthy aspects of GIPS verification include the following:

- A single verification report is issued to the entire firm; *GIPS verification cannot be carried out for a single composite.*
- Verification cannot be partial: it is all or nothing. In other words, verification cannot enable a firm to claim that its performance presentation is in compliance with GIPS "except for ..."
- Verification is not a requirement for GIPS compliance, but it is *strongly encouraged* and may eventually become mandatory.
- The initial minimum period for which verification can be performed is one year of a firm's presented performance. The recommended period over which verification is performed will be that part of the firm's track record for which GIPS compliance is claimed.
- After performing the verification, the verifier may conclude that the firm is not in compliance with GIPS or that the records of the firm cannot support a complete verification. In such situations, the verifier must issue a statement to the firm clarifying why a verification report was not possible.

GIPS Advertising Guidelines

All advertisements that include a claim of compliance with the GIPS Advertising Guidelines must include the following:

1. A description of the firm.

2. How an interested party can obtain a presentation that complies with the requirements of GIPS standards and/or a list and description of all firm composites.

3. The GIPS Advertising Guidelines compliance statement:

   [Insert name of firm] claims compliance with the Global Investment Performance Standards (GIPS®).

4. A description of the strategy of the composite being advertised.

5. Period-to-date composite performance results in addition to either:
   a. 1-, 3-, and 5-year cumulative annualized composite returns with the end-of-period date clearly identified (or annualized period since composite inception if inception is greater than one and less than five years). Periods of less than one year are not permitted to be annualized. The annualized returns must be calculated through the same period of time as presented in the corresponding compliant presentation.
   b. Five years of annual composite returns with the end-of-period date clearly identified (or since composite inception if inception is less than five years). The annual returns must be calculated through the same period.

6. Whether performance is shown gross and/or net of investment management fees.

7. The benchmark total return for the same periods for which the composite return is presented and a description of that benchmark. If no benchmark is presented, the advertisement must disclose why no benchmark is presented.

8. The currency used to express returns.

9. The description of the use and extent of leverage and derivatives if leverage or derivatives are used as an active part of the investment strategy of the composite. Where leverage/derivatives do not have a material effect on returns, no disclosure is required.

10. When presenting noncompliant performance information for periods prior to January 1, 2000 in an advertisement, firms must disclose the period(s) and which specific information is not compliant as well as provide the reason(s) the information is not in compliance with the GIPS standards.

The Advertising Guidelines also suggest that firms may present other information, though this supplemental information should be of equal or lesser prominence than the required information previously described.

ESSENTIAL EXAM STRATEGIES

GAME PLAN

This document is different from our other review materials for the CFA® exam, but as always, the objective is to enhance your chances of passing the CFA exam. However, our other review materials cover what you need to know to pass the exam. In this book, I give you some important guidance on how to pass the exam. By this time, you have studied the entire Level 3 curriculum, and have a solid grasp of the content. I won't spend time here reviewing or quizzing you on material. Instead, I provide guidance on how to successfully demonstrate your knowledge on exam day.

Level 3 stands alone in 2008 with two different types of questions. As you no doubt already know, the morning half of the exam will be constructed response (essay). Many of these will provide a template in which you will select and/or compose your answer. An example of this type of constructed response question is one in which someone has made several statements. The template will have the statements listed in the first column and the words "correct" and "incorrect" in the second. You are asked to circle either correct or incorrect, and if you circled incorrect, you must explain in the third column why the statement is incorrect.

There will also be short essay questions. I say short because you will never be asked to construct a long, intricate response. Oftentimes the answer can be put into bullet form, and you should do this whenever possible. Be careful with bullets, however. Be sure you include enough in each bullet to demonstrate to the grader that you know the answer. By all means, never leave a short answer question blank! Write something…you might get partial credit.

In addition to template and short essay, you will probably see calculation questions. They are typically short calculations, such as calculating the income return on a real estate investment. More than likely, you will have to perform calculations related to derivatives, and I have demonstrated just about every possible type of derivatives calculation in Books 3 and 4 of our Study Notes. Just be careful and evaluate your answer for the correct magnitude and sign before moving on.

The afternoon portion of your exam will be selected response, item set. These will include a vignette with six 3-point selected response (multiple choice) questions, just like those at Level 2. Never leave one of these unanswered. Always try to eliminate any incorrect choices and mark the most likely of the remaining answers.

The main difference between Level 2 and Level 3 is that most Level 3 questions require a more thoughtful response. The Level 2 exam covered a large amount of material and required you to demonstrate your knowledge of that material. The Level 3 exam asks you to take your knowledge and apply it to given situations. You will be expected to demonstrate a greater depth of understanding than on the Level 2 exam. Many candidates expect to "coast" through Level 3 after succeeding at Level 2. While the Level 3 exam is generally less challenging than Level 2 from a content perspective, do not let yourself get complacent in your exam preparation!

I will begin by showing you some proven approaches to mastering the CFA curriculum for Level 3. Next, I will walk you through a plan for the last week before the exam. I will offer important suggestions to make sure you are prepared on exam day—that you're not so flustered by the time you begin the exam that your performance is negatively affected. I will also spend some time discussing strategies for taking the exam and how to approach individual questions.

THE PRACTICE FIELD

Over the past few months, you have studied a lot of material. The CFA Institute assigned readings for the Level 3 curriculum include about 2,200 pages and more than 400 learning outcome statements (LOS). The bad news is that remembering every detail in such a vast amount of material is impossible. The good news is that you don't have to remember every detail. This guide will help show you how to get the most benefit from the short time remaining until the exam.

As you prepare for the CFA exam, try to focus on the exam itself. Don't add to your stress level by worrying about whether you'll pass or what might happen if you don't. There is ample stress from remembering the material—you certainly do not need to add to that stress level. Many of the tips I have included are proven stress reducers on exam day. Your grasp of the content combined with these tips should have you very well prepared for the exam.

As the Level 3 manager, I have earned the CFA charter and have extensive experience teaching the topics covered in the CFA curriculum. As such, I know what you are going through from personal experience, and have witnessed several thousand candidates go through the process of earning the right to use the CFA designation. I've been there and done it. Now, I want to share with you some time-honored strategies that lead to success on the Level 3 exam.

I'll start with some overall thoughts. You should follow two basic strategies in learning the CFA curriculum. First, you should *focus on the big picture*; second, you should *know the main concepts*.

The Big Picture

By focusing on the big picture, I mean you should know *something* about as many concepts as possible. The Level 3 exam is more of a "big picture" exam than the preceding levels—this exam brings together much of what you have learned previously. By remembering some basic information on exam day, you will be able to narrow your answer choices in an item set, or earn a few extra points on an essay question. You probably won't answer many questions correctly with only a basic grasp of the concept, but you can help yourself out. For example, you can improve your odds on a multiple-choice question from 25% to 50%! On an essay question, you'll be able to earn some points. In addition, you will be able to distinquish between relevant and irrelevant information in a question.

Another component of focusing on the big picture is covering as many topics as possible. Even if you never use futures, and you know you never will, *at least try to get a basic grasp of important concepts*. It is simply a very poor exam strategy to ignore significant pieces of the curriculum. I've known candidates in the CFA program who thought that as long as they knew a few topics really well, they could bluff their way through the rest of the exam. They were smart, but their exam strategy wasn't.

Know the Main Concepts

By knowing the main concepts, I mean those concepts *most likely* to be on the exam. These are the concepts that are tested most consistently on the CFA Level 3 exam. In any given year, some concepts might be omitted, but if you can answer questions on these concepts, you may increase your odds of passing dramatically. Generally, the idea is to be correct on most of the questions on important concepts, and then rely on your "big picture" knowledge to get points on the remaining material.

Calculations

To determine whether you will be asked to calculate an answer on the exam, look at the command word(s) in the LOS. The command word *calculate* is obvious, but others like *demonstrate* could lead to using calculations.

You may have noticed that in some sections of the Study Notes, an LOS with the command word *discuss* is followed by calculations or mathematical expressions. In those cases, the formulas and calculations were included to help your studying only. You will not be asked to perform the calculations on the exam.

Characteristic Lists

Another common source of specific questions is identifying the characteristics of various securities, models, and valuation methods. A typical question format would be "Which of the following *most accurately* describes...?" Here, the big picture approach can help you weed out bad answers. Also, some candidates use mnemonics to help remember lists of characteristics or lists of pros and cons. Although they will not ask for an entire list, essay questions sometimes ask for a few advantages/disadvantages, et cetera, with brief descriptions of each.

Know Your Strengths

Everyone has his or her own style of learning. Some people can sit down and study for hours at a time. Some people do better learning small pieces of the curriculum each day. Be aware of your study habits, and do not place unrealistic burdens on yourself. Be especially aware of problems with certain topics. For example, if you have always struggled with options, look at ways to improve your grasp of that material. Spend more time with it, attend a review course, or join a study group. Do not expect that you can ignore some topic and make up for lost points in that area by blowing the top off another area. Similarly, do not skip an area because you think you already know it. Every year there are options traders who fail the derivatives questions or consultants who fail the performance evaluation questions. *You need to review all the material in the assigned CFA curriculum to give the CFA answer and pass the CFA exam.*

RULE BOOK

Prior to exam day, be sure to visit the CFA Institute Web site and thoroughly read the information listed under Candidate Resources. I have reproduced some of that material below, and you can go to www.cfainstitute.org and click on *CFA Program* and then *Candidate Resources* for the complete list and text. As Level 3 candidates you are probably aware of most of this, but it never hurts to be sure. You don't want any surprises on exam day!

Candidate Responsibilities

Source: www.cfainstitute.org/cfaprog/resources/examdetails/responsibilities

When you enroll in the CFA Program, you are committing to the CFA Institute Code of Ethics and Standards of Professional Conduct. As part of the enrollment and registration process, you must sign a Candidate Responsibility Statement and agree to adhere to the policies and procedures in force, including the testing policies.

This commitment is not to be taken lightly: The code requires that you act with integrity, competence, and dignity, and in an ethical manner, and the standards require that you not engage in professional conduct involving dishonesty, fraud, deceit, or misrepresentation. There is nothing that CFA Institute does as an organization that is of greater importance than promoting the use of our code and standards by investment professionals and enforcing the code and standards among CFA Institute members and CFA candidates. These are the standards of integrity that you must abide by as long as you are a CFA candidate and/or a CFA Institute member.

Reviewing Your Exam Confirmation E-mail. It is your responsibility to review your exam confirmation e-mail to confirm your exam date and test center selection. Carefully review your chosen test center to ensure that you have requested the correct test center location and code (i.e., the test center code LND represents London, ONTARIO, not London, England).

Changing Your Personal Information. You must notify us of any personal information changes. Make updates online for address, e-mail, phone number, or name changes. Failure to do so may prevent or delay receipt of important information. Changing your address will not change your test center.

Changing a Test Center Location. We accept requests to change test center locations up until 75 days before exam day. Any requests received after that date will be considered on a case-by-case basis. Find out how to request a test center change.

Exam Day Experience

Source: http://www.cfainstitute.org/cfaprog/resources/examdetails/ examdayexperience

A standard exam day follows this format (exact times may vary):

8:00 a.m. Candidates arrive for morning session and begin the check-in process.

8:45 a.m. Approximate time that doors to testing rooms will close to begin announcements. (Once doors close, candidates will not be allowed to enter the testing room until the timed portion of the examinations has started.)

9:00 a.m. Morning session begins.

12:00 p.m. Morning session ends.

Lunch break for candidates.

1:00 p.m. Candidates arrive for afternoon session and begin the check-in process.

1:45 p.m. Approximate time that doors to testing rooms will close to begin announcements. (Once doors close, candidates will not be allowed to enter the testing room until the timed portion of the exams has started.)

2:00 p.m. Afternoon session begins.

5:00 p.m. Afternoon session ends.

At the conclusion of each session, candidates must remain seated until all exam materials are collected and reconciled. Because of enhanced exam security, this process may require candidates to remain seated for additional time after the 12:00 p.m. and 5:00 p.m. end times.

Candidates must attend both the morning and afternoon sessions to have their exams graded.

Exam Admission Ticket Policy

Source: www.cfainstitute.org/cfaprog/resources/examdetails/policies/ticketpolicy

Candidates are required to present an exam admission ticket for admittance to the test center (along with a current government-issued photo identification). Be sure to review your personal information (name, test center) and inform CFA Institute immediately of any errors. The name on your admission ticket must match the name as it appears on your current government-issued photo identification (ID); submit a change to CFA Institute if necessary. If the names do not match, your exam results may be voided.

Testing facilities may change from year to year; therefore, it is important to note the address on your exam admission ticket and become familiar with the test center location.

Exam admission tickets are only available to candidates **online** and will be posted on this Web site in late April (for all levels of the June CFA exam) and late October (for the December Level 1 CFA exam). CFA Institute does not distribute paper admission tickets.

Once the tickets are available, an e-mail announcement will be sent to each candidate who has a valid e-mail address on file with CFA Institute.

Before viewing your ticket, you will be prompted to read, and must agree to abide by, the conditions, requirements, policies, and procedures for the CFA

Program. CFA Institute strongly encourages you to take the time to carefully read and understand these policies. Violation of any of the rules and regulations of the CFA Program will result in CFA Institute voiding your exam results and may lead to suspension or termination of your candidacy in the CFA Program.

It is your responsibility to print one copy of your admission ticket on clean, unused paper and bring it with you to the test center on exam day. If you do not have internet access, please contact us to obtain your ticket by facsimile. You will not be admitted to the testing room without an admission ticket.

Candidates must not write on the front or back of their admission ticket at any time before, during, or after the exam. The ticket must display the correct exam date and test center. Your ticket will only allow you admittance to the test center shown on the ticket.

Personal Belongings Policy

Source: www.cfainstitute.org/cfaprog/resources/examdetails/policies/belongings

Only a limited number of items are allowed in the testing room. You are strongly encouraged to leave your personal belongings at home or in your car; however, as a courtesy, your test center will have an area away from the testing room designated for personal belongings.

Proctors and security personnel will ask to inspect your belongings at check-in to ensure that prohibited items are not carried into the testing room. If proctors or security personnel find items that are not permitted in the testing room, you will be required to place them in the Personal Belongings Area. You will not have access to these items during the examination, but may access them during the lunch break and at the conclusion of the examination.

Please note that it is not the responsibility of the proctors or security personnel to ensure the safety of the materials in the Personal Belongings Area. Neither CFA Institute nor the test center, testing personnel, or vendors will assume responsibility or liability for stolen, lost, or damaged personal property left in this area.

You must follow these guidelines at your test center. With your cooperation, we will ensure that candidates are checked in promptly and seated on time.

The following items must be kept on your desk during the exam:

- Exam admission ticket.
- Current government-issued photo identification.
- Approved calculator(s), including calculator case(s).
- Writing instruments (pencils for Levels 1 and 2, pens and pencils for Level 3).

The following items may be kept on your desk, if needed:

- Erasers, calculator batteries (and screwdriver for battery replacement), pencil sharpeners (no knives), eyeglasses, earplugs, and wristwatches (analog and digital) are acceptable.
- Audible alarms and/or timers must be turned off.

The following items are permitted in the testing room but must remain in your pockets or under your chair when not in use:

- Wallet (money purse).
- Medicine, tissues, and other necessary medical or personal items.

The following items are not permitted in the testing room:

- Food or drinks.
- Baggage of any kind including transparent bags, backpacks, handbags, tote bags, briefcases, luggage, carrying cases, or pencil cases.
- Study materials including notes, papers, textbooks, or study guides.
- Scratch paper, present/future value tables, or calculator manuals.
- Highlighters, correction fluid, correction tape, or rulers.
- Knives of any type, including box cutter and X-ACTO® knives for use as pencil sharpeners.
- Cell phones, MP3 players, BlackBerrys®, cameras, pagers, headsets, computers, electronic organizers, personal data assistants, or any other remote communication or photographic devices.
- Any type of desk clock or timer.

Misconduct and Rules Violations

Source: www.cfainstitute.org/cfaprog/resources/examdetails/policies/misconduct

It is your responsibility to read and understand all testing policies set forth by the CFA Program. Testing personnel will report to CFA Institute any violations of testing rules or policies that occur during the exam.

If you engage in any misconduct during the exam, you may be dismissed from the test center and subject to other penalties, including **voiding of exam results and suspension or termination of your candidacy** in the CFA Program.

Misconduct includes:

- Creating a disturbance.
- Giving or receiving help.
- Opening, working on, or reading the exam during a time not authorized by the testing personnel.
- Writing or erasing after instructed to stop.
- Removing exam materials or notes from the testing room.
- Taking part in an act of impersonation or other forms of cheating.

- Failing to follow the directions of testing personnel.
- Using books, unapproved calculators, headsets, rulers, listening devices, paging devices (beepers), cellular phones, recording or photographic devices, papers of any kind, or other aids.
- Writing on the front or back of your exam admission ticket at any time (before, during, or after the exam).
- Failing to follow CFA Institute conditions, requirements, policies, or procedures.

Candidates are "covered persons" under CFA Institute Bylaws (PDF) and the Rules of Procedure for Proceedings Related to Professional Conduct (Rules of Procedure) (PDF). Therefore, any proceeding/investigation of a candidate's alleged misconduct is considered a professional conduct matter.

Exam Results

Source: www.cfainstitute.org/cfaprog/resources/examdetails/examresults

Exam results are reported as "pass" or "fail" within 90 days (60 days for Level 1) of the exam date.

Results are only available online and are never released over the telephone. Individual candidate results are only released to the candidate and are never released to a third party. A summary of exam results may be distributed to the CFA Institute member societies, CFA exam prep course sponsors, and others.

Actual exam scores are not released. The score matrix provided on the exam results is an indicator of overall performance and cannot be used to determine approximate scores or pass/fail status. The "<=50%" range is considered poor; "51% – 70%" is considered poor to average; ">70%" is considered average to above average.

Retabulation. If you are uncomfortable with the grading process after receiving your results, you may request that your exam be manually retabulated by CFA Institute staff at a cost of US$100.00. To request an exam score retabulation, complete a request form, or contact us to request a copy of the form. Your form and payment must be received by CFA Institute **within 30 days of the release of exam results**. All exam materials, including answers, are the property of CFA Institute and will not be returned to you in either original or copied form.

These policies will apply to you. Every year, numerous candidates have problems on exam day because they assumed their cases would be legitimate exceptions. There is no such thing. I can't tell you how many stories I have heard of people sprinting back to their cars to put stuff away and get back in time to start the exam. If you read the rules and follow them, you reduce the potential for unexpected stress on the day of the exam. That's a good thing!

FINAL WARM-UPS

You should have a definite strategy for the last week before the exam. If possible, it is best to take at least some of the week off from work. You should save at least two practice exams for this last week. To simulate the real thing, you should avoid looking through them or studying questions in them until you are ready to sit down and take them for the first time. Take one of these exams early in the week, and time yourself. Use your results to determine where to focus your study efforts over the last few days. You should devote most of your time to areas where you performed poorly, but spend enough time on your stronger topics to keep them fresh in your mind—this is a definite confidence booster!

At some point in the week before the exam, it is a good idea to visit the actual exam center. Figure out how long it will take to get there on exam day and where you can park. Even if you are returning to the same site where you took the Level 2 exam, it is a good idea to be sure nothing has changed due to construction or a move to a different floor or room. It might even be helpful to locate a lunch destination in the area. The fewer surprises and distractions on exam day, the better. If the exam center has multiple entrances, try to find out where you will enter for the exam.

As a Level 3 candidate, you know by now to expect problems on exam day. They may not be major problems, but be prepared for things like cold/hot rooms, noise, lines, et cetera. There are likely to be distractions that you cannot control, but if you are prepared for them, they are less likely to affect your exam performance.

The evening before the exam, try to avoid studying. Try to relax and make a concerted effort to get a good night's sleep. Tired candidates make silly mistakes on the CFA exam. If you are not rested, you will more than likely miss easy points. This seems like an obvious and trite point, but it is difficult to overemphasize the importance of going into the exam well rested.

A final note: During the lunch break eat a healthy, light lunch and get some exercise. I found that a brisk 15-minute walk reinvigorated me for the afternoon. A heavy lunch (or no lunch) coupled with lying down under a tree can lead to a lack of energy. The afternoon portion of the exam is going to be a challenge. You will need a clear head to perform up to your capabilities.

GAME DAY

Answering a Level 3 Selected Response Item Set Question (Multiple Choice)

Here are some tips to keep in mind as you work through selected response item set questions:

- You will have 18 minutes for each 6-question selected response item set, but answering the questions themselves should not take that long. You should read the vignette after first quickly reading the questions. This will make you more focused on the relevant information.
- In some cases you will be given information that seems unrealistic. That's okay. Unless you are specifically asked to critique the information, accept it as given and use it to answer the questions.
- Focus on the individual words in the question and watch for double negatives, like "All of the following are disadvantages except:" It is very important not to misread words by reading too quickly (e.g., reading "most likely" instead of "least likely"). There will be distracters aimed at this type of mistake.
- Be careful to answer the question as written. Sometimes a distracter looks good because it is consistent with information in the case, but it is actually irrelevant to the question you're answering.
- Try to restate the question in your own words (i.e., what you think the question is really asking). This can help you filter out extraneous information and focus quickly on appropriate answer choices.
- On calculation questions, don't mark an answer too quickly just because it agrees with your answer. Pause for a moment and think about whether the magnitude or sign of the answer seems logical. For example, in hedging a bond portfolio with futures, did you forget to use the total futures price? Did you forget to divide the dollar duration of the CTD by its conversion factor? Did you mark a positive answer when you are long the bonds and should short (negative sign) the futures? I can guarantee there will be distracters that incorporate these and other common mistakes.
- Make sure that you are marking your answer in the right place on the answer sheet. If you skip questions or do the questions out of order, be careful to check yourself.
- Don't be afraid to rely on first impressions. It is okay to change an answer, but only do so if you have a sound reason. When you come back to a question, you will most likely be tired and not thinking as clearly. You may even be biased by a later question that made you think differently.
- As for the format of the selected response item set questions, you know now to expect the unexpected. That sounds cliché, I admit, but it's quite appropriate for the CFA exam. Regardless of the format of the selected response questions, they can be attacked in the same manner as always.

- Finally, do not lose confidence. No one has ever received a perfect score on the CFA exam. Remember, the passing score is around 65% to 70%. That means you can miss 30% to 35% and still pass. So even if you know you have struggled on a few questions (maybe even five or six in a row), do not lose confidence. The worst thing you can do is start second-guessing yourself—you will take longer to answer every question, and you will start changing correct answers.

What to Do With a Difficult Item Set Question

You will run into questions that give you trouble. You might not understand the question, you may think none of the answers makes sense, or you just might not know that concept. Here are some tips to follow if you find yourself facing a difficult question:

- If the question does not make sense or if none of the answers looks even remotely correct, reread the question to see if you missed something.
- Look at the other questions in the item set and see if they shed any light on the question. There might be a logical progression in the questions that will become apparent.
- Never leave an answer blank. A blank answer has a maximum point value of zero. A randomly marked answer has an expected value of $0.25 \times 3 = 0.75$ points, and if you eliminate at least one bad answer that value increases. You are not penalized for wrong answers!
- If you are unable to determine the best answer, you still should be able to help your odds by eliminating one or two answer choices and guessing.
- Also, take some comfort from the fact that the CFA exams are graded on a curve. If the question gave you trouble, it is quite possible that other candidates had trouble with it as well.
- As I said earlier, do not lose confidence. There are 59 other questions.

Answering a Level 3 Essay Question

Here are some tips to keep in mind as you work through constructed response essay questions. You should consider these tips in tandem with the next section on how essay questions are graded—there is an obvious connection between how your paper will be graded and how you should approach your answer.

Answer the question that is asked, not the question you wanted. Sometimes candidates see a concept they know and build their answer around that concept, disregarding other important aspects of the question. You do not get points for demonstrating knowledge beyond the scope of the question! In fact, you will probably irritate the grader, which is not a good idea.

Allocate points to various parts of the question. If Part A asks you to list and describe three characteristics, and it is worth six points, then assume you will get one point each for naming the characteristic and one point each for a description. Another guideline would be to write one sentence for each minute the question is worth, so a 1-point description should not be half a page long! One sentence, or part of a sentence, will be fine.

If the question asks you to choose, select, recommend, et cetera, be sure that you do so. Many times candidates write a good answer, defending their choice, without ever explicitly stating the choice. The choice itself is usually worth a point or two, and if you do not explicitly state it, you will not get those points. On a template question, remember to circle a choice if you are asked to do so.

Write down the equation, and show your calculations! Sometimes the question specifically asks you to do this, but you should show your work anyway on calculation questions. If the grader sees that you set it up right but miscalculated, you will get partial credit. Also, if you had some pieces of a formula in the wrong place and some in the right place, you will get partial credit. If you only write down your final answer, you will get points only if that is the exact answer.

Don't be afraid to repeat yourself in your answer. Candidates sometimes feel that their answer can't be right because they are just restating something they have already said in another part of the question, or possibly rewriting part of the question itself. Do not second-guess yourself just because you feel like your answer is redundant. This repetition is often worth points.

Do not worry about spelling or grammar. Try to write legibly, but do not take too much time to do so. Graders are used to seeing the handwriting of candidates under stress, and yours is probably no worse than most. If you cross out part of your answer and replace it with text from somewhere else on the page, just be sure to draw an arrow so the grader can follow what you did. Write in blue or black ink. Do not use red or green. Graders use red and green, and if you use those colors, you will upset everyone who reads your exam.

Never leave an essay answer blank. You would be amazed at how many points can be earned with a very sketchy or vague answer. Sometimes just restating the question in your own words can earn a couple of points. On most essay questions, the first few points are pretty easy to get. For example, on a 12-point question, an answer with anything resembling a relevant response could probably get three or four points. Give yourself a chance at these points.

What to Do With a Difficult Essay Question

By taking a big-picture approach in preparing for the Level 3 exam, you should be able to write something relevant on just about any concept. If you hit a brick wall trying to answer an essay question, keep these tips in mind.

If the question itself is confusing, try and rephrase it in your own words. This may help you come up with a plausible answer. If you simply do not know the material, take a common sense approach to an answer. Write down a few thoughts that you think may be relevant. For example, assume you are asked to describe an option straddle, and you skipped that material because you did not think it would appear on the exam. Do not be afraid to use common sense. An option straddle obviously combines multiple options on a single underlying asset. The name "straddle" suggests that you are buying or selling options with the same strike prices, "straddling" the current price. Try to sound knowledgeable but vague. The grader will not award full credit, but you will get at least a few of the available points.

This same logic applies to a template question, or an essay question that asks you to make a choice or reach a conclusion. Make the choice, even if you have little or no supporting argument. You might get some points. A blank answer never gets any points.

How an Essay Answer is Graded

Let us begin by offering some reassuring words about the CFA exam grading process. All graders are CFA charterholders, so they have all been candidates at some time. These graders cannot take points away from you. They can only award points. There is a thorough system of checks and balances in the grading process that assures that essay answers are graded as consistently and as fairly as possible. Exams that are near the passing mark are audited to be sure nothing was missed. This audit is not just performed on a sample of exams, it is performed on all exams that are near passing, and it is performed by the more experienced graders. In short, the grading process is structured to give all candidates a fair and reliable assessment of their exams.

Here are some facts about the grading process that might help you formulate essay answers.

Each question is graded by a team of graders who grade only that question, so they are familiar with the assigned material related to that question. Because these graders will review hundreds of exams, they will quickly learn to look for certain features in answers, such as key words or phrases. Remember, because graders see only one question, they will not be aware of things you said on other parts of the exam. Do not be afraid to repeat a point you feel you have already made—this may be new information to the grader of this question.

A grader key is established for each question, identifying the key components of a correct answer and allocating the points to be awarded to each component. These keys usually break the answer down into 1- or 2-point pieces that can be evaluated quickly and objectively. Some answers may earn two points with a brief phrase, while some answers might earn the same two points for a 2- or 3-sentence explanation.

Graders do see a version of the "guideline answer." In fact, this guideline is often revised and refined during the grading process. The grader key is usually derived from this guideline answer. Rest assured, however, that graders do not see any candidate answers that are very similar to the guideline. The guideline answer is written by the authors of the question, who have all of the assigned materials in front of them and hours to work on it. Graders do not expect to see anything resembling the guideline answer, and you should not expect your answer to be as comprehensive. Do not hesitate to use very short, incomplete sentences, phrases, or even bullet points, as long as you convey the answer.

Time Management

Candidates who fail the CFA exam cite time management as their biggest downfall. Do not let poor time management determine your exam results. The following will help you manage your time wisely:

- Take at least one practice exam where you time yourself. This will give you some indication of whether you will have time problems on exam day. However, do not let positive results here lull you into overconfidence. The stress of exam day, plus possible distractions like noise, unpleasant and/or changing room temperature, or other candidates' noises can make a big difference in how fast you work.
- One way to alleviate time pressure is to bank a few minutes by doing an easy topic first. Select a topic with which you feel comfortable, and go there first. If you start to struggle there, move to a different topic. This strategy should help you gain some confidence as you progress through the exam, and will also allow you to get a little ahead with your time allocation.
- I like the idea of doing an easy topic or question first to get going, but I do not recommend skipping around excessively as you work through the exam. Skipping back and forth could break your concentration and consume valuable time as you try to figure out what you have and have not done. Also, skipping around increases the chance of marking the wrong space on the answer sheet or even forgetting to answer a question altogether. There is no feeling worse than discovering an unanswered essay question two minutes before time is called!
- Remain calm. Even if you fall behind, panic will only make things worse. You won't think clearly and you'll miss easy questions. If you need a short break, put down your pencil and take a few deep breaths. This will take about 30 seconds, and may very well help you think clearly enough to answer several additional questions correctly. In fact don't be afraid to take a mind-clearing water break. Just don't overdo it.

Time Management for Constructed Response Essay Questions (Morning Session)

Monitor your progress. Keep an eye on the time as you work through the exam. There will typically be 10 to 15 questions worth 15 to 20 points each. The total points equal the minutes available (180). You may deviate some as you work through easy and more difficult questions, but be careful not to ever let yourself fall too far behind. Also, bear in mind that you do not have 15 minutes to answer a 15-point question—you will need some of that time to read the question and think about your answer.

Pay attention to the points allowed for each question, and do not get carried away with a topic you know very well. If you spend ten minutes on a 4-point answer you are not helping yourself. In fact, you may be penalizing yourself by reducing the time you have available for other, more difficult questions.

Time Management for Selected Response Item Set Questions (Afternoon Session)

Again, monitor your progress. There will be 60 questions in 10 item sets, each of which should take 18 minutes. As with essays, you may deviate some as you work through the easy and more difficult questions, but be careful to not let yourself fall behind.

Remember that the length and difficulty of ethics questions make this topic a bad one to start with, even though it will probably be first. Also, the gray areas covered by ethics questions often make you start to second-guess yourself, which is a very bad precedent to set early in the afternoon. Be *very* careful if you jump around between topics to be sure you are marking the correct blanks on the answer sheet.

Finally, catch your breath at lunch. As previously mentioned, it is a good idea to have a lunch destination planned beforehand. You may or may not want to join other candidates for lunch. If you do talk to other candidates, do not let their comments influence you. They may be saying the exam is easier or more difficult than they expected, but they may or may not be correct about how well they are doing. If you want to review a little at lunch, that is fine, but if you need to relax for a few minutes, that relaxation may do you just as much good as an additional 30-minute cram session. Do what you are comfortable with. I found taking a brisk 15-minute walk did wonders for clearing the cobwebs out of my brain.

Types of Item Set Questions to Expect

It is very difficult to generalize about item set questions, but there are certainly some formats you should be prepared for. Most item set questions require some thought and will definitely be more difficult if you are not well rested, or if you are really stressed out. I have listed several general types of questions and provided an example item set. The example shows some of the general types of questions you might expect, along with some commentary.

©2008 Kaplan Schweser

Long Questions

Look out for these. They are major time-burners. There are two possible ways you may see long questions: (1) the vignette might be long or (2) the questions themselves might be long. Be prepared for extraneous information and irrelevant facts in every item set. The exam authors want to be sure you can identify the relevant information to demonstrate your grasp of the material.

Two-Column Questions

You might see some questions like this on the exam. There are a few things to keep in mind with this type of question:

- One question actually tests two concepts.
- These questions can combine qualitative and quantitative components.
- By determining that half of the answer is incorrect, you can usually eliminate one or more choices.
- These questions can be of two general types:

 1. A list of statements with choices like:
    A. Statement i is correct; statement ii is correct.
    B. Statement i is incorrect; statement ii is correct.
    C. Statement i is correct; statement ii is incorrect.
    D. Statement i is incorrect; statement ii is incorrect.

 2. An answer with a single sentence that doesn't appear to be two separate concepts, like:
    A. A non-collateralized loan, such as a repo.
    B. A collateralized loan, such as a repo.

Even though the correct answer might be to use a repo, Answer A is incorrect because repos are collateralized. Read the answers carefully. Don't mark the incorrect answer because you are in a hurry!

Answer Choices That are Direct Opposites

You will see some questions where there are pairs of answer choices—either one pair with two other different answers, or two pairs. By pairs we mean answers that are identical except for one word, for example, substituting "increase" for "decrease." There may be critical information in these paired answers. One of them is likely to be correct, and the difference between the two answers may be the key to answering the question correctly. If you see paired answers, check to see if the difference between them is critical to the question at hand.

"Distracter" Answers That are True or Sound True but are Not Correct

These are answer choices that sound good. They may sound good for any of several reasons:

- They might be true, but not appropriate answers (or at least not the best answer).
- They might be consistent with irrelevant information provided in the case.
- They might include "buzzwords" or common concepts.

Be very careful with these types of distracters. You always want to try and select the best answer that would apply in the specific case. Distracters may make sense. They may also make you think you could defend them as an answer choice. You might think, "Well, they want me to answer 'A,' but I think 'B' is okay, and I can argue the point with anyone." Think again. You will never get the chance to argue the point. Take the safe bet and choose the CFA Institute answer.

Answer Choices That Can Be Eliminated

It is important to read every answer choice before making your selection. This strategy will help you avoid missing a better answer. Similarly, when you are struggling with a question, eliminate the worst answers to narrow your choices and improve your odds of earning some points.

SAMPLE ITEM SET

DEBT INVESTMENTS ITEM SET #1 HAS SIX PARTS FOR A TOTAL OF 18 MINUTES

Use the following information to answer Questions 25 through 30.

Wilson Partners, an investment advisory firm, has a $10,000,000 mortgage-backed securities position that it needs to finance for one month. Assume that the 30-day repo rate is 5.50% and that Wilson Partners is able to finance 95% of its position with a dealer.

In its corporate bond portfolio, Wilson holds $5,000,000 worth of Elm Corp. bonds. They are considering selling the Elm bonds and replacing them with Oak Corp. bonds. Wilson uses a 2-year time horizon for evaluating both bonds. Currently, Wilson assumes a flat yield curve with 5% yields on bonds comparable to Elm and Oak. Wilson expects yields on such bonds to be 4% in two years, again with a flat yield curve. The two bonds are comparable in terms of credit risk. Both bonds have semiannual coupon dates of June 1 and December 1. Other characteristics are given in Exhibit A.

Exhibit A: As of 6/1/2004

Issuer	Maturity	Coupon	Current Price	Duration	Est'd Price 6/1/2006
Elm Corp.	6/1/2014	6.00%	$1,077.90	7.8	$1,135.80
Oak Corp.	6/1/2019	5.00%	$1,000.99	10.8	$1,100.60

25. In order to achieve its objective of borrowing against the mortgage-backed securities position, Wilson should enter into a type of:
    A. collateralized loan, commonly called a repurchase agreement.
    B. collateralized loan, commonly called a reverse repurchase agreement.
    C. non-collateralized loan, commonly called a repurchase agreement.
    D. non-collateralized loan, commonly called a reverse repurchase agreement.

26. The repo rate on this transaction would be determined by all of the following **EXCEPT** the:
    A. term to maturity of the collateral securities.
    B. prevailing Fed funds rate.
    C. credit quality of the collateral securities.
    D. requirement that the collateral securities be delivered to the lender of funds.

27. The dollar amount of the repo margin on this transaction is *closest* to:
    A. $550,000.
    B. $500,000.
    C. $27,500.
    D. $41,667.

28. The total maturing amount of the loan at the end of the repo term will be *closest* to:
    A. $10,045,833.
    B. $9,545,833.
    C. $9,543,542.
    D. $9,500,000.

29. What is the expected total return on a bond equivalent basis over a 2-year time horizon on both the Elm bond and the Oak bond, assuming a reinvestment rate of 3% annually?

	Elm	Oak
A.	2.65%	4.91%
B.	5.37%	10.06%
C.	7.90%	9.45%
D.	8.17%	9.78%

30. Assume that Wilson's objective in the Elm/Oak trade is to alter the duration exposure of their portfolios to take advantage of their interest rate forecasts. Based on the information in Exhibit A and on your answer to the previous question, Wilson should:
    A. sell the Elm bonds and buy the Oak bonds because the dollar duration of the Elm bonds is greater than the dollar duration of the Oak bonds.
    B. not sell the Elm bonds because their duration is less than the duration of the Oak bonds.
    C. sell the Elm bonds and buy the Oak bonds, but only buy enough Oak bonds to match the dollar duration of the current Elm bond position.
    D. sell the Elm bonds and buy equivalent market value of the Oak bonds.

ITEM SET ANSWERS

25. **B** A repo is the sale of a security with the agreement to repurchase it later at a higher price. A reverse repo is the purchase of a security with the agreement to sell it back later at a higher price. The difference between the two is the counterparty who initiates the transaction. In the reverse repo, the investor effectively invests short-term funds. A repo is used by dealers and others to purchase securities (i.e., use the securities as collateral).

26. **A** The term to maturity of the underlying securities will not affect the repo rate. The better the credit quality, the lower the rate, and a delivery requirement would also lower the repo rate. The Fed funds rate will determine the general level of all repo rates.

27. **B** Financing 95% of the position implies a repo margin of 5%: $10,000,000 × 5% = $500,000.

28. **C** $10,000,000 – $500,000 = $9,500,000 = loan amount

    $9,500,000 × 5.50% × 30 / 360 = $43,541.67 = total interest

    $9,500,000 + $43,541.67 = $9,543,541.67 = maturing amount

29. **C** Elm:

    Coupon + reinvest: PMT = 30; N = 4; I/Y = 1.5;

    CPT FV = $122.73

    Horizon price = $1,135.80

    Total future dollars = $1,258.53

    Total return = (1,258.53 / 1,077.9)0.25 – 1 = 3.95%

    Bond equivalent = 3.95 × 2 = 7.90%

Oak:

Coupon + reinvest: PMT = 25; N = 4; I/Y = 1.5;

CPT FV= $102.27

Horizon price = $1,100.60

Total future dollars = $1,202.87

Total return = (1,202.87 / 1,000)0.25 – 1 = 4.73%

Bond equivalent = 4.73 × 2 = 9.45%

30. **D** Wilson's forecast for a decline in rates from 5% to 4% should lead them to try and increase the duration of their portfolio, so they can benefit more from the decrease in rates. If they want to take advantage of this forecast, Wilson should not try to match the dollar duration of the Elm position, because they would be limiting their potential gain. The dollar duration of the Elm bonds is less than the dollar duration of the Oak bonds.

Sample Essay Questions

Following are some sample essay questions taken from past Level 3 exams. The guideline answers have been highlighted to show the portions needed to earn points. I have developed grader keys for each question, but I have no knowledge of what the real grader's key looked like for any of these questions. This allocation is just an educated guess of how points might have been awarded. There are two sample questions from the prior exams, just to show you how points may be allocated to the guideline answers. Following these first questions, there are two more from more recent exams. On these last questions, I have created a few "sample" answers to show what real candidate answers may have looked like and how they would have been scored. These illustrations should help you assess your own answers as you work practice problems yourself.

QUESTION 1 HAS TWO PARTS FOR A TOTAL OF 12 MINUTES

Required CFA Institute Disclaimer: Due to CFA curriculum changes from year to year, published sample exam questions and guideline answers prior to the current year may not reflect the current curriculum.

Charles Investment Management, Inc., a fixed-income manager of U.S.-only portfolios, has provided significant excess returns for its clients through duration and sector management. The firm defines sectors as either government bonds or corporate bonds. Several of the manager's clients have asked the firm about the possibility of investing in international fixed-income markets. These clients mention the favorable performance of these markets, as exemplified by the "international fixed-income aggregate index" in Table 1. The clients are asking

Charles to transfer the same management techniques that it has successfully applied in the U.S. market to international fixed-income markets.

Table 1: Annualized Rates of Return

Bond Index	One Year	Five Years
International fixed-income aggregate index, unhedged	1.0%	15.9%
International fixed-income aggregate index, hedged	6.5%	7.2%

A.   Infer from Table 1 the effect of changes in the U.S. dollar on international fixed-income returns for U.S. investors in the past 1-year and 5-year periods.

(6 minutes)

B.   Explain why the firm's techniques to generate excess returns through duration and sector management in U.S. fixed-income markets may not be transferable to international fixed-income markets.

(6 minutes)

QUESTION 1 ANSWER

A.   Effect of changes in U.S. dollar:

The difference between the hedged and unhedged returns is a function of fluctuations in the currency return over the time period studied. *Over the 5-year period, the U.S. dollar was relatively weak against other currencies, causing the unhedged index to outperform the hedged index by 8.7 percentage points. For the recent 1-year period, the U.S. dollar strengthened against other currencies. The index returns hedged into U.S. dollars increased by 5.5 percentage points because of the relative dollar strength.*

B.   Transferability of duration and sector management:

Duration management is more difficult in international fixed-income investing because few non-U.S. bond markets have liquid issues with maturities greater than ten years. Most non-U.S. bond markets also lack the broad range of instruments, such as STRIPS and repos, that allow low-cost duration management in the U.S. market. Although interest rate futures are available in most non-U.S. markets and offer a low-cost vehicle, they are limited typically to the short end of the term structure. Swap markets are liquid and generally available but pose challenges in counterparty credit and technical and operational barriers. A U.S. bond portfolio's duration, benchmarked to the U.S. yield curve, is managed in the aggregate. *Managing the durations of international portfolios against an aggregate benchmark can be difficult because of the differing volatility and correlation characteristics among the markets composing the index.*

Sector management is also difficult outside the United States. A scarcity of corporate bonds often exists outside the United States because of policies favoring the raising of capital through bank financing and equity issuance. Market anomalies can arise from differing tax treatments among markets. *Implementing some sector management strategies may be difficult because mortgage markets and the derivative instruments produced by that sector may not exist to the extent available in the United States.*

POSSIBLE GRADER'S KEY

Note that if your answer included only the *italicized* text, you would probably have earned the full 12 points.

A. 2 points – for 1-year period, U.S. dollar appreciated.
    1 point – appreciated dollar penalized unhedged returns.
    2 points – for 5-year period, U.S. dollar depreciated.
    1 point – depreciated dollar penalized hedged returns.

B. Duration management:
    1 point – limited availability of securities.
    1 point – identifying securities that would be in short supply long-term, low-cost swaps with no credit risk.
    1 point – difficult to manage against benchmark.

    Sector management:
    2 points – limited availability of corporate bonds.
    1 point – for other sectors possibly not available—MBS, derivatives.

A few thoughts on this answer:

- In Part A, both the 1-year and 5-year horizons would need to be addressed, each with three points allocated.
- In Part B, both duration and sector management would need to be addressed, each with three points allocated. There is more to say about duration management, but the sector management probably got the same number of points.

QUESTION 2 HAS TWO PARTS FOR A TOTAL OF 18 MINUTES

Required CFA Institute Disclaimer: Due to CFA curriculum changes from year to year, published sample exam questions and guideline answers prior to the current year may not reflect the current curriculum.

Lindsay Corporation Pension Plan:

Michel Dumont is Chief Financial Officer of Lindsay Corporation, which is located in the United States, and chairs the Investment Committee for its $100 million defined-benefit pension plan. Lindsay operates exclusively in the U.S. market and has recently completed a 5-year early retirement program. As a result of this program, many long-time employees decided to retire early at age 60 and receive full pension benefits. Lindsay's actuary has determined the following:

- 60% of all participants in Lindsay's defined-benefit pension plan are now retired and receiving their pensions.
- The required real rate of return based on actuarial assumptions for the pension fund is 5.5% annually.
- The average age of active employees who will eventually collect retirement benefits is 45 years.
- Inflation has been stable at 2% annually, as measured by the U.S. Consumer Price Index (CPI), and is forecasted to remain at this level for the foreseeable future.
- The pension plan is currently fully funded, and Dumont would like to minimize the amount of company contributions required in the future.

A. Formulate and justify investment policy objectives for the Lindsay pension plan in the following three areas:
    i.   Return objective.
    ii. Risk tolerance.
    iii. Time horizon.

(9 minutes)

Mountaintop College Endowment Fund:

Dumont is also a member of the Board of Trustees of the endowment fund at Mountaintop College. The fund was established to provide scholarships and currently has assets of USD 1 billion. In addition to its U.S. campus, the college has recently established campuses in Europe and Japan. Its spending policy was recently amended as follows:

- The new payout level will increase the spending rate from 4% to 6% of assets each year.
- 35% of the new payout level will be awarded in local currencies to students attending the college's foreign branches.

The fund's current asset allocation was structured to balance the objectives of near-term funding of scholarships and longer-term, inflation-adjusted preservation of capital. The overall volatility of the current portfolio is similar to the volatility of a domestic-only balanced portfolio. Annual increases in college tuition are forecasted to average 3% globally over the long term, and inflation is forecasted to remain at 2% annually as measured by U.S. CPI.

B. Discuss each of the following for the endowment fund. Specifically address the impact of the change in the fund's spending policy, where applicable.
    i.   Return objective.
    ii. Risk tolerance.
    iii. Time horizon.

(9 minutes)

QUESTION 2 ANSWER

A.   Investment policy objectives for the Lindsay pension plan in the three areas are:

    i.   Return objective:

        The return objective for this mature U.S. corporate pension plan is the sum of the plan's required real rate of return (5.5%) and the expected rate of inflation (2%) for a total of 7.5%. An alternate approach would be to multiply, rather than add, the two rates, which produces a return objective equal to 7.6%, as follows:

$$[(1 + 0.055) \times (1 + 0.02)] - 1 = 0.076$$

    ii.   Risk tolerance:

        The level of risk tolerance for the pension plan is quite low, well below average. The plan is quite mature, as indicated by the high percentage (60%) of employees already retired and receiving pension payments and by the relatively advanced average age of active employees (45 years). In addition, the plan is currently fully funded.

    iii.   Time horizon:

        The time horizon for the pension plan is substantially shorter than average. The horizon is relatively short because payments must be made now (and into the future) to the 60% of employees already retired and must be made in the near future to many of the active employees because their average age is 45 years. This combination of circumstances markedly reduces the time horizon as compared with most corporate pension plans and reinforces the minimum risk, limited return objectives of the plan.

B.   The nature of the three investment policy elements, and the impact of the change in spending policy on each, is:

    i.   Return objective:

        The return objective for the Mountaintop Fund will change to the sum of the new spending policy (6%, up from 4%) and the annual college tuition inflation rate (3%) for a total of 9% (up from 7%).

    ii.   Risk tolerance:

        The level of risk tolerance for the Mountaintop Fund is high. A spending rate of 6% and a tuition inflation rate of 3% is fairly common among

U.S. university endowment funds and a high level of risk tolerance is commonly assumed for such funds. *The increased spending rate, which raised the total return to 9%, would require the fund to increase its risk tolerance.* In addition, *the new exposure to currency risk may alter the risk profile of the fund.*

   iii. Time horizon:

The fund's time horizon is very long term; there is no change in the fund's time horizon as a result of the change in the spending rate.

POSSIBLE GRADER'S KEY

Note that if your answer included only the *italicized* text, you would probably have earned full credit of 18 points.

A.   i.   1 point – return must cover required real rate of 5.5%.
           1 point – return must cover inflation of 2%.
           1 point – return must be greater than or equal to 7.5%.

    ii. 1 point – risk tolerance is low.
           1 point – high percentage of retired employees.
           1 point – high average age of active employees.

  iii. 1 point – time horizon is relatively short.
           1 point – plan must be able to pay current retirees.
           1 point – plan must be able to pay active employees with high average age.

B.   i.   1 point – return must cover 6% spending rate.
           1 point – spending rate has increased from 4% to 6%.
           1 point – return must cover 3% tuition increases.

    ii. 1 point – risk tolerance is high.
           1 point – risk must be high to achieve required return of 9%.
           1 point – currency risk introduced under new spending policy.

  iii. 2 points – time horizon is long.
           1 point – no change in time horizon due to change in spending policy.

A few thoughts on this answer:

- Part A asks you to formulate and justify. So, your answer must include a justification. For example, if your answer on the return requirement was: "Return must be >7.5%," you probably only got 1 point. You would need to justify where the 7.5% came from in order to get full credit.
- The justifications for risk tolerance and time horizon seem redundant. However, you would need the explanation in both places in order to earn the points. Don't be afraid to repeat yourself if you are supporting an answer to a different part of a question. There is often overlap in these policy statement questions.

           ©2008 Kaplan Schweser

- Part B asks you to specifically address the change in spending policy. If you did not justify your answers in terms of the changes, you would not earn full credit. Read questions closely, and do what the question asks you to do. It may seem like you are stating the obvious to say "the spending rate went up so the return requirement must also go up." But unless you tie the two together, you would not get the points.

Questions 3 and 4

Required CFA Institute Disclaimer: Due to CFA curriculum changes from year to year, published sample exam questions and guideline answers prior to the current year may not reflect the current curriculum.

Questions 3 and 4 relate to Robert Taylor. A total of 44 minutes is allocated to these questions. First review the introduction below and Exhibit 3-1. Candidates should answer these questions in the order presented.

Introduction

Robert Taylor, age 50 and a U.S. resident, recently retired and received a $500,000 cash payment. He also obtained $700,000 through the exercise of stock options. Both figures are net of tax. Taylor is not entitled to a pension; however, his medical expenses are covered by insurance paid for by his former employer. Taylor is in excellent health and has a normal life expectancy.

Taylor's wife died last year after a long illness, which resulted in devastating medical expenses. All their investments, including a home, were liquidated to fully satisfy these medical expenses.

Taylor has no assets other than the $1,200,000 cash referenced above, and has no debts. He plans to acquire a $300,000 home in three months and insists on paying cash given his recent adverse experience with creditors.

When presented with investment options, Taylor consistently selects the most conservative alternative.

After settling into his new home, Taylor's living expenses will be $2,000 per month and will rise with inflation. He does not plan to work again.

Taylor's father and his wife's parents died years ago. His mother, Renee, is 72 years old and in excellent physical health. Her mental health, however, is deteriorating and she has relocated to a long-term care facility. Renee's expenses total $3,500 per month. Her monthly income is $1,500 from pensions.

Her income and expenses will rise with inflation. She has no investments or assets of value. Taylor, who has no siblings, must cover Renee's income shortfall.

Taylor has one child, Troy. Troy and a friend need funds immediately for a start-up business. First year costs are estimated at $200,000. The partners have no assets and have been unable to obtain outside financing. The friend's family has offered to invest $100,000 in the business in exchange for a minority equity stake if Taylor agrees to invest the same amount.

Taylor would like to assist Troy; however, he is concerned about the partner's ability to succeed, the potential loss of his funds, and whether his assets are sufficient to support his needs and to support Renee. He plans to make a decision on this investment very soon. If he invests $100,000 in Troy's business, he insists that this investment be excluded from any investment strategy developed for his remaining funds.

With this information, portfolio manager Sarah Wheeler prepared the investment policy statement for Taylor shown in Exhibit 3-1.

Exhibit 3-1

Return objective	• Income requirement is $2,000 monthly. • Total return requirement is 2.7% annually ($24,000 / $900,000).
Risk tolerance	• Substantial asset base and low return requirement provide ample resources to support an aggressive, growth-oriented portfolio.
Time horizon	• Client is 50 years old, recently retired, and in excellent health. • Time horizon exceeds 20 years.
Liquidity needs	• $300,000 is needed in three months for the purchase of a home. • Modest additional cash is needed for normal relocation costs. • $100,000 may be needed for possible investment in his son's business. • A normal, ongoing cash reserve level should be established.
Tax	• There is little need to defer income. • Mother's expenses may have an effect.
Legal and regulatory	• No special considerations exist.
Unusual circumstances	• Client desires to support mother. • Client insists that any investment in son's business be excluded from long-term planning. • Client has strong aversion to debt.

QUESTION 3 HAS TWO PARTS FOR A TOTAL OF 20 MINUTES

A. Evaluate the appropriateness of Taylor's investment policy statement in Exhibit 3-1 with regard to the following objectives:
   i. Return requirement.
   ii. Risk tolerance.

(12 minutes)

B. Evaluate the appropriateness of Taylor's investment policy statement in Exhibit 3-1 with regard to the following constraints:
  i.   Time horizon.
  ii. Liquidity needs.

(8 minutes)

QUESTION 3 ANSWER

A.   i.   *The return objective section of the investment policy statement (IPS) is inadequate.*
  - Although Wheeler accurately indicates Taylor's personal income requirement, *she does not recognize the need to support Renee.*
  - Wheeler does not indicate the need to protect Taylor's purchasing power by increasing income by at least the rate of inflation over time.
  - *Wheeler does not indicate the impact of income taxes on the return requirement.*
  - Wheeler calculates required return based on assets of $900,000, appropriately excluding Taylor's imminent $300,000 liquidity need (house purchase) from investable funds. However, Taylor may invest $100,000 in his son's business. If he does, Taylor insists this asset be excluded from his plan. In that eventuality, Taylor's asset base for purposes of Wheeler's analysis would be $800,000.
  - Assuming a $900,000 capital base, Wheeler's total return estimate of 2.7% is lower than the actual required after-tax real return of 5.3% ($48,000 / $900,000).

  ii. *The risk tolerance section of the IPS is inappropriate.*

  - *Wheeler fails to consider Taylor's willingness to assume risk as exemplified by his aversion to loss, his consistent preference for conservative investments,* his adverse experience with creditors, and his desire not to work again.
  - Wheeler fails to consider Taylor's ability to assume risk, which is based on Taylor's recent life changes, the size of his capital base, high personal expenses versus income, and expenses related to his mother's care.
  - *Wheeler's policy statement implies that Taylor has a greater willingness and ability to accept volatility (higher risk tolerance) than is actually the case.* Based on Taylor's need for an after-tax return of 5.3%, a balanced approach with both a fixed income and growth component is more appropriate than an aggressive growth strategy.

B.   i.   *The time horizon section of the IPS is partially appropriate.*

  - Wheeler accurately addresses the long-term time horizon based only on Taylor's age and life expectancy.
  - Wheeler fails to consider that Taylor's investment time horizon is multistaged.

- *Stage one represents the life expectancy of Renee,* during which time Taylor will supplement her income.
- *Stage two begins at Renee's death,* concluding Taylor's need to supplement her income, and ends with Taylor's death.

ii. *The liquidity section of the IPS is appropriate because Wheeler fully discloses all potential liquidity needs.*

POSSIBLE GRADER'S KEY

Note that if your answer included only the *italicized* text, you would probably have earned full credit of 20 points.

A. i. 2 points – return objective is inadequate.
2 points – each for any of the following, up to six points maximum: ignores Renee's support; does not consider inflation; does not consider taxes; includes the $100,000 to be invested in son's business; total return estimate too low.

ii. 2 points – risk tolerance is inappropriate.
2 points – each for any of the following: does not consider Taylor's stated aversion to risk, does not consider Taylor's ability to assume risk, allows for too much potential volatility.

B. i. 1 point – time horizon is partially appropriate.
1 point – long time horizon acceptable for Taylor himself.
2 points – time horizon should be multi-stage with Renee's life expectancy being first stage, stage two beginning upon her death.

ii. 2 points – liquidity section is appropriate.
2 points – all liquidity needs addressed.

A few thoughts on this answer:

- When points are given in blocks of two or three, the grader will have some discretion as to what is needed for a 2-point versus a 1-point explanation. The 2-point answers will not necessarily be the longest ones. The 2-point answers will just clearly state the rationale.
- Investment policy statements are on the exam every year in some form. Remember a few important points to look for:
  - Do returns include inflation adjustment?
  - Have taxes been addressed?
  - Are return objectives and risk tolerance consistent?
  - Have all specific cash flows been covered (liquidity), in this case, the home purchase and the investment in the son's business?
  - Don't worry if some issues show up in more than one place. In this case Renee's needs affect the return requirement, the risk tolerance and the time horizon.

SAMPLE ANSWERS

Some sample answers follow. These are answers we wrote to give you an idea of what real answers might look like, and how they might be scored.

A. i. Income requirement should be $4,000 per month.

        Total return requirement should be 48,000 / 800,000 = 6%.

    ii. Return requirement of 6% is about average.

        Balanced portfolio more appropriate than aggressive portfolio.

B. i. Time horizon looks good.

    ii. Liquidity needs look good also.

Observations:

This weak answer got 7 of 20 possible points. This candidate may have felt he did well on this question. However, these explanations are far too brief for the points available and the lack of additional analysis is mainly what cost this candidate points. Also, in Part A, the candidate lost four points just because he failed to evaluate the risk and return (i.e., state whether they were adequate or appropriate).

A. i. Income requirement is too low—should include $2,000 to cover Mother's shortfall.

        Income will need to increase in line with expected inflation.

        Taylor wants to exclude investment in son's business, so there is only $800,000 available to cover required return.

    ii. Taylor wants low risk, Wheeler is suggesting high risk approach.

        Taylor's expenses will require a portfolio biased toward current income rather than capital appreciation.

B. i. Taylor has a long time horizon. His expenses will decrease if his mother dies.

    ii. Wheeler has addressed all liquidity needs.

Observations:

This answer addressed many of the relevant issues, but still only got 14 points, missing the points for clearly stating whether the policy statement was adequate. Notice how brief this answer is, but the candidate still earns most of the points.

A.   i.   Wheeler has written a poor investment policy. The return objective is missing several important components. It does not address Renee's expenses that exceed her income by $2,000 per month. Instead, it only uses the $2,000 Taylor needs for himself to live on. In reality, Taylor has probably underestimated his own expenses and should reconsider whether his budget is accurate. Taking into account inflation, Renee's needs, and a more realistic expense level for someone in Taylor's station in life, I think the return requirement should be $6,000 per month at least.

   ii.   Wheeler has also done a lousy job on Taylor's risk profile. Taylor will need $6,000 per month ($72,000 per year) on a base of $800,000 (not $900,000 like she said). This is a 9% return, which would involve a high current income portfolio. The focus should be on income, not on aggressive growth.

B.   i.   The 20-year time horizon is not appropriate. The time horizon should be split into two parts. The first horizon should be Renee's life expectancy, which is relatively short term. After that, Taylor has a long time horizon.

   ii.   Finally, with the liquidity needs, Wheeler did something right. She mentions all of the various liquidity needs that Taylor has: the $300,000 for the home, the $100,000 for the son's business, and some extra cash for unexpected expenses.

Observations:

This answer earned 17 points, largely by clearly evaluating the policy statement. Even though the candidate largely missed the point on the risk tolerance, he aced Part B and covered the critical issues to earn points.

QUESTION 4 HAS ONE PART FOR A TOTAL OF 12 MINUTES

After revising the investment policy statement and confirming it with Taylor, Wheeler is now developing a long-term asset allocation strategy for him. Wheeler will use the following revised information to recommend one of the allocations in Exhibit 4-1:

- Taylor has decided to invest $100,000 in his son's business but still insists that this investment be disregarded in making his allocation decision.

- Taylor's total cash flow needs have changed to $4,200 a month.
- The available asset base is $800,000.
- Wheeler estimates that the inflation rate will be 1% next year.
- Taylor is determined to maintain the real value of his assets because he plans to set up a charitable foundation in the future.
- Taylor insists on taking no more risk than absolutely necessary to achieve his return goals.

Exhibit 4-1: Potential Long-Term Asset Allocation Strategies

	Allocation A	Allocation B	Allocation C	Allocation D
Asset class weighting:				
Stocks	20%	40%	60%	80%
Bonds	75%	55%	35%	15%
Cash	5%	5%	5%	5%
Expected annual:				
Return	6.7%	7.5%	8.2%	9.1%
Standard deviation	9.0%	11.5%	15.3%	19.0%
Potential for:				
Asset growth	very low	low	moderate	high
Income growth	very low	low	moderate	high
Current income	high	high	low	very low
Stability	very high	high	moderate	low

Select the allocation strategy from Exhibit 4-1 that is most appropriate for Taylor, and justify your selection with two supporting reasons related to the revised information shown in Exhibit 4-1.

(12 minutes)

QUESTION 4 ANSWER

Allocation B is most appropriate for Taylor. Taylor's nominal annual return requirement is 6.3% based upon his cash flow (income) needs ($50,400 annually) to be generated from a current asset base of $800,000. After adjusting for expected annual inflation of 1%, the real return requirement becomes 7.3%. That is, to have $808,000 ($800,000 × 1.01), the portfolio must generate $58,400 ($50,400 + $8,000) in the first year, and $58,400 / $800,000 = 7.3%.

Allocation B meets Taylor's minimum return requirement. Of the possible allocations that provide the required minimum real return, Allocation B also has the lowest standard deviation of returns (i.e., least volatility risk), and by far the best Sharpe ratio. In addition, Allocation B offers a balance of high current income and stability with moderate growth prospects.

Allocation A has the lowest standard deviation and best Sharpe ratio, but does not meet the minimum return requirement, when inflation is included in that requirement. Allocation A also has very low growth prospects.

Allocation C meets the minimum return requirement and has moderate growth prospects but has a higher risk level (standard deviation) and a lower Sharpe ratio, and less potential for stability than Allocation B.

Allocation D also meets the minimum return requirement and has high growth prospects but has the highest standard deviation and lowest Sharpe ratio of the allocations that provide the required minimum real return.

Thus, of the three allocations meeting the minimum return requirement, Allocation B presents the lowest level of risk as indicated by its lower expected standard deviation. Given Taylor's stated desire to assume "no more risk than absolutely necessary" to achieve his return goals, Allocation B is the appropriate selection.

POSSIBLE GRADER'S KEY

Note that if your answer included only the *italicized* text above, you would probably have earned full credit of 12 points.

1 point – return objective includes $4,200 per month or $50,400 annually.
1 point – return objective includes inflation of 1% annually (0.01 × $800,000 = $8,000).
1 point – return objective based on $800,000 in assets.
2 points – Allocation B meets return requirements.
2 points – Allocation B is lowest risk alternative that meets return needs.
2 points – Allocation B has lower risk (either lowest standard deviation or highest stability).
3 points – Allocation B the is best choice.

A few thoughts on this answer:

- Achieving the required return is the first priority, and so five points were allocated there.
- Minimizing risk was second priority, so four points allocated there.
- Selection of B gets three points, and would need to be specifically stated in the answer. The question did ask you to select one allocation.

SAMPLE ANSWERS

Following are some sample answers. These are answers we wrote to give you an idea of what real answers might look like, and how they might be scored.

4.   Taylor wants to minimize his risk. The lowest risk allocation is A. Allocation A also has the highest stability, and Taylor wants to maintain the real value of his assets. Taylor's return on Allocation A will be 0.067 × $800,000 = $53,600, which exceeds his cash flow needs of $4,200 × 12 = $50,400 annually.

Observations:

This answer got 5 points out of 12 possible. The candidate ignored inflation as part of the required return and so made the wrong selection. Still, because the candidate correctly minimized risk, he earned some points.

4. Taylor needs to decide whether he wants to take the lowest risk available, and sacrifice his return objective, or meet his return objective and accept slightly more risk. Allocation A is the lowest risk choice, based on its low standard deviation and high stability. However, this allocation does not meet Taylor's inflation adjusted required return, which is:

$$[(\$4,200 \times 12) + (800,000 \times 0.01)] \, / \, \$800,000 = 7.3\%$$

In order to get 7.3%, Taylor must move to Allocation B and accept a higher standard deviation.

So Taylor has to choose—more risk or less return. He can eliminate choices C and D, since they are even higher risk.

Observations:

This answer got 9 points out of 12 possible. The only missing points were for selecting the correct allocation. The question asks YOU to choose, not Taylor.

4. Allocation B is the way to go. It is the lowest risk allocation that meets Taylor's required return. Taylor insisted on taking no more risk than required to achieve his return goals. He also wants to maintain the real value of his assets, so his return would have to include an inflation adjustment of 1% per year.

Observations:

This answer got 8 points out of 12 possible. This candidate identified B as the lowest risk choice that met the return requirement, but gave no evidence of what the return requirement was or how it was derived.

CONCLUSION

Hopefully these examples have shown you some things to look for on exam day. Obviously, you will not see any of these specific questions on the real exam. But if you see some of these structures, they will now look familiar to you, and you should feel more comfortable addressing them.

I wish you the best on June 7!

INDEX

1/n diversification 42

A

absolute-return vehicles 163
accounting manipulations that benefit
    managers 146
account structure effectiveness 52
accrued benefits 95
active equity managers 134
active investor 147
active management by larger risk factor
    mismatches 98
active management decisions 206
active participants 95
active return 134, 169
active risk 134
acute market inefficiencies 46
additional compensation arrangements 7
adjustments to the immunized portfolio
    102
ad valorem 144
Alex Kaye 28
algorithmic trading 198
aligning risk exposures 100
allocating shareholder capital to pension
    plans 71
allocating to managers 142
allocation/selection 209
almost right defense 42
alpha 98
alpha and beta separation approach 143
alpha correlations 130
alpha hunters 46
alpha research 73
alternative investment benchmarks 157
alternative investment groups 153
alternative investments 152
alternative investments portfolio
    management 152
American option 172
analytical VAR 170
anchoring 37

anchoring-and-adjustment 39
angel investors 159
appreciating currencies 227
Argent Capital Management 28
aspirations 40
asset allocation 87
asset categories 208
asset classes 88
asset class returns 82
asset-liability management (ALM)
    efficient frontier 90
Asset/Liability Management (ALM)
    strategic asset allocation 87
asset/liability mismatch 71
Asset Manager Code of Professional
    Conduct 38
asset-only approach 94
asset-only strategic asset allocation 87
asset segregation 49
assets-under-management fee
    (AUM fee) 162
asset valuation reserve (AVR) 66
asset-weighted returns 232
assuming parallel rate shifts 107
assurity of completion 193
auction market 194
automated auctions 194

B

backfill 158
backwardation 167
balanced mandate 222
banks 67
barbell strategy 106
basis risk 119
Bayesian Rigidity 46
bear call spread 180
bear put spread 180
behavioral finance 49
benchmarks 206
beta grazers 46
beta research 73